HOW TO CLEAN PRACTICALLY ANYTHING

THIRD EDITION / UPDATED

The Editors of
Consumer Reports Books
with Monte Florman
and Marjorie Florman

CONSUMER REPORTS BOOKS
A Division of Consumers Union
Yonkers, New York

Published by Consumers Union of United States, Inc., Yonkers, New York 10703.

Library of Congress Cataloging-in-Publication Data
How to clean practically anything / the editors of Consumer Reports Books ; with Monte Florman and Marjorie Florman. — 3rd ed. updated
p. cm.
Rev. ed. of : How to clean practically anything / Monte Florman, Marjorie Florman, and the editors of Consumer Reports Books. c1989.
Includes index.
ISBN 0-89043-753-x
1. House cleaning. 2. Cleaning. I. Florman, Monte. II. Florman, Marjorie. III. Florman, Monte. How to clean practically anything. IV. Consumer Reports Books. V. Consumer reports.
TX324.H69 1992
648'.5—dc20 32-5431
CIP

This book is printed on recycled paper.
Design by GDS/Jeffrey L. Ward
Fifth printing, December 1994
Manufactured in the United States of America

How to Clean Practically Anything: Third Edition/Updated is a Consumer Reports Book published by Consumers Union, the nonprofit organization that publishes *Consumer Reports,* the monthly magazine of test reports, product Ratings, and buying guidance. Established in 1936, Consumers Union is chartered under the Not-for-Profit Corporation Law of the State of New York.

The purposes of Consumers Union, as stated in its charter, are to provide consumers with information and counsel on consumer goods and services, to give information on all matters relating to the expenditure of the family income, and to initiate and to cooperate with individual and group efforts seeking to create and maintain decent living standards.

Consumers Union derives its income solely from the sale of *Consumer Reports* and other publications. In addition, expenses of occasional public service efforts may be met, in part, by nonrestrictive, noncommercial contributions, grants, and fees. Consumers Union accepts no advertising or product samples and is not beholden in any way to any commercial interest. Its Ratings and reports are solely for the use of the readers of its publications. Neither the Ratings, nor the reports, nor any Consumers Union publication, including this book, may be used in advertising or for any commercial purpose. Consumers Union will take all steps open to it to prevent such uses of its material, its name, or the name of *Consumer Reports.*

CONTENTS

HOW TO USE THIS BOOK

Ratings of individual brands and models are based on Consumers Union (CU) laboratory tests, controlled-use tests, and expert judgments. Although the Ratings are not an infallible guide, they do offer comparative buying information that can greatly increase the likelihood that you will receive value for your money.

While you may be tempted to buy whatever brand appears at the top of the Ratings order, it is best to read the full product or appliance report. Then read the section that precedes the Ratings and the notes and footnotes. In those sections you will find the features, qualities, or deficiencies shared by the products in the test group.

The introduction to the Ratings tells you the basis on which the order of the Ratings was decided. When products are listed in order of estimated quality, CU judged the model listed first to be best, the next listed second best, and so on. Sometimes, when the differences among the products were judged to be small and of little practical significance, products are listed alphabetically or by price. In some cases, small differences appear in a subgroup of products within the Ratings. These subgroups are bracketed and also listed alphabetically or in price order. Each Ratings chart includes the month and year in which the test group was published in *Consumer Reports*.

Check-rated models (✓) are high in quality and appreciably superior to the other products tested. Best Buy Ratings are given to products that rate high and are also relatively low-priced.

Prices. The prices for cleaning products are what was paid, or an average of what was paid, in the store by CU shoppers. It's unusual for such products to carry "list" prices, which are established and published by the manufacturer. Therefore, the price you pay will almost certainly be different, possibly substantially different, from the Ratings' price.

Appliances generally carry list prices, although they are often a fiction that enables retailers to appear to be offering a bargain by advertising prices discounted from the "list." Even so, list prices are still a useful guide when you are comparing prices of competing models. Keep in mind, however, that most prices have changed since they were published in *Consumer Reports.*

Product and model changes. Manufacturers frequently change the packaging and formulations of disposable cleaning products. Perhaps the "new" version will be more eye-catching or smell better and compete better with its rivals.

You should take advantage of sales and specials as they occur in your neighborhood. (The savings on specials offered several miles away from where you usually shop may be offset by what it costs to get there.) When you encounter a sale, you often have to consider giving up some quality in favor of price. But you may find that the lesser product still suits your needs.

Cleaning appliances are marketed quite differently from disposable cleaning products. Manufacturers commonly introduce "new" models once a year, and sometimes even more frequently. The objectives are to match the competition; to boost sales by offering new styles, colors, or features; and sometimes to incorporate technological changes. As a practical matter, however, retailers carry over the older models until their inventories run out. It may take months, even years, for all of the old merchandise to disappear from warehouse stocks. This slow evolution tends to keep information about models in the Ratings useful for a considerable period.

On the other hand, the particular brand and model you select from the Ratings chart may be either out of stock or superseded by a later version when you try to buy it. The Ratings should still prove useful to help you decide what features and performance characteristics are the more important ones, and which are simply frivolous or may actually detract from a product's usefulness.

We hope *How to Clean Practically Anything* will steer you toward safe, practical, and inexpensive home cleaning products. Keep it handy, thumb through it, and use it as a reference to cope with stubborn cleaning problems and to help you choose products that work for you.

ORGANIZED CLEANING

Many people find that frequent, systematic light cleaning has advantages over periodic upheaval. For one thing, the concept of continuous processing applied to cleaning chores is far easier on household surfaces. It minimizes the need for scrubbing that causes unnecessary wear and tear on wall, floor, and furniture finishes. In addition, dust on wooden surfaces, as well as on upholstery, draperies, and so forth, may be easier to remove before it builds up and combines with other soil such as body oils and tiny airborne droplets of cooking grease. Frequent vacuuming will also minimize the need for professional cleaning. Some find it easier to do a chore or two a day rather than let tasks accumulate and become overwhelming.

PLANNING

Develop a list of all tasks that need to be done during the year and group them under frequency headings—daily, weekly, monthly, semiannually, and annually. It may be possible to budget your time so that weekly chores are spread out over several days. For householders with weekday responsibilities other than cleaning, house maintenance must be on a catch-as-catch-can basis. But even within limits of available time, it's a good idea to plan to accomplish household tasks on a regular schedule.

What you clean and how often you clean depend upon your personal preferences and tolerances. The following schedule is meant as a guideline to suggest how a home can be cleaned with well-defined tasks.

Divide responsibilities among all family members. Make certain that everyone knows who does what and when.

Daily. Dishes should be washed, dried, and put away, and kitchen counters wiped. Clean the kitchen sink and wipe the range surfaces (including the microwave oven) once a day or, even better, after each use. Picking up should become second nature.

Once a week. Dust furniture and shelves; vacuum and, where applicable, brush upholstered furniture. Vacuum rugs and floors. Clean under furniture and behind it. Damp mop the kitchen floor. Empty wastebaskets. Wash bathroom basins, fixtures, and floors. Dust radiators, woodwork, pictures, and mirrors. Wipe windowsills, and brush shades and blinds. Clean kitchen range burners. Wipe the refrigerator and kitchen cabinet fronts. Polish bright metal surfaces.

Monthly. Do one or more of the following special jobs in several rooms on the same day: vacuum and, where applicable, brush curtains and draperies. Wipe wood trim and, where needed, walls and around doorknobs. Wash windows. Wash and, if necessary, wax the kitchen floor. Polish wood furniture and vacuum upholstered furniture as necessary, paying special attention to cleaning under cushions and in crevices between the back and the cushion support. To prolong their life, turn over mattresses, end to end and side to side, which will help equalize their wear. In hot weather, clean air-conditioner filters according to the manufacturer's recommendations.

Seasonally or semiannually. Take inventory of the items in closets and drawers that are no longer useful. (The more clutter, the harder it is to clean.)

Rearrange clothes closets by season, hanging clothes by type for easy access. Weed out unused clothing that can be contributed to appropriate agencies. Pack winter and summer clothing where it will remain clean and free from moth damage until needed again. (Dry-cleaning establishments commonly offer free storage for items that are given to them for cleaning.)

Wash mattress covers. Wash curtains and draperies or have them dry cleaned. Dust the coils behind or underneath the refrigerator.

Annually. Have the furnace cleaned and tuned in late spring or early fall. A central air-conditioning system and room air conditioners should be checked for proper operation before the onset of hot weather. Shampoo rugs as needed, or have them cleaned professionally. Put power and hand gardening tools in good order—cleaned, oiled, and greased—before storing them for the winter. The same applies to snow removal equipment in the spring.

EQUIPMENT AND STORAGE

If everything is kept organized, it will be easier for you to work in the space and you won't waste time looking for something when you need it. If you live in a two- or three-story dwelling, it might be worth the investment of duplicating supplies, such as vacuum cleaners, so that you can have them on the same level where they are used. Keep special bathroom cleaning equipment and supplies in or near the bathroom, if space permits.

Keep cleaning equipment as clean and dry as possible, so that it's ready for the next use. Be sure that any enclosure where cleaning materials are stored has ventilation holes in the door to allow volatile materials to evaporate from cloths, sponges, and mops. Brooms and brushes should not rest on their bristles. Hang them to prevent premature wear, deformation, and loss of usefulness. Since cleaning products are often hazardous, make sure the shelves on which they are stored are high enough to be out of reach of young children.

Avoid cluttering a cleaning closet with rarely used supplies and equipment, but keep a supply of paper vacuum-cleaner dust bags on hand. Use the brand that is recommended for your particular vacuum; off-brand bags may not work well. You may also want to stock spare sponge-mop refills, as well as a package or two of hand sponges.

Good dust cloths can be made from cast-off soft cotton garments and bedding. (Although they are costlier to use, less effective than cloth, and harsh on some surfaces, some people find paper towels convenient.) Cloths will hold dust better if they are pretreated. A simple method is to put a cloth into a screw-cap glass jar that has been coated on the inside with furniture polish. Put about two teaspoons of liquid polish into a container and turn it until a thin layer of polish covers the inside surface. Let the cloth stand in the jar for a day or two.

ANOTHER SOLUTION

Housecleaning takes up time and effort. One obvious way to escape it, although the solution can be expensive, is to employ a qualified, reliable, and courteous home-cleaning service. Some people use a professional service once or twice a year; others employ a cleaning person once a week or every two weeks or so. If you decide to use professional help, ask for referrals from reliable neighbors and friends. If that fails, check the Yellow Pages under Housecleaning. Always ask for and check references.

DISHES

DISHWASHER DETERGENTS

Liquid dishwasher detergents may be convenient to use, but the first such products had two major drawbacks: The liquid was so thick that it could be squeezed out only with some difficulty; and the detergent that did make its way into the dishwasher didn't do a stellar job of cleaning.

The new "liquid gel" detergents taking over in the supermarkets seem to solve both problems.

The main difference between a liquid and a liquid gel is the substance used to thicken the product so it won't dribble out of the dishwasher's dispenser cup. Liquids are thickened with insoluble clays. The gels contain soluble agents that make them slippery enough to slide easily out of the bottle yet thick enough to stay in the dispenser.

The gels are respectable cleaners, some comparable with the best powders. Gels are easier to dispense than the liquids, so less detergent goes to waste.

COSTS

These products cost between 8 and 18 cents per washload, based on national average selling prices and a typical dose of four tablespoons. Store-brand powders tend to be the cheaper products to use. The liquids and gels tend to be the more expensive.

Cost-per-use figures for liquids and gels assume that you can squeeze all of the detergent out of the bottle. As a practical matter, both liquids and gels require some coaxing. Even when emptied by repeated squeezing and draining, the liquids' containers may still hold more than a cup of detergent—a fourth of the total contents. The gels retain no more than one third of a cup. You should be able to recover most of that if you let the bottle stand on its head.

Two powders that are not sold in stores deserve special mention because of their extraordinarily high cost. *Shaklee Basic-D* and *Amway Crystal Bright* cost 38 cents and 52 cents per four-tablespoon dose, respectively. Both products suggest using small amounts—four teaspoons for *Shaklee,* two tablespoons for *Amway.* But if you follow *Amway*'s suggestion, you'll see reduced performance and still pay 26 cents per wash—more than twice what you'd pay for a four-tablespoon dose of *Cascade* powder. And you can't stint on the *Shaklee* in hard water. The company recommends four tablespoons or more in hard water.

ENVIRONMENTAL EFFECTS

All dishwasher detergents contain phosphorus. Just as it enhances the cleaning ability of laundry detergents, phosphorus helps dishwasher detergents do their job better, especially in hard water. But phosphorus also poses an ecological concern because of its role in promoting the growth of algae in streams and lakes.

Over the years, manufacturers have tried to reduce the amount of phosphorus in dishwasher detergents, but they haven't been able to eliminate it altogether. So dishwasher detergents with phosphorus are tolerated even in areas where laundry detergents are required to be phosphorus-free.

As a rule, a four-tablespoon dose of dishwasher detergent contains about as much phosphorus as half a cup of phosphate laundry detergent.

The detergent containers themselves may pose another environmental problem. Most powders come in foil-covered cardboard boxes that could be hard to recycle. Liquids and gels come in jugs made of high-density polyethylene, one of the most widely recycled plastics. Many communities, however, still don't recycle plastic at all.

Ratings of Dishwasher Detergents

◉ ◓ ○ ◒ ●

Better ←——→ **Worse**

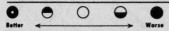

Listed by types; within types, listed in order of overall cleaning ability. As published in a **February 1992** report.

Price. The estimated average, usually for a 50-ounce container, based on prices paid nationally. A * denotes the price paid (a national average price wasn't available).

Cost per use. A calculation, based on the package price and a measured dose of four tablespoons of detergent.

Phosphorus. The **percentage** comes from product labels; **grams per use** is a calculation. Phosphorus can enhance a detergent's performance by softening water, dispersing dirt, and emulsifying greasy soil. Phosphorus also contributes to the growth of algae in streams and lakes. The amount of phosphorus in a four-tablespoon dose of a typical dishwasher detergent is about the same as that in one-half cup of a phosphate laundry detergent.

Cleaning. Each product was used to wash full loads in four identical dishwashers, using hard water and plates purposely coated with a tenacious soil of hominy grits and milk. Three key areas of performance were tested: **Dishes** scores show how well each product removed the dried hominy grits from glass plates. None of the products removed all the dried-on grits all the time; but the best cleaned the dishes completely about half the time. **Glass film** and **glass spots** scores show how well the products prevented hard-water minerals and soil from the wash water from leaving spots and overall haze on drinking glasses, in repeated washings.

Features in Common

Except as noted, all: • Powders come in cardboard container. • Liquids and gels come in plastic jug with childproof cap.

Key to Comments

A–Container has flip-top cap; not childproof.
B–Much less effective when used at lower dose, as suggested on label.
C–Damaged metallic decoration on china more than most.
D–Came in wide-mouth plastic container with screw cap.
E–Childproof cap fairly hard to open.
F–**Shaklee** purchased in 47-oz. container; **Amway,** in 48-oz.; **Palmolive** gels, in 65-oz. size.

Product	Price	Cost per use	Phosphorus: Percentage	Phosphorus: Grams per use	Cleaning: Dishes	Cleaning: Glasses, film	Cleaning: Glasses, spots	Comments
Powdered and liquid detergents								
✓Cascade	$2.79	12¢	8.1	5	◉	◉	◉	—
Lemon Cascade	2.81	14	8.1	6	◉	◉	○	—
Electrasol	2.20	11	7.1	5	◓	◉	◓	—
Kroger Bright	1.91	8	8.7	5	◉	◓	◓	—
Shaklee Basic-D	9.00*	38	8.7	5	◉	◓	◉	B,C,F
A&P Liquid	2.20	14	5.9	5	◓	◉	○	A
All	2.16	9	6.1	4	◓	◓	◉	—
Sunlight Lemon	2.82	11	6.1	3	◓	◓	◉	—
White Magic Lemon	2.47	11	8.7	5	◉	○	○	—
Albertson's Lemon	1.99	8	8.3	5	◓	◓	◓	—

Product	Price	Cost per use	Phosphorus		Cleaning			Comments
			Percentage	Grams per use	Dishes	Glasses, film	Glasses, spots	
Powdered and liquid detergents								
Top Crest	2.15	10	8.7	6	◓	◓	◓	—
Amway Crystal Bright	9.20*	52	8.7	7	●	●	◒	D,F
White Magic	2.42	11	8.7	5	◓	○	◓	—
A&P	1.93	9	8.7	6	○	○	◓	—
A&P Liquid Lemon	2.32	15	5.9	5	○	◓	◒	A
A&P Lemon	1.89	9	8.7	6	○	◒	○	—
Gel detergents								
Palmolive Liquid Gel Lemon	2.70*	17	5.8	5	●	●	●	A,F
Palmolive Liquid Gel	2.70*	17	5.8	5	◓	●	●	A,F
Cascade LiquiGel	2.80*	18	4.2	4	◓	●	○	E
Cascade LiquiGel Lemon	2.80*	18	4.2	4	◓	◓	○	E

DISHWASHERS

Most dishwashers offer some variation on the basic wash-rinse-dry. A dishwasher's Normal or Regular cycle typically includes two washes interspersed with two or three rinses. A Heavy cycle can entail longer wash periods, a third wash, hotter water, or all of the above. A Light cycle usually includes just one wash.

These basic cycles are probably all that is needed. Additional washing and drying options abound, necessary or not.

The common Rinse and Hold option can be useful for small families. Instead of stacking dirty dishes in the sink or the dishwasher, you can gradually accumulate a full load, rinsing the dishes as you go.

Don't expect a machine that offers a Pots-and-Pans cycle to do the work that requires abrasive cleaners and elbow grease. And think twice before subjecting good crystal or china—especially sets with gold trim—to a dishwasher's China/Crystal setting. The harsh detergents and possible jostling could etch or otherwise damage fine china.

WASHING AND DRYING

Fancy electronic controls don't necessarily translate into better cleaning. Most machines, electronic or not, work pretty well overall. Most machines also use their water-heating element to dry the dishes; some have a blower or a separate duct-mounted heater. Whatever the method, your machine should do an excellent job of drying china and glasses. Drying flatware is a bit more demanding for some.

No-heat air drying, which works on evaporation and heat retained from the wash, produces reasonably dry dishes provided you can wait a few hours. You may be able to speed up drying by propping open the door.

ENERGY AND NOISE

If you don't rinse dishes before you load—and you needn't—a dishwasher actually uses no more water than hand-washing in a dishpan; in fact, a dishwasher uses less water than you would if you washed dishes under a running faucet. The machines themselves use a small amount of electricity, consuming between 0.6 and 1.1 kilowatt-hours of electricity when supplied with 140° water, which works out to between 4½ and 8½ cents of electricity at average power rates. No-heat drying saves a penny or two.

Heating water to feed the dishwasher accounts for the bulk of its energy costs. An electric water heater will consume about 18 cents of electricity to provide the 11 gallons of 140° water typically used for one load; the total comes to about $90 a year, assuming you run the dishwasher once a day. The hot-water cost for a gas- or oil-fired heater will be about 6 cents a load, or a total of about $45 a year. Setting the water heater's thermostat to 120° should cut those totals by a few dollars a year. Using cooler water will cut the household's overall hot-water costs by about $11 to $32 a year.

Quiet operation has become a dishwasher's main selling point, second only to washing performance and durability. Dishwashers have become quieter over the years.

SAFETY

If you should open a dishwasher in mid-cycle—to add a forgotten plate, perhaps—don't worry about getting splashed. All models have a safety interlock that will turn off the power when the door is opened, and most have latches that prevent you from opening the door too quickly. Ail models have a float switch, which senses accidental overfilling and also cuts power. Some models with electronic controls go even further. If they overfill, they automatically drain themselves and display a warning signal.

Many dishwasher accidents involve people cutting themselves, usually on knives or forks as they reach over a flatware basket into the machine's dish rack. It's always a good idea to load flatware with their points down. In addition, a machine's heating element can inflict a serious burn. Make sure that the appliance has cooled before you reach into the bottom of the tub to clean a filter or retrieve an item that has dropped.

Door vents, often at a toddler's eye level, can emit steam, so keep children away while the dishwasher is running. Some electronic models have a hidden touchpad that locks the controls to discourage children from playing with them—a worthwhile feature.

DISHWASHER RELIABILITY

The Repair Index below, based on more than 154,000 responses to Consumers Union's 1991 Annual Questionnaire, shows the percentage of

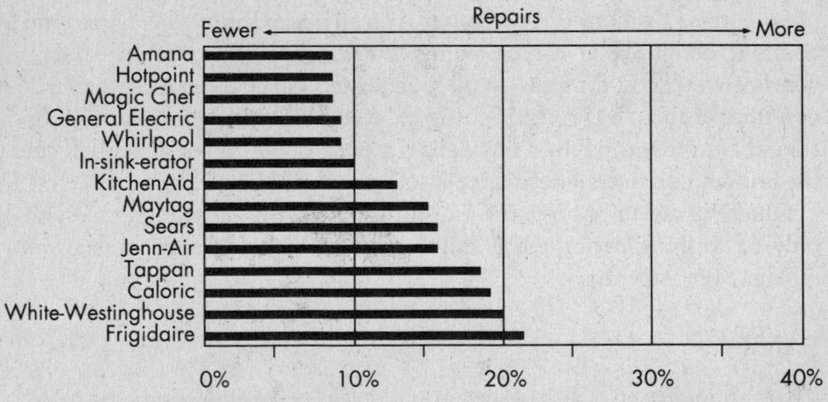

As published in the *Consumer Reports 1993 Buying Guide Issue.*

under-the-counter dishwashers purchased new between 1986 and 1991 that have ever needed repair.

Brands with the shortest bars have been the most reliable. Differences of three or more percentage points are meaningful.

The oldest machines in the survey were, as a rule, increasingly more likely to have needed repairs than the newest, and machines used more frequently were also more likely to have needed repairs. Consequently, the data have been adjusted to eliminate differences among brands due solely to age and how much the dishwashers were used.

Note that the index includes all models of a given brand, not just models tested by CU. In addition, the data deal with past performance and cannot anticipate design and manufacturing changes companies may make in the future. However, the data have been consistent enough over the years, so your chances of buying a trouble-free dishwasher are increased if you choose a brand that's been reliable in the past.

Check *Consumer Reports* for a Ratings report on dishwashers, scheduled for publication in the August 1993 issue.

HAND DISHWASHING LIQUIDS

Dishwashing liquid works well for those items that cannot be subjected to the stresses of a dishwasher—fine crystal, overglazed china, and other tableware that could be damaged by the harsh chemicals found in dishwasher detergents. Many people use dishwashing liquid outside the kitchen as well, where it excels at washing fine fabrics and even the family car.

The foam and suds in dishwater provide physical evidence of a detergent at work. When they subside, the cleaning potential of the detergent has been exhausted. The depletion of suds tells you that it's time to add more detergent. In laboratory tests done by Consumers Union, the depletion of suds was considered an indicator of which dishwashing liquids were effective the longest.

Ratings of Hand Dishwashing Liquids

Listed in order of increasing calculated real cost. As published in a **September 1991** report.

Product. We bought national and store brands. Most are color-tinted; some were tested in as many as three different tints, but color had no bearing on effectiveness, we judged.

Price. The average price paid for 32-ounce bottles (or the closest to that size).

Usage factor. The number was derived by testing and statistical analysis to determine how much grease and flour could be added to sudsy water before the suds went away. The lower the factor, the less detergent needed to wash a load of dishes.

Real cost. Average price per quart multiplied by the usage factor. If you know a product's usage factor, you can calculate its real cost yourself. Just multiply the selling price by the usage factor.

Product	Price	Usage factor	Real cost
Kroger	$1.35	1.0	$1.35
Sunlight	1.82	1.0	1.82
Ajax	1.86	1.0	1.86
A&P	1.42	1.4	1.99
Pathmark	1.49	1.4	2.09
White Magic	2.29	1.0	2.29
Dove	1.69	1.4	2.37
Sweetheart	1.16	2.1	2.44
Crystal White Octagon	1.22 [1]	2.1	2.55
Palmolive	2.56	1.0	2.56
Dawn	2.70	1.0	2.70
Dermassage	1.49	2.1	3.13
Joy	2.26	1.4	3.16
Ivory	2.46	1.4	3.44
Lux	1.73 [2]	2.1	3.63
Cost Cutter (Kroger)	.78	4.7	3.67
No-Frills (Pathmark)	.79	4.7	3.71
Amway Dish Drops	6.80	0.8	5.44

[1] *Price calculated from 40-oz. size.*
[2] *Price calculated from 22-oz. size.*

The testers put a measured amount of detergent into a bowl of moderately hard water, warmed it to 120°F, and stirred it into a foam. Then they added pellets of fat and flour until the suds stopped forming, an indication that the detergent had run out of cleaning power.

The strongest, most concentrated products could cope with six to eight pellets before becoming exhausted. The weakest liquids were largely spent after absorbing just a single pellet.

A statistical analysis of these tests assigned a numerical value to each level of strength—the "usage factor." Nearly all the strongest cleaners had a usage factor of 1.0. Less effective detergents had a higher factor. If a teaspoon of one of the strongest cleaners was necessary to wash a certain number of dishes, 1.4 to 4.7 teaspoons of the other detergents would be required to do the same.

But strength alone is not the full measure of a detergent. When you multiply a liquid's usage factor by its price, you can determine the product's real cost—what you actually pay for a given amount of cleaning power.

RECOMMENDATIONS

The strongest dishwashing liquids are often the most economical, but not always. You can get the best use of them by measuring small amounts (less than a teaspoonful at a time) into a dishpan and washing until the suds are almost gone. If you squirt an overdose of detergent into the dishpan or directly onto a sponge or the plates before scrubbing, you're apt to use far more than necessary.

Using any of these products will have only a minor effect on the environment. The detergents themselves are largely biodegradable and contain no phosphates. Of course, if you buy a product with a low usage factor, you'll send fewer empty bottles to a landfill.

FLOORS

CARPET CLEANING

Typical supermarket carpet-cleaning products include powders, foam shampoos that come in a pressurized can, and liquids sprayed straight from the container. A few concentrated products—powder or liquid—must be mixed with water, an extra step.

Most manufacturers recommend that you scrub the cleaner into the carpet with a brush and remove the residue with a regular vacuum cleaner (liquids, of course, need time to dry first).

Manual carpet cleaning isn't as unpleasant as it might sound. The powders minimize the mess, and the job goes quickly. The powders are dry, so the room can be used immediately afterward. (Actually, "dry" powders are moist, but they're drier than liquids and foams.)

Stains are likely to be a problem for supermarket carpet-cleaning products. None were better than fair in treating any of the test stains.

CLEANING WITH A MACHINE

Machines are usually sold or rented with a recommended cleaning product. The majority of machines are steamers (the "steam" is a hot detergent solution that the machine sprays on the rug). Steamers not only apply the solution but also use suction to remove it. They require water, however, which complicates matters, and they aren't all that convenient to use.

Some steamers get their water supply via a long hose that you attach to a hot-water faucet. As you clean, the hose is dragged along. In other models, you fill a reservoir with hot water. With both kinds, you will eventually need to pour out the dirty water, which is collected either in the base of the machine or in a removable container. When full, the part you empty can weigh as much as 46 pounds.

With any machine that uses water, or with any wet cleaner you scrub yourself, you must wait for the carpet to dry, which can take at least overnight. There's also a risk of wetting the carpet too much. Water can seep through and damage a hardwood floor or the jute backing on an old rug (it won't hurt the polyolefin backing of most new rugs).

Instead of water and detergent, some machines use powder. They may apply the powder, scrub it in, and use suction to remove it, or they may merely apply the powder and provide agitation. You then use your own vacuum cleaner to clean it up. Follow the manufacturer's recommendations regarding the length of time to leave the powder on the carpet.

Rented machines are likely to be larger than those sold to homeowners, which can pose transportation problems if you don't have access to a vehicle with adequate cargo space.

PROFESSIONAL CLEANING

If you take a 9 × 12-foot rug to a professional cleaner, expect to pay at least $40 or $50 and wait a week or two for your rug's return. For an extra $15 or $20, some cleaning companies will pick up and drop off a rug.

If you call a service that comes to your home, try to arrange a definite appointment or you might have to wait at home all day.

The ideal sequence of events would be for the cleaning service to visit the home to carefully evaluate the carpet's condition before rendering an estimate, but this often does not happen. Some cleaning services will provide a preliminary price pending closer inspection in the home. This is perfectly acceptable if the cleaners do a careful inspection and requote (if necessary) before cleaning begins.

The cleaning service should discuss its procedures in detail. Depending on the carpet's condition, it may not be possible to clean the carpet completely. The company should inform the customer if its cleaners will not be able to remove a stain without damage. There shouldn't be any surprises.

Ratings of Carpet Cleaners

◉ Better ◓ ○ ◒ ● Worse

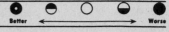

Listed by types; within types, listed in order of ability to remove ground-in dirt from white nylon carpeting. Products judged equally effective are bracketed and listed alphabetically. As published in a **January 1991** report.

Brand and model. Includes carpet-cleaning machines, purchased and rented, and chemicals you apply by hand, scrub in, and vacuum up with a conventional vacuum cleaner. Machines generally come with a recommended chemical.

Type. **SM**=a steamer machine. Most clean with a detergent; the *Vax* and *Carpet Magic CM-3H* use a cleaner and defoamer, which you have to mix. **PM**=a machine that uses moist powder. **P**=powder; no machine needed. **F**=foam. **LS**=liquid spray. **C**=concentrated powder or liquid.

Brand and model	Type	Price: machine/chemical	Size, oz.	Coverage, sq. ft.	Dirt removal
Machines					
Host H Type AV-1A (rental, with Host chemical)	PM	$10 day/$17	232	432	◉
Sears 87781 (with Capture chemical)	PM	200/19	64	—	◓
Vax 121/2	SM	400/6	35	—	○
Bissell 1631	SM	190/11	64	—	◒
Bissell 1640-4	SM	110/11	64	—	◒
Genie SH600	SM	140/5	32	—	◒
Regina ES278	SM	85/7	15	—	◒
Regina S-300	SM	99/7	15	—	◒
Sears 85792	SM	200/5	32	—	◒
Shop-Vac 700C	SM	140/4	5½	—	◒
Carpet Magic CM-3H (rental)	SM	18 day/10	32	—	●
Eureka 2820 Type A	SM	200/5	32	—	●
Genie SH859	SM	170/5	32	—	●
Chemicals					
Host Dry Carpet Cleaner	P	—/17	232	432	◓
Capture Dry Powder Cleaner	P	—/19	64	—	○
Amway Magic Foam Carpet Cleaner	F	—/7	21	140	◒
Amway Rug and Upholstery Shampoo #E-822	C	—/7	32	—	◒
Fuller #99621 Kit	C	—/25	34	—	◒
Glamorene Spray 'N Vac	F	—/4	24	108	◒
Lestoil Deodorizing Rug Cleaner	F	—/3	19	108	◒
Resolve Carpet Cleaner	LS	—/4	22	100	◒
Turtle Wax Carpet Cleaner	F	—/2	16	80	◒
Woolite Deep Cleaning Rug Cleaner	F	—/4	22	140	◒
Woolite Self Cleaning Carpet Cleaner	F	—/4	22	240	◒
Carbona 1-Hour Rug Cleaner	F	—/3	24	140	●
Formula 10 Concentrated	C	—/6	6	240	●
Johnson Glory Unscented	F	—/4	22	100	●
K-Mart Carpet Cleaner	F	—/3	22	140	●

Price. Machine prices are list. Cost per day is given for rented machines. Cleaning-agent prices are the average paid for the size listed.

Size. Of purchased chemical.

Coverage. Based on manufacturer's statement, when available.

Dirt removal. The basis of the Ratings order. With stains, professional carpet-cleaning firms were far more successful than these products. Spot-cleaning with home brews also did the trick.

Filled weight. You usually lift the bottom of the machine to dispose of dirty water, but some machines (see Comments) have a removable tank. Filled weight refers to the part you must lift.

Dirty-water capacity. To nearest half-gallon. The smaller the capacity, the more often you have to empty the container; the larger, the harder it is to lift.

Noise. The quietest machines sounded like a good vacuum cleaner.

Kool-Aid	Coffee	Tea	Red wine	Motor oil	French dressing	Spaghetti sauce	Filled weight	Dirty-water capacity	Noise	Comments
◒	◒	○	○	◓	◒	○	—	—	◉	A,C,I,S,U
◒	◒	◒	◒	◒	◒	◒	—	—	○	A,C,I,S,U,BB
◒	●	●	○	◒	◒	◓	13 lb.	1 gal.	◉	B,G,I,P,T
◒	◒	◒	◓	◒	◒	○	19	1½	○	C,S,U,Y
◒	◒	◒	○	◒	◒	○	29	3	●	E,S,Y
●	●	●	◒	●	●	◒	42	4½	●	F,H,I,V,Y,BB
◒	◒	◒	○	●	◒	◒	7	½	○	A,B,C,D,L,N,Q,S,U
◒	●	◒	◒	●	◒	○	7	½	○	A,B,C,D,K,N,Q,S,U
●	●	●	○	◒	◒	○	20	2	○	B,J,L,N,V
◒	●	●	○	○	◒	◒	46	5	●	F,H,Y
●	●	●	●	◓	◓	○	32	3	◉	B,F,M,O,R,U
◒	●	●	◒	●	●	●	42	4½	◉	H,I,Y
◒	●	◒	◒	◒	●	◒	26	2½	○	G,H,I,Y,BB
●	●	●	●	◒	●	◒	—	—	—	—
◒	●	●	●	●	●	●	—	—	—	AA
●	●	◒	●	◒	◒	◒	—	—	—	—
◒	◒	○	○	◒	◒	◒	—	—	—	—
●	●	●	◒	◒	◒	◒	—	—	—	Z
◒	●	●	●	●	●	●	—	—	—	W
●	●	●	●	●	●	●	—	—	—	W
◒	●	●	◒	●	◒	◒	—	—	—	—
●	●	●	●	●	●	●	—	—	—	—
●	●	●	●	●	●	●	—	—	—	—
●	●	●	●	●	●	●	—	—	—	X
●	●	●	●	◒	●	●	—	—	—	W
◒	◒	◒	○	◒	◒	◒	—	—	—	—
●	●	●	●	●	●	●	—	—	—	W
●	●	●	◒	●	●	◒	—	—	—	W

Features in Common

Except as noted, all machines: • Are canister-style. • Have an 8- to 8½-foot suction hose. • Have a 17- to 18-foot power cord. • Have one speed. • Have a nonremovable container to collect dirty water. • Can also be used as a wet or dry vacuum cleaner. • Can be used to clean upholstery.

Except as noted, all cleaning-agent manufacturers: • Recommend scrubbing.

Key to Comments

A–Upright design.
B–Water reservoir, no hose; must be filled.
C–Easier to maneuver than most.
D–Easier to assemble than most.
E–Unwieldy base; judged likely to spill.
F–Has 7-foot suction hose.
G–Has 6- to 6½-foot suction hose.
H–Suction hose attachment may come apart.
I–Power cord at least 20 feet long.
J–Power cord interferes with disassembly.
K–Has 3 speed settings.
L–Has 2 speed settings.
M–Difficult to distinguish Off setting.
N–Has removable container with handle.
O–Has removable container without handle.
P–Must remove 2 pieces of machine to empty container.
Q–Removable container extremely difficult to empty completely.
R–Can be used to vacuum wet areas, not dry.
S–Cannot be used as vacuum cleaner.
T–Vacuum nozzle beater bar helps loosen dirt.
U–Cannot be used to clean upholstery.
V–Upholstery-cleaning part sold separately.
W–Manufacturer says scrub for heavy soil only.
X–Manufacturer doesn't recommend scrubbing.
Y–Faucet connection; 50-foot hose.
Z–Kit includes several products—only carpet shampoo tested.
AA–Product is identical to **Amway Easy Magic Dry Powder Carpet Cleaner.**
BB–Although this model has been discontinued and is no longer available, the information has been retained to permit comparisons.

Ask the company what it will do if its cleaners damage the carpet, and ascertain how they will protect adjacent furniture. Be sure to check references to determine if the cleaning service adheres to these precautions during the job.

RECOMMENDATIONS

Whether you do the work yourself or hire professionals, be sure to clean your carpet before it becomes very soiled. Many products should be able to handle a lightly soiled carpet. Ground-in dirt is much more difficult to remove.

In general, when a rug has been soiled by garden-variety dirt, it's better to send it out to professionals or to call in a professional cleaning service.

Stains need special attention. You might have some luck with a home brew Consumers Union tried (see First Aid for Carpet Stains, below).

FIRST AID FOR CARPET STAINS

Wherever possible, blot up spills immediately using a *clean white* absorbent material to avoid the possibility of dye transfer and to facilitate visualization of the stain removal process, since stains transfer to the towel. With some spilled substances—children's fruit drinks, for instance—you have only minutes before the stain sets permanently.

If a spot has remained on the carpet for a long time and has become a dry mass, scrape off as much as possible using the side of a spoon or a *blunt* spatula before attempting to remove the remainder. For chewing gum or wax, freeze with an ice cube before scraping.

Before attempting any stain removal, always pretest *with each of the cleaning agents.* To do this, dampen an inconspicuous area of the carpet—in the corner of a closet, for example—with the chemical, leave it on for about 10 minutes, and then blot with a clean white towel. Inspect the towel for dye transfer and the carpet for damage. If bleeding, color change, or other damage occurs, consult a cleaning expert.

Have on hand an oil solvent (see Selected Glossary in the Stain Removal Chart for Fabrics, page 206) for greasy, oily stains. But be careful about using a solvent-based cleaner on a rug that has a plastic or rubber foam backing or separate padding. The solvent could soften such materials and ruin them. Be careful, too, about inhaling vapors from these solvents. Use them in a well-ventilated room.

Stain removal often requires several steps. Proceed through the following series of cleaning steps (one at a time) until the stain is completely removed. There is no need to use all the steps if the stain comes out early in the process.

When using an absorbent powder (cornstarch or a commercial product), sprinkle a thick layer of it over the stain. Brush in the resulting "mud," let it dry completely, then vacuum. Use a detergent solution (one teaspoon dishwashing liquid to one cup of water) for water-soluble spills. Follow, if necessary, with one tablespoon of ammonia to half a cup of water. As a last effort, use one part white vinegar to two parts water. Apply these solutions directly on the carpet. Do not overwet.

For spills that are both greasy and water-soluble, apply small amounts of a dry-cleaning solvent with a clean white absorbent towel and blot or tap (do not scrub). Work from the outer edge of the stain to the center to avoid spreading it. Then use the detergent solution. Do the same for unidentified spills. Reapply each agent until the stain is no longer transferred to the towel. Rinse lightly.

Blot (don't rub) or scrape up as much as possible. Then cover the spill with a pad of several paper towels and stand on the towels for a minute or so. When the stain has been removed, lightly rinse the area with water (do not soak). Cover the wet spot with several layers of clean white toweling or a half-inch pad of paper towels, weight it down, and allow to dry for at least six hours.

For stains with an offensive odor such as pet urine, use the vinegar solution first. Then use the detergent solution. For acidic stains such as vomit or fruit drinks, use the ammonia mixture to neutralize the acid (but don't use ammonia on wool; it sets stains on that material).

Soda water can be effective on water-soluble stains, especially if the stains are fresh.

Copious spills that penetrate through the carpet to the backing and even to the floor are a special problem. If the substance is one that smells, you may have to get the carpet lifted and cleaned professionally.

If none of the recommended steps work, which we found to be a real possibility, you might wish to enlist the services of an expert. Be aware that do-it-yourself cleaning efforts might render the stain difficult for even an expert to remove. On a nasty stain especially, consider hiring professional carpet cleaners rather than attempting to do the job yourself. Just blot it up and get help.

Household products that contain bleach, hydrogen peroxide, or some other oxidizing agent can cause irreversible damage. A leaking container of laundry bleach is an obvious villain. Other products are more insidious. The damage caused by acne medications containing benzoyl peroxide, for instance, often doesn't show up right away. Those medications, typically hard to wash off hands, have ruined many a carpet. Other products to watch out for include swimming pool chemicals, mildew removers, liquid plant foods, and pesticides.

FLOOR POLISHERS

"Self-polishing" floor wax may meet some people's standards all year round on floors that can take—and need—a water-based polish. As a once-

or twice-a-year proposition, wood floors can be polished with a rented machine or a service company can be called in.

If you take pride in near-perfect floors and want to keep them buffed to a mirror sheen, you should have a machine of your own. You should have little trouble buying one that works well enough at polishing bare floors or hard-surface floor coverings. Differences are more likely to be in convenience features than in performance.

SHAMPOOING AND SCRUBBING

Floor polisher attachments can work quite well for wet shampooing rugs, but their use may entail some risk of damage to the rug from the abrasive action of the brushes. Therefore, you should always try shampooing a small inconspicuous area of rug or carpet first to find out whether the rug can withstand the machine. Better still, rent one for a trial run. As well as checking for damage, see whether you're satisfied with the shampooing process: You may find the technique difficult—and the results may not satisfy you. Also check how easily the machine can be converted from polisher to shampooer and back.

If shampooing sounds like trouble, remember that rugs may not require shampooing very often. When they do, if you can take them up easily enough, they may be sent out for cleaning. Alternatively, a commercial rug-cleaning firm can shampoo them in place. (See section on carpet cleaning, page 10.)

A floor-polishing machine, with or without special attachments, can be used for wet scrubbing on hard-surfaced floors. It can be a real boon on extremely dirty floors—much better than hand scrubbing or wet mopping. Damp mopping is easier and quicker for tidying up a slightly dirty floor.

A machine with vacuuming action offers a special advantage: It can suck up the dirty water, thereby eliminating tedious mop-up. Don't be surprised if the holes in the water-pickup entrance of these machines become blocked by particles of dirt. You can minimize this problem by sweeping or vacuuming the floor before you scrub. Dirty water may also continue to drip from the machine even after you have emptied it, and even a little water on a polishing pad or brush can smear a newly waxed surface. To help prevent this, be sure the machine has dried before you use it for polishing.

WAXING

Two-brush models, the most common type, tend to leave a narrow strip of less-polished floor in the space between the brushes. To get reasonably even polishing, you have to push the machine through overlapping strokes.

Most machines have dispensers for wax and sudsy water. Nevertheless, it's easier and probably more effective to spread wax—liquid or paste—with an applicator and use your machine only for polishing and buffing.

RECOMMENDATIONS

Price is not a guide to effectiveness, since even a cheap polisher will do the job. As you move up the price ladder you get more accessories and more features (more than one speed, for example). Whether these items are needed is best left up to the individual buyer, based on his or her needs and preferences.

FLOOR POLISHES

No-wax resilient flooring promises liberation from the nuisance of periodic polishing, particularly important for people who insist on shiny floors in their homes. Judging by the popularity of no-wax flooring—much of which is relentlessly shiny—consumers are glad to avoid the polishing chore.

But as more and more no-wax floors were installed in kitchens, companies found out from consumers that no-wax floors weren't shiny enough to suit some people, and there were complaints about dirt building up on such floors. People were using regular polish on no-wax floors. A new product category emerged from the dissatisfaction: a combination cleaner and polish formulated for use on no-wax floor coverings.

COMBINATION PRODUCTS

If you have new no-wax flooring, you don't need to use a polish—even for cleaning. If you have very shiny, polyurethane-finished wood floors, a polish won't make any real difference in appearance. But on no-wax vinyl-surfaced floors, whose shine is a bit less glaring, a polish can add a touch of gloss.

If you have a new vinyl no-wax floor and feel compelled to use a polish, you won't be doing anything but boosting the shine. The amount of protection offered by a thin film of polish is insignificant compared with the protection offered by a layer of vinyl on the flooring.

Still, even rugged plastics such as polyurethane and vinyl can get scratched and worn over time. It is also reasonable to assume that an accumulation of tiny scratches will eventually dull no-wax flooring a little. Polishes do have some ability to fill in tiny scratches, which would tend to improve the shine of worn areas. Until a no-wax floor is worn, however, floor polish is a waste of money. You'd be better off saving that money to make up for the extra cost of the no-wax flooring.

Although no-wax floors resist dirt well, they still get dirty. Should you buy a one-step, wash-and-wax product that "cleans as it shines," simply as a way to clean your no-wax floor? Products for no-wax floors are usually labeled as "self-cleaning"—that is, a new coat of polish wholly or partly dissolves the previous layer, and dirt is picked up on the mop along with the excess polish. Products sold for no-wax floors are excellent at cleaning if the floor isn't terribly dirty to begin with, particularly if you damp mop once a week.

WAXING FLOORS THAT NEED IT

While no-wax flooring has a smooth, sealed surface, the surface of older vinyl composition tiles and other plain resilient flooring is relatively rough and porous. On such floors, polish keeps a floor cleaner and shinier partly by sealing the surface.

Polishes for resilient flooring are water-based emulsions that impart more of a satin luster than a mirror finish to a dull surface like that of resilient tiles. No product is likely to keep resilient tiles pristine. Like a polish

Maintaining Wood Floors

A lot of people have ripped up their carpets, rented floor sanders, and now have hardwood floors graced with area rugs. But there's been no resurgence in the sale of wood-floor waxes. Most people who redo wood floors make them into no-wax wood floors by giving them several coats of polyurethane varnish. The polyurethane finish requires nearly as little maintenance as a no-wax resilient flooring—vacuuming or dusting and maybe a refinishing every few years.

Because water can damage and discolor wood, wood-floor waxes are formulated with a petroleum solvent. Consequently, they are much more noxious substances than water-based polishes and should be used with good ventilation. (A few water-based polishes claim to be usable on wood floors, too, but it's not worth the risk: If the finish has been breached for any reason, the wood could be damaged by the water.)

Buffing waxes must be buffed after they have dried. Doing this by hand is theoretically possible, but using a machine is easier. A one-step wood wax that requires no buffing is likely to be noticeably duller and look dirtier than a buffing wax after it's been on the floor for a while.

So if you are willing to go to the trouble of moving the furniture to wax a wood floor, you might as well do it right, which means using a little extra effort and a buffing wax.

A wax with a coloring agent should be used only on very dark floors—those the color of end-grain walnut or rosewood. Otherwise, wax applied after some use can make scratches stand out because the wax is darker than the wood.

for no-wax flooring, a product intended for regular flooring is usually resistant to water and vulnerable to alcoholic beverage spills.

Polishes that aren't good at self-cleaning require a clean floor before they're applied—otherwise, you encase the dirt and old polish in plastic.

Long ago, when floor waxes were really waxes, they required buffing in order to develop any shine at all. Then self-polishing floor waxes came along. They were the waxes that dried to a satin luster without buffing. Today, self-polishing floor polishes may still have real wax in them, but more often they are principally vinyl, acrylic, or some other plastic that dries to a shinier finish. The new formulations are better than the old waxes in one important respect: They are less slippery.

A few products say that you can use them diluted to restore shine in between full-strength applications. The diluted polishes do add some shine, but not as much as a full-strength polish would. Diluted polishes remove some dirt, but not as effectively as using them at full strength. These products are useful as damp-mopping aids only if the floor is slightly dirty or dull.

REMOVING OLD WAX

Technology has produced polishes that don't need buffing but has been less successful in eliminating the chore of stripping off old polish as the layers build up. Even polishes labeled as self-cleaning leave a small amount of old polish behind. The problem is usually most noticeable in corners, where the polish isn't worn away by traffic. While you may be content to let the layers of wax accumulate for a long time before trying to remove them, floor polish instructions generally say that "for best results" you should strip the polish after every five or six coats, or once or twice a year.

The typical recipe for removing old floor wax is one half cup of powdered floor cleaner and two cups of ammonia in a gallon of cool water, some fine steel wool, and a lot of elbow grease. There are also wax removers on the market, which are often recommended on the labels of their brand-mate floor polishes.

RECOMMENDATIONS

For taking care of new or fairly new no-wax floors, use a plain damp mop or a little detergent and a rinse. When the floor is so worn that it looks as if it really needs a polish, choose among the no-wax products by their price.

Hard-Surface Floor First Aid for Stains from Spills

When using any household chemicals, handle them with care and store them out of the reach of children. Never mix chemicals with each other or with household cleaning products unless there are specific directions to do so. Wear rubber gloves when working with alcohol, hydrogen peroxide solution, household ammonia, acids, or chlorine bleach. To be on the safe side, it's a good idea to work in a well-ventilated room: Establish cross ventilation with open windows and doors and a window fan to exhaust air.

Before using any chemical, test it on a small corner of the stain. If your procedure is wrong, the chemical damage will be limited to that one area. If you use steel wool on a stain, use grade 00 and rub gently. On wood, rub with the grain.

After you have tried ordinary liquid detergent (dishwashing liquid or laundry liquid) and water applied with a rag or sponge—or an all-purpose liquid cleaner sprayed from its container—try these suggestions to remove a variety of potentially stubborn stains. Whenever possible, work on a wet stain before it has had a chance to soak in and/or dry.

Alcoholic beverages. Try rubbing with a clean cloth dampened with rubbing alcohol.

Blood. Try clear, cold water first (before any detergent). If the stain remains, use caution in applying a solution of ammonia and cold water—and rinse quickly to avoid discoloration.

Candle wax or chewing gum. Use ice cubes to chill the material to brittleness. Then, using a plastic spatula, carefully scrape the wax or gum from the floor.

Cigarette burn. For heavy stains, try scouring powder and a piece of steel wool or a plastic scouring pad dipped in water. For hard-surface floors, rub with a cloth dampened with a solution of lemon juice and water.

Coffee or fruit juice. Saturate a cloth with a solution of one part glycerine to three parts water and place it over the stain for several hours. (Glycerine is available in drugstores.) If the spot remains, rub it gently with scouring powder and a cloth dampened in hot water.

Dyes. Rub with a cloth dampened in a solution of one part chlorine bleach and two parts water. If this doesn't work, try scouring powder and a cloth dampened with hot water.

Grease and oil. Remove as much as possible with newspaper, paper towels, or a plastic spatula. On resilient tile, rub with a cloth dampened in liquid detergent and warm water (or an all-purpose cleaner). On wood and cork, place a cloth saturated with dry-cleaning fluid on the stain for no more than five minutes. Then wipe the area dry and wash with detergent and water.

Ink. Try a commercial ink remover, following instructions carefully, or rubbing alcohol.

Lipstick. Try steel wool wet with detergent and water. If the floor is hard surfaced or has a no-wax finish, or is embossed vinyl composition, use a plastic scouring pad instead of steel wool.

Mustard. Place a cloth soaked in hydrogen peroxide solution over the stain. Over that place an ammonia-soaked cloth. Leave in place until the stain has faded, sponge with water, and wipe dry.

Paint or varnish. On resilient tile, use liquid or all-purpose detergent with a cloth or sponge or steel wool applied very carefully. On a hard-surface floor, scrub with a concentrated solution of powdered detergent and water or apply undiluted liquid laundry detergent.

Rust. Use a commercial rust remover intended for your particular type of floor.

Shoe polish or nail polish. If concentrated detergent solution doesn't work on resilient flooring, try scouring powder or steel wool. On wood and cork, steel wool should do the trick. Don't use nail polish remover; it may soften resilient flooring.

Tar. Use ice cubes to chill the tar to brittleness. Then scrape the tar carefully with a plastic spatula. To remove the tar stain, apply a damp cloth wrapped around a paste made of powdered detergent, chalk, and water. Leave the paste on the stain for several hours.

Tobacco. Rub with a cloth dampened in a solution of lemon juice and water. If that isn't effective, place a cloth soaked in hydrogen peroxide over the stain and cover that with an ammonia-soaked cloth. Leave in place until the stain has faded, sponge with water, and wipe dry.

Urine. Rub with a hot, damp cloth and scouring powder. For increased effectiveness, place a cloth soaked in hydrogen peroxide over the stain and cover that with a cloth soaked in ammonia. Leave in place until the stain has faded, sponge with water, and wipe dry.

After you have successfully removed a stain, rinse the area well and allow it to dry before you apply any new finish (polish, for example). The newly finished area should blend in with the rest of the floor within a day or two.

For taking care of a regular resilient floor, if shininess is important to you, buy a product that is known to give a high gloss.

FURNITURE

FURNITURE CARE

Some say furniture should require an absolute minimum of care, asserting that the oil or lacquer finish normally used on furniture protects the wood by sealing it. Others feel that the original finish itself needs a protective layer—usually a wax—that should be renewed periodically. Between those who opt for no wax and those who recommend lots of wax are those who temporize with a little wax sometimes.

At one time, a key part of spring cleaning involved giving the furniture a fresh coat of wax: paste wax, no less, applied with plenty of muscle. The wax was supposed to "feed" the wood and help protect it. No doubt, some people still hew to that ritual. Many others forgo the paste wax but spritz the furniture with a cleaner like *Pledge* or *Endust* whenever they dust. Chances are, those people are wasting their effort and money.

Consumers Union's testers have found that, in general, the need for waxing and cleaning furniture with a brand-name product is often quite unnecessary. Most furniture won't benefit from waxing because its surface has been sealed at the factory with a durable finish that keeps the wood from drying out and, to some degree, protects against spills and minor scratches. Oils and waxes don't penetrate the finish. The minuscule residue that remains from most polishes after application and buffing contributes nothing to damage control.

Modern furniture does need cleaning, however. Dust, smoke, and greasy cooking fumes combine to create a dulling film. Fingerprints begin as small smudges and grow to a grimy coating.

You can choose among dozens of furniture cleaners at the supermarket. Many, like the familiar *Pledge, Behold,* and *Endust,* are intended primarily to help remove dust. Others, such as *Kleen 'N Shine* and *Murphy Oil Soap,* are intended for cleaning wood and other surfaces. Hardware stores carry still other furniture cleaners and polishes, generally oil-based products such as *Old English Red Oil* and *Scott's Liquid Gold.* Only a few actually contain wax.

Except for old furniture whose original finish may not have sealed the wood very well—or newer furniture that has been used a lot and whose finish may be worn thin—regular dusting with a soft rag slightly dampened with water may be all you need to keep furniture looking new and clean. It's still true, however, that finely finished wood and wood with a modern, well-sealed finish should be treated with respect when it comes to water. Indeed, *Murphy Oil Soap*'s label carries an admonition that the product, when used on furniture, should first be tested on an inconspicuous area. The maker of *Fantastik,* an all-purpose cleaner, advises against using it on varnished surfaces. See following paragraphs for a discussion about caring for valued furniture—old or antique, and especially teak varieties.

The mirror finish on a piece of furniture is there courtesy of the furniture maker. The shine you get from a product depends almost entirely on the nature of the furniture's original finish. For instance, no polish is likely to increase the luster of a "piano top" high-gloss mahogany. It is already mirrorlike. Furthermore, the finish isn't likely to be protected to any degree by using furniture polish.

Waxing won't improve the shine of furniture whose original finish is still intact. In fact, a furniture polish may muddy the finish. A buildup of wax can darken the wood and mask its grain. Some oils (such as lemon oil) applied to a previously waxed surface can make the surface sticky, vulnerable to fingerprints, and a magnet for dust. Wax-containing products applied over some oils won't adhere properly. Cleaning up the mess may require a lot of elbow grease.

Stains. Consumers Union's tests showed that a supermarket furniture cleaner isn't likely to protect a wood finish against common stains. Moreover, a fresh application of the product is by no means guaranteed to remove any new stains. A bit of ordinary dishwashing liquid and water should do the job just as well.

Water. Any furniture cleaner should be able to wipe away water spots. But water that's allowed to stand on wood furniture is likely to penetrate most finishes, except for plasticized ones like urethane. When you wipe away the water, a cloudy white mark often remains. You may be able to buff out a light mark with a product that has a high oil content. But some rings on certain kinds of furniture finish won't yield—meaning it's time to call in the refinisher.

Scratches. Most furniture-care products don't contain dye, so they aren't meant to cover up deep scratches. Products that claim to hide surface scratches are worth a try. Tests showed that one product, *Oz Cream Polish,* managed to fill in scratches and make them less visible.

RECOMMENDATIONS

Check *Consumer Reports* for a Ratings report on furniture polishes, published in the May 1993 issue. But for relatively new furniture that's been maintained in good condition, there's no practical reason to add another cleaning product to the clutter under the kitchen sink. It's easy enough to use a little plain water and dishwashing liquid to take care of dirtier surfaces, first trying the mixture's effectiveness on an out-of-the-way area on the piece of furniture. Again, it's a good idea to try *any* furniture-treatment product on an inconspicuous area before plunging into the job full tilt.

Do you want to protect furniture finishes against heat and solvents such as alcoholic beverages, aftershave lotion, perfume, cough syrup, and the like? The best protection is a nonabsorbent barrier, such as a dish or a coaster.

CARING FOR VALUED OR TEAK FURNITURE

Older furniture that still bears its original finish, and modern-day teak furniture, both require special care. Regular dusting is important for antiques, say the experts. Tools of the trade include feather dusters, soft cotton cloths laundered without harsh detergents, and small vacuum cleaners.

The experts also recommend waxing, but generally only once or twice

Home Brews

In addition to plain water and dishwashing liquid, Consumers Union tested the following home brews:

- One-half teaspoon light olive oil added to one-quarter cup white vinegar, with enough water to make a pint. This proved to be as effective as any store product.
- One-quarter cup walnut oil plus four drops of lemon extract. This was only as effective as the better oil-based products.

a year. One antiques dealer recommends waxing at the beginning and end of the heating season. Changes in temperature and humidity can be very damaging to wood furniture because wood shrinks and expands in response to those changes. According to the dealer, waxing unfinished surfaces allows the raw wood to absorb the wax, thereby minimizing the chance that the wood will crack or the veneer will lift or separate. You should wax the underside of a table, for example, as well as the unfinished interior of highboys, breakfronts, and other so-called case pieces.

Some experts recommend against waxes that contain silicone. They say such products compromise the wood's ability to respond to changes in temperature and humidity, and increase the risk of cracking.

Teakwood, which is an oil-finished product, has special needs, too. One industry expert said frequent dusting is important. Furniture that's used fairly often may need oiling every month or two. The expert recommends a solution of mild detergent for cleaning and tung oil (or some other type of oil) for restoring the sheen in dry areas.

Teak furniture not subject to much wear may need oiling only a few times a year. If the wood looks pale and the surface feels dry, the furniture probably needs oiling. One teak furniture retailer suggests using a clean, soft cloth to oil the entire piece, then letting the oil sit for three to four hours or, better, overnight. Afterward, buff with another clean, soft cloth to remove excess oil.

UPHOLSTERY CLEANERS

Regular vacuuming is about the best way to keep upholstery looking fresh. But you may not be motivated to vacuum upholstered furniture often enough; dust isn't as obvious on an armchair as it is on a table top. Eventually, the upholstery becomes so dirty that drastic measures are necessary.

A surprisingly large number of people take the most drastic measure of all—they just throw out the soiled furniture and replace it with new. According to a survey, that's how a significant number of *Consumer Reports* subscribers dealt with the problem. Some took a less drastic approach, opting for reupholstering or slipcovers. Others chose heavy-duty, overall cleaning—a far more economical solution, if it works.

There are three ways to clean upholstery: You can buy a cleaning product and apply it to the fabric by hand. You can buy or rent a machine that cleans carpets and upholstery. You can call in a professional cleaning service, usually listed under "Carpet Cleaners" or "Upholstery Cleaners" in the Yellow Pages.

Consumers Union testers tried all three methods.

CLEANING

Generally, cleaning by hand means spraying the upholstery cleaner on the fabric; gently rubbing the resulting foam with a damp sponge, cloth, or brush; and vacuuming the residue. The job can be time-consuming, and the furniture may not turn out clean enough.

In laboratory tests, only *Blue Coral Dri-Clean Upholstery and Carpet Cleaner,* bought at an automotive-supply store, did a good job on the light-colored test furniture, which had been soiled with hard-to-clean substances commonly found in offices. The other products tested for a February 1992 report were Bissell Upholstery Shampoo; Blue Coral Velour and Upholstery Cleaner; Blue Lustre Dry Upholstery Cleaner; Blue Lustre Upholstery Cleaner; Carbona Shampoozer for Rugs and Upholstery; Glamorene Spray 'n Brush Upholstery Cleaner and Deodorizer; a homemade brew (4 teaspoons of Joy dishwashing liquid in a quart of water); Kmart Upholstery

Shampoo; Scotchgard (Auto-Pak) Upholstery Cleaner + Protector; and Woolite Upholstery Cleaner. These products might have done better on darker, less soiled upholstery. And any cleaning product is likely to work better if the job is done before upholstery is truly filthy.

Even subscribers who cleaned with a machine weren't always happy with the result, and some found a machine difficult to use. The *VAX* steamer used in the tests, with *VAX Carpet Cleaner* and *VAX De-Foamer*, did a good job on a desk chair. But setting up the machine, cleaning the chair, and then disassembling and cleaning the machine was quite complicated. *Blue Coral Dri-Clean* worked about as well, and with a lot less fuss.

Most subscribers left the cleaning to a professional, but a substantial number indicated that even the pros couldn't get their furniture clean. The service hired to clean the desk chair did only slightly better than the *Blue Coral Dri-Clean* and the *VAX* steamer. Asked to rate its results on a five-point scale from poor to excellent, the firm awarded itself a three. Had it been doing the job for a private customer, it would have cautioned that the chair was too dirty to come out perfectly clean.

PROFESSIONAL CLEANING

Cleaning a six-foot sofa can cost anywhere from $40 to $100, depending on where you live and whom you hire. Replacing a damaged sofa with a new one can cost between $600 and $6,000, so price shouldn't be the most important criterion when you're hiring a professional; competence should be.

One way to find an upholstery cleaner, of course, is to look in the phone book, where you'll find listings for big national companies such as Stanley Steemer and Sears, large regional companies like Macy's, and local companies. If you come up empty, the International Institute of Carpet and Upholstery Certification can recommend firms that have passed a test on cleaning upholstery. When you call the institute's toll-free number (800-635-7500), a representative will use your zip code to locate two or three cleaning firms in your area.

The firm should give a preliminary estimate over the phone, then come to the house to evaluate the furniture and spot-test it—by applying a bit of cleaner to an inconspicuous piece of the fabric—before giving a firm price quote.

The company should explain the procedure and what the furniture should look like after cleaning.

They should outline their guarantee and voluntarily offer references.

Most professionals prefer to steam clean upholstery because the results are generally better than with dry cleaning. But cleaning with water, even when it's done by a pro, can be risky. Therefore, a careful cleaner will spot-test when they come to your home to assess furniture and quote a firm price. If problems appear as a result of a spot test, most companies will switch from steam cleaning to dry cleaning.

Some professional cleaners spot-test on the scheduled cleaning day. That's also an acceptable approach, as long as the tested material has time to dry thoroughly before work begins.

Professional carpet and upholstery cleaners often raise the subject of chemical fabric protectors. There is, of course, an extra charge for such treatment, and therefore there are extra profits for the seller. According to the 3M Company, which makes Scotchgard, if a fabric protector is applied at the mill where the fabric is made, subsequent applications aren't likely to help fight stains. Fabric does need to be retreated but only after every third cleaning.

Although there are many brands of stain repellent, there are basically two types: fluorocarbons and silicones. Fluorocarbons protect against both oil- and water-based stains; silicones protect only against water-based stains.

If you don't know whether your upholstery has been treated with a stain protector, you might consider having one applied after cleaning. Two caveats: It's important that the protector be applied evenly. (Electric sprayers and aerosol cans are likely to create a more even coat than is possible with a pump sprayer.) And it's important to check the label for precautions and to spot-test. Chemspec, which makes Chemspec's All Fabric Stainshield with Teflon, a brand often used by professional cleaners, advises applying a bit of protector on a hidden area of the upholstery to make sure the dye doesn't bleed. And 3M recommends Scotchgard for only certain types of fabrics.

RECOMMENDATIONS

Preventive maintenance—vacuuming regularly and catching spills before they become stains—can go a long way toward postponing the need for an overall cleaning. Vacuum all surfaces of the furniture, including the back and sides, the skirt, the arms, the platform underneath the cushions, and both sides of loose cushions.

If you're working on arms that are narrower than the vacuum cleaner's nozzle, cover the exposed section of the nozzle to improve suction. When vacuuming a delicate fabric—velvet, nubby silk, or crewel embroidery, for instance—you can avoid snagging the fabric by placing a piece of nonmetallic window screen between the nozzle and the fabric.

Once furniture is too soiled for vacuuming, your best bet is to hire a professional. Choose one who will evaluate the furniture and spot-test the fabric before cleaning. Make sure the company warns, in writing, of any problems anticipated during the cleaning and promises to pay for any unanticipated damage.

You'll save money by doing the job yourself, but your success will depend on your own cleaning skills, and the work takes a lot of time. According to the manufacturer, *Blue Coral Dri-Clean,* which did almost as well as professional cleaning, should not be used on silk or velvet. Spot-test it before you submit your whole sofa to a cleaning, and apply it in a well-lighted area so you can see how the job is going.

A steamer can only be used on fabrics that can tolerate a water-based cleaner. Additionally, the machine isn't easy to set up, use, and clean.

A GUIDE TO UPHOLSTERY FABRICS

Wool, cotton, linen, silk, rayon, nylon, and polyester are among the fibers that are turned into coverings for sofas and chairs. The fabric may be made of a single fiber or a blend, and it may have a special finish, such as the starchy glaze that gives linen its soft glow.

Steam cleaning with detergent and water is the most effective way to clean most fabrics. But not all fabrics relate well to water. Some shrink; some become mottled by water spots; some turn brown.

To clean fabric successfully, you must first find out just what fabric you're dealing with. If the furniture was purchased within the last few years, it probably has a cleaning code on its label. (Look under the cushions for a tag affixed to the platform.) A "W" means that the fabric can be cleaned with a water-based product. An "S" indicates that a solvent-based cleaner (dry cleaning) is required. If the code reads "W-S," the choice is yours. An "X" is bad news: Any cleaning other than vacuuming isn't recommended. More and more furniture manufacturers are putting an "X" on upholstered furniture—not necessarily because the fabric can't be cleaned by either method but to limit their liability if something goes wrong.

This guide provides information about the cleaning of materials commonly used in upholstery textiles and can help you decide whether to dry clean with solvents or "wet clean" with a water-based solution. If your fabric is a blend of different fibers, base your decision on the most sensitive one in the blend.

Spot-testing a cleaning product (in an inconspicuous area, of course) before you clean is a good idea, even if you know the recommended cleaning method or the fiber content of the textile. Apply a bit of cleaner where different colors meet and let it dry thoroughly. Check to see if colors have changed and if the fabric's finish remains.

UPHOLSTERY STAINS

For some furniture, the problem isn't widespread soil but a sudden spill. If you're quick enough, blotting the spill with a clean white towel may do the trick. (A white towel lets you see what you're removing and eliminates the chance of introducing another stain in the form of a dye.) Once a spill becomes a stain, cleanup can still be successful, if you use the right approach. Certain basics apply to all stain-removal efforts. If the spill has dried to a hard glob, as spaghetti sauce can, scrape up as much as possible with the side of a spoon. If you're dealing with chewing gum or wax, freeze the stuff with an ice cube to make scraping more effective. Of course, for any stain, quick action is ideal; you'll achieve the best results by treating the stain immediately.

Several steps are often required to remove a stain. (Of course, if the stain is gone after one step, there's no need to go on to the next.) Use a small amount of each cleaning solution, and try to avoid soaking the fabric. Apply the cleaner with a white towel, blotting from the outside of the stain toward the center. Avoid scrubbing, which can spread the stain and abrade the fabric. When the towel is no longer picking up any of the stain, rinse the fabric with water (use a spray bottle, and avoid wetting the fabric more than necessary), and move on to the next cleaning agent.

For recommended solutions and techniques for removing a variety of stains from both washable and unwashable fabrics, refer to the Stain Removal Chart at the end of this book.

DEALING WITH SPILLS AND STAINS ON LEATHER

Leather dyers either apply a pigmented coating to the leather's surface or treat the hide with aniline dye. Pigmented leather is more resistant to water-soluble spills and stains. Aniline-dyed leather is exceptionally soft and exceptionally porous. Spills soak up quickly, becoming stains that can be almost impossible to remove.

You can test your leather furniture to find out which type of dye was used. Place a drop of water in a spot that's not often seen (under the cushion, for example). If the water doesn't soak in, the leather is pigmented. If it does soak in, the leather is aniline-dyed—and vulnerable.

Suede is another vulnerable leather—not just because of the dyeing process, but because it's porous and quick to sop up stains. In addition, suede has a nap that's flattened by liquid spills and by use. Sit on suede often enough over the years and you'll smooth the nap so much that the arms and, perhaps, the front edge of the seat will look dirty and shiny. Only a professional leather refinisher can restore the nap to suede.

Vacuuming is an important part of routine maintenance of leather furniture, whether it's pigmented, aniline-dyed, or suede. You can also wipe pigmented leather periodically with a soft white cloth dampened with water. And you can brush suede with a terry-cloth towel to spiff up its nap. Beyond vacuuming, there isn't much you can do for aniline-dyed leather except to treat it with tender loving care. When it becomes stained or soiled, your only recourse is professional cleaning.

If you spill something on leather, the faster you clean it up, the better. Consumers Union applied test stains to swatches of pigmented leather and

Upholstery Stains

◉ ◓ ○ ◒ ●

Better ⟷ Worse

Stain Guide

As published in a **February 1992** report.

Stains. For **ketchup, coffee, juice, milk,** and **mustard**, the Association of Specialists in Cleaning and Restoration International recommends using an enzyme detergent as a last resort, but we found that enzyme detergents can bleach certain fabrics, so we didn't use them.

Stain type. WS=water-soluble; **SS**=solvent-soluble.

Steps. As recommended by the Association of Specialists in Cleaning and Restoration International, to be used on cloth upholstery in the sequence shown in the table.

1: Dry-cleaning solvent (use it with adequate ventilation).
2: One tsp. dishwashing liquid per cup distilled or soft water (hard water won't work as well).
3: One tbsp. household ammonia per half-cup distilled or soft water.
4: One-third cup white vinegar per two-thirds cup distilled or soft water.

Materials. Wool, Haitian cotton, and **linen** had no stain protection. **Cotton** was protected with Wyngard. **Nylon, olefin** (polypropylene), **cotton velvet,** and **acrylic velvet** were protected with Scotchgard. **Polyester** was protected with Covgard.

Key to Comments
A–Water stains appeared.
B–Fabric shrank.
C–Some color was removed.
D–Blotting alone removed stain.
E–Stain came out during first step.
F–Stain came out during second step.
G–We tried all recommended steps.

			Materials								
Stains	Stain type	Steps	Wool	Haitian cotton	Cotton	Nylon	Linen	Olefin	Polyester	Cotton velvet	Acrylic velvet
Ketchup	WS	2,3	◉ A,G	● A,G	○ G	◉ G	○ B,G	◓ G	◉ G	◓ C,G	◓ G
Cola	WS	2,3,4	◉ D	◉ D	◉ E	◉ D	◓ A,B,G	◉ D	◉ D	◓ A,B,E	◉ E
Coffee with sugar	WS	2,4,1	◉ B,E	◉ A,G	◉ E	◉ E	◉ B,G	◉ E	◉ E	◓ E	◉ E
Crayon	SS	1,2	● B,G	◒ B,G	● G	● G	● B,G	○ G	● G	● G	● G
Ballpoint-pen ink	SS	1,2,3	● G	● G	● G	● G	● B,G	● G	● G	● B,G	● G
Grape juice	WS	2,3,4	◉ D	◉ D	◉ D	◉ D	● B,G	◉ A,D	◉ D	◓ A,E	◉ D
Milk	WS	2,3,4,1	◉ D	◉ D	◉ D	◉ D	◉ B,E	◉ D	◉ D	◉ D	◉ D
Mustard	WS	2,4	◒ G	● A,G	● G	● G	● G	● G	○ G	● G	● G
Lipstick	SS	1,2,3	● G	● A,G	● A,G	● G	● A,G	● G	● G	● B,G	● G
Italian salad dressing	SS	1,2,3,4	◉ A,F	◉ B,E	◉ F	◉ E	◓ A,B,F	◓ F	◉ F	◓ D	◓ D
Cream shoe polish	SS	1,2,3	● B,G	● A,G	● G	● A,G	● B,G	● G	● G	● B,G	● G
Red wine	WS	2,4,3	◉ F	◒ A,E	◉ E	◉ E	● B,G	◉ E	◉ D	◓ E	◉ D

A Guide to Upholstery Fabrics

This guide was published in a **February 1992** report.

Fiber. Cotton refers to all cotton except Haitian, which may release a brown dye and stretch when wet. All the fibers are likely to be stained by oil-based spills. **Cotton, linen, rayon, silk, wool,** and **nylon** are also likely to be stained by water-based spills. Dry cleaning is acceptable for all the fibers. Wet cleaning, which often works better, is generally OK for all, but check under "wet-cleaning flaws" to see what problems can arise, and be sure to spot-test.

Tendency to bleed. On a scale from 1 to 5, with 1 most likely to bleed; 5 least likely. Bleeding can occur with either wet or dry cleaning.

Wet-cleaning flaws. The tendency for fibers to water-spot, brown, or shrink during cleaning with a water-based solution. These columns can help you determine whether dry or wet cleaning is more appropriate for your upholstery.

		Wet-cleaning flaws			
Fiber	**Tendency to bleed**	**Water-spot**	**Brown**	**Shrink**	**Comments**
Cotton	2	Low	High	Moderate	A
Linen	2	Low	High	High	A,B
Rayon	2	High	High	Very high	A,D
Silk	1-3	High	High	Low	E,F
Wool	2-3	Low	Moderate	Moderate	B
Acetate	4-5	Low	Low	Low	D,G
Acrylic	5	Low	Moderate	Low	C
Nylon	4-5	Low	Moderate	Low	H
Olefin	5	Low	Low	Low	C,I,J
Polyester	5	Low	Low	Low	C

Key to Comments

A–May contain glazing, sizing, or other finishes that can run or be removed during cleaning.
B–Turns dark when wet; hard to assess quality of cleaning.
C–Spots may reappear after cleaning.
D–Tends to shrink even when preshrunk.
E–Water marks may be difficult to remove without damaging fabric.
F–May stretch with excessive agitation.
G–Dissolves in acetone. Avoid nail-polish remover and commercial ink removers.
H–Dissolves in strong acids.
I–Latex backing may be weakened by age, sunlight, and chlorinated solvents.
J–Resists bleach.

blotted them up a minute later with a damp washcloth. The water-based stains (ketchup, cola, coffee, grape juice, milk, mustard, and red wine) disappeared. There was less success with oil-based stains: Crayon, ballpoint-pen ink, lipstick, Italian salad dressing, and cream shoe polish did not come off.

For those stains, three leather cleaners were tried, first pretesting them in a hidden spot. All the cleaners removed some dyes.

Don't consider using cleaning solvents, ink removers, or paint removers on pigmented leather. Since the dye is essentially painted on the leather, those products can remove it.

When you are faced with stains that won't come out, find a professional. Call the store where you purchased the furniture. If it can't help, check the Yellow Pages or ask a local dry cleaner for advice. Cleaners who handle leather clothing don't always work on leather furniture, so it may take a few calls to find a leather-furniture cleaner.

Expect the cleaning to be costly, and expect to be without your furniture for a while: Often, professionals prefer to clean leather in the shop. Removing dirt and stains can also remove dyes, so the furniture may need to be recolored.

HOUSE CLEANING

ALL-PURPOSE CLEANERS

A good all-purpose liquid cleaner should be able to handle a variety of chores. Indeed, all-purpose cleaner labels variously claim that their products are suitable for an ambitious list of cleaning tasks: appliances, cabinets, countertops, dishes, pots and pans, stove tops, laundry, screens and blinds, vinyl and aluminum siding, whitewall tires, and boats.

Yet the main target for all-purpose cleaners would appear to be small areas of concentrated dirt. Convenience in cleaning spots and smudges with a full-strength cleaner seems to be the objective of flip-top squeeze bottles, pull-out dispensing caps, and trigger-spray pumps. Tests conducted by Consumers Union concentrated on the products' ability to conquer three tough, typical kinds of dirt: pencil, crayon, and grease. Few cleaners performed well on all three. Black grease was the most intractable soil. The best products did a decent job on crayon or pencil; a couple just smeared the black grease.

Pine oil, a solvent that is a relative of turpentine, helps penetrate and loosen greasy dirt. It is found in substantial amounts in some of the good all-purpose cleaners. Pine oil also confers a certain psychological benefit: A pine scent has come to be associated with cleanliness.

At full strength, an all-purpose cleaner should be used gently, then promptly and carefully rinsed off. Otherwise, you may risk marring the surface. Check the label for precautions; if in doubt, first test an inconspicuous spot for marring. Most cleaners may be diluted for cleaning walls and floors with a sponge or a mop and bucket, and all should do a respectable job.

SAFETY

Some products are caustic enough to warrant your using rubber gloves when cleaning, or at least avoiding prolonged contact with the skin. Since the solvents and other ingredients that dissolve, emulsify, suspend, or otherwise loosen grime are powerful chemicals, any cleaner should be used carefully and kept out of the reach of children. To avoid potentially hazardous chemical reactions, never mix different cleaners together.

RECOMMENDATIONS

Many everyday spots and stains are fairly easy to remove. Most products can be diluted for washing floors or walls and should be up to the task. Spot cleaning can always be improved, within limits, with the application of elbow grease.

It is a waste of money to pay extra for products that claim disinfectant properties. A disinfecting cleaner cannot sterilize every surface in a home or sterilize the air. At best, such a cleaner can temporarily reduce populations of some germs in a very limited area for a limited time. Keeping a sickroom clean—with any cleaner—and washing hands after contact with a sick person are usually sufficiently hygienic. If you need stronger germicidal protection, ask your doctor for advice.

Check *Consumer Reports* for a Ratings report on all-purpose cleaners, scheduled for publication in the August 1993 issue.

BATHROOM CLEANERS

Some of the products promoted as bathroom cleaners derive their strength from old-fashioned pine oil; others rely on a mix of powerful chemicals.

Ratings of Bathroom Cleaners

◉ ◓ ○ ◒ ●
Better ⟵⟶ Worse

Listed in order of estimated quality, based on cleaning ability and effectiveness at retarding mildew growth. As published in a **September 1991** report.

Product. Most are formulated and marketed specifically for bathroom use. Also included are several "all-purpose" cleaners as well as chlorine bleach and detergent-laced towelettes.

Dispenser. Cleaners usually come in convenient aerosol cans (**A**) or in squirt bottles that dispense the cleaner in various ways: A pump spray (**P**) tends to be easier to use than a flip-top cap (**F**). Products that pour from a screw-cap bottle (**S**) are least convenient. Another option is towelettes (**T**) laced with cleaner. They come stacked in a tissue-type box for quick removal.

Price/size. Average prices for the size (in ounces or fluid ounces) most commonly available. Based on a survey conducted in mid-1991. Prices marked with an * are average prices paid. For towelettes, the size is the number of sheets per box.

Cost per use. For 2 tablespoons—about an ounce—of an aerosol or liquid, or one towelette. Based on price paid.

Cleaning. How well each cleaner removed laboratory-prepared **soap scum** and **mildew** from ceramic tile and grout when applied, rinsed, and wiped according to label instructions. Products judged ◉ did a thorough job; those judged ○ removed about half the film; those judged ● were ineffectual.

Inhibiting mildew. Fungi favor damp bathrooms. Any cleaner judged at least ○ should help keep mildew at bay.

Surface damage. To see what could happen if cleaner spattered and was not wiped off right away, a small amount of each product was applied to common bathroom surfaces. The cleaners were left overnight, then rinsed off. Products that passed the test left no damage. Those that failed left the surface dull or discolored. No cleaner marred ceramic tile, grout, chrome, plastic laminate, fiberglass-reinforced plastic, or DuPont's Corian. One or more products marred brass, semigloss paint, stainless steel, or a vinyl shower curtain.

Product	Dispenser	Price/size	Cost per use	Cleaning: Soap scum	Cleaning: Mildew	Cleaning: Inhibiting mildew	Surface damage	Comments
Spic and Span Pine [1]	S	$2.82/28	10¢	◓	◒	◉	brass, paint	—
Top Job With Ammonia 2000 [1]	S	2.58/28	9	◉	◒	○	brass, paint	—
Woolworth Bathroom	A	1.54*/17	9	◉	◒	○	paint	*D,G*
Easy-Off Instant Mildew Stain Remover	P	2.48/16	16	◓	◓	●	brass, paint	*B,C,F,G*
Clorox Regular Bleach	S	1.25/128	1	◉	◓	●	brass, paint	*C,G*

Earth Rite Tub & Tile	P	2.52/16	16	◉	○	●	paint	*H*
Tilex Instant Mildew Stain Remover	P	2.70/16	17	◉	○	●	brass, paint, steel	*B,C,F,G*
Descale-It Bathroom Tile and Fixture	P	2.95/16	18	◓	○	●	brass, paint	*G*
X-14 Instant Mildew Stain Remover	P	2.76/16	17	◓	◓	●	brass, paint, steel	*C,F*
Eliminate Shower Clean Tub and Tile	P	2.99/16	19	◓	○	●	brass, paint	*G*
Dow Bathroom II	P	2.15/17	13	◉	◒	●	paint	*G*
Tough Act Bathroom	P	2.30/17	14	◓	◒	●	paint, steel, vinyl	*G*
Pine Power [1]	S	2.63/28	9	○	◒	○	paint	—
Ecover Cream [1]	F	3.19/34	9	◓	◒	●	brass, paint	—
Fantastik Swipes [1]	T	2.90/24	12	◓	◒	●	paint	*H*
Lime A-Way Bathroom	P	3.34/22	15	◓	◓	●	paint	*A*
Dow Bathroom	A	2.18/17	13	○	◒	○	paint	—
Lysol Bathroom Touch-Ups	T	2.06/36	6	◓	●	●	—	*H*
Lysol Basin Tub & Tile	P	2.13/17	13	◓	◒	●	paint, steel	*H*
Spiffits Bathroom	T	2.85/24	12	○	◒	○	paint	*H,I*
Scrub Free Bathroom Lemon Scent	P	2.20/16	14	○	○	●	brass, paint	*A,E,H*
K Mart Bathroom	A	1.66*/17	10	○	◒	●	paint	*G*
Lysol Basin Tub & Tile	A	2.19/17	13	○	◒	●	paint	—
A&P No-Scrub Bathroom	P	1.87/22	9	◒	○	●	brass, paint, steel	*A,E,H*
Pine Sol Spruce-Ups Lemon Scent [1]	T	2.46/22	11	◒	◒	●	—	*H*
Not Acceptable								
■ *The following product was judged Not Acceptable because some containers bought for testing leaked or became swollen within a few months.*								
Tile Plus Instant Mildew Stain Remover	P	2.11/20	11	◉	○	●	brass, paint	*B,C,F,H*

[1] *All-purpose cleaner.*

Key to Comments

A–Strongly acidic; avoid contact with skin. Gloves advised.
B–Strongly alkaline; avoid contact with skin. Gloves advised.
C–Contains bleach; avoid contact with bath mats, rugs, and fabrics.
D–Label warns of extreme flammability and several other hazards.
E–Severe eye irritant, label warns.
F–Not recommended for people with heart or respiratory problems, label warns.
G–Tested container harder to use than some for people with limited hand or arm function.
H–Tested container much easier to use than most for people with limited hand or arm function.
I–Left streaks after cleaning.

Because damp bathrooms are fertile ground for fungi, bathroom cleaners often contain an antimildew agent, an ingredient many all-purpose cleaners lack.

There are other distinguishing characteristics as well—price, for instance. Per use, some bathroom cleaners cost twice as much as all-purpose cleaners. Manufacturers try to justify the higher cost with fancy packaging—trigger-spray pumps, aerosol cans, flip-top containers, and colorful boxes instead of the screw-cap bottles that hold many all-purpose cleaners. Admittedly, these fancy packages are more convenient—there's no pouring involved, so spills are less likely.

EFFECTIVENESS

Despite label claims, few bathroom cleaners are very effective at removing mildew or inhibiting its growth. Many products—including all-purpose cleaners—are largely ineffective in getting rid of mildew that accumulates in the grout on a tiled surface. A better approach is to apply a cleaner *before* mildew has accumulated: Some products are more effective at preventing mildew than at removing it.

Many cleaners claim to disinfect, and they may indeed get rid of some microorganisms for a while. But trying to kill microorganisms in an unsterile environment is futile. As soon as you eliminate some germs, they're replaced by others.

SURFACE DAMAGE

You may spill a bit of cleaner and not notice the spill for hours. Quite a few products dull or discolor brass and painted trim. Some also mar stainless steel surfaces and vinyl shower curtains.

Many cleaning products can irritate skin and eyes. A few are alkaline or acidic enough to warrant the use of rubber gloves.

Many pump sprays can irritate lungs. A few specifically warn against use by anyone with heart or respiratory problems. One of the ingredients in some cleaners is sodium hypochlorite, a substance that generates chlorine gas. It is merely odorous when poured from a bottle. When sprayed, however, it can be more easily inhaled and may cause a severe reaction in some people.

Generally, cleaners are not too hazardous for a healthy, reasonably cautious person to use, but read labels carefully.

A cleaner containing bleach shouldn't be mixed with a product containing ammonia or acid. Such combinations can produce dangerous fumes.

RECOMMENDATIONS

Specialized bathroom cleaners are convenient to use, and some are very effective on soap scum and mildew. But a good all-purpose cleaner can cost less, clean soap scum at least as well, and do a better job of inhibiting the growth of mildew.

Towelettes are unnecessarily disposable, even if they are handy for small jobs. Most are fairly expensive, considering that you're likely to use them only for light cleaning on small areas.

CLEANSERS

It used to be that the more abrasive a scouring powder was, the more effectively it cleaned—and the more surely it eroded porcelain-enamel finishes and the decorative polish of cookware.

Liquid cleansers, introduced in the 1970s, replaced gritty particles, such as silica, with softer abrasives like calcium carbonate. Today, both liquids and powders derive much of their cleaning strength from detergent, bleach, and alkaline or acidic chemicals. The detergent in the cleanser helps loosen soil and cut grease; the bleach aids in removing many stains, especially from scratched and dented surfaces; and the other chemicals enhance a cleanser's ability to get rid of certain difficult stains.

Today's cleansers (the word "scouring" has disappeared from the labels) claim to remove soil and stains without damaging the surface being cleaned.

CLEANSER EFFECTIVENESS

The gentlest cleansers will leave few or no marks even on a piece of glass (similar in hardness to the porcelain in bath tiles and sinks).

A slightly abrasive cleanser leaves light hairline scratches on glass panels and is more likely to erode surfaces over time. Moderately abrasive cleansers leave a silky smooth frosting of scratches—although nothing like the deep marks left by old-time abrasive cleansers.

A good product shouldn't leave marks on chrome, imitation marble, fiberglass, glass, or glazed tile. But watch your pots and pans: A number of cleansers dull or discolor aluminum, copper, or stainless steel.

Since most cleansers are alkaline, one would expect them to do well on difficult-to-remove soil, as well as on a variety of stains such as pot marks on a kitchen sink, rust, and tea stains. And most products do, but some are especially effective on particular types of stains.

SAFETY

Cleansers containing bleach or acid shouldn't be mixed with ammonia or even with other cleansers: The combination can produce dangerous fumes. A number of bleach-containing cleansers warn about this on the label.

Some cleansers are strongly alkaline and could irritate your skin. You might want to wear rubber gloves when cleaning with them.

You might also want to remove your jewelry. Cleansers can dull the polish on a ring and scratch soft gems such as pearls and opals, and the chlorine bleach in some products can discolor silver.

CLEANSER VARIETIES

When you're cleaning a new surface, try a cleanser first on an inconspicuous corner, wipe it off, and check for marring. Over time, of course, even the gentlest product can cause some damage, which is why it's important to use a light touch and a soft applicator.

If a light touch fails on a very soiled surface, cautiously try a more aggressive applicator, a plastic mesh pad, or a reinforced sponge.

Light-duty plastic mesh pads are probably the best choice for cleaning highly polished metals. Light-duty pads are generally safe to use on plastic-laminate countertops. Light-duty products are often labeled for use on nonstick-coated cookware as well, but repeated scourings may reduce the nonstick properties of the coated surface.

Overall, light-duty pads require a lot more rubbing than heavy duty. They are less efficient with baked-on oven grime than powdered cleansers.

Removing gooey food residue is another kind of chore—messy but light duty. Plastic mesh pads and metal spirals are the most suitable type of pad for this job; they pick up the sticky remnants and part with them easily when they are rinsed. Use metal spirals with care, depending on the surface's sensitivity to scratching.

It's safest to clean porcelain enamel with a cellulose sponge and powdered or liquid cleanser than any kind of scouring pad. Light-duty cleansers (plus detergent) are suitable for cleaning porcelain in good condition.

RECOMMENDATIONS

A barely abrasive product is safe on delicate surfaces. It can do an excellent cleaning job, even on tough soils, and yet it doesn't damage surfaces if you don't wipe it all up.

If you have some very demanding jobs, like scraping crusted soil off old pots and pans or cleaning a badly abraded porcelain sink, you will probably need a much more abrasive product.

If you have rust or hard-water stains, you might consider one of the special—and expensive—cleansers: *Zud Heavy Duty* and *Bar Keepers Friend.* They cost about twice as much as most of the other cleansers on the supermarket shelves but claim to be especially effective on rust and other difficult stains.

The two were tested for abrasiveness and for cleaning power. They proved to be moderately abrasive and excellent at removing baked-on soil, tea stains, and "pot" stains made by aluminum, copper, and stainless steel. They worked quite well on rust, and they should also do an excellent job of removing hard-water stains.

On the other hand, if the two cleansers spatter and aren't wiped up, they can dull or discolor a variety of surfaces, including plastic-laminate countertops and pots made of aluminum, copper, or stainless steel. In addition, they contain oxalic acid, a potent poison. Keep them out of the reach of young children.

Cleansers are not appropriate for all chores in the kitchen and bathroom. You'll want a good all-purpose cleaner to take care of ordinary soil on floors, walls, countertops, range surfaces, and the like.

DRAIN CLEANERS

Most chemical drain openers open blocked drains by eating and boiling their way through the clog. Obviously, chemicals strong enough to dissolve grease, hair, paper, and other debris can severely damage your eyes, lungs, and skin. Accidentally swallowing even a small amount of drain opener can result in appalling injuries or death.

To say that you should use these products with extreme caution is an understatement. It's best not to use chemical drain openers at all. The mechanical devices described below are much safer than chemicals and just as effective.

MECHANICAL METHODS

Often the best way to clear a drain is to push or pull on the clog. You can buy a plunger, a plumber's snake, or a drain auger at any hardware store. None of these tools require special expertise to use, and you can depend on any of them to eliminate most clogs. Another type of product uses pressurized air or gas to push an obstruction around the bend in the drainpipe and into the clear.

Some devices are meant to be used with a garden hose. They are available at hardware stores and look a little like a canvas pastry bag. Attach one to the end of a garden hose that you feed down the drain. Water pressure expands the bag, sealing it in place and pushing the clog free. The bags should work well, provided you can reach the sink with the hose.

CHEMICAL CLEANERS

When most chemical drain cleaners contact standing water in a blocked drain, they release heat that liquefies congealed grease. Alkalies break down grease chemically as well, gradually converting it into a water-soluble soap. Sulfuric acid dissolves such debris as paper or hair.

These chemicals may also damage plumbing and surrounding surfaces. If you have plastic (PVC) pipes, the heat liberated by these products may soften them, perhaps enough to loosen a cemented joint. If you have metal pipes that are old and corroded on the inside, the heat and chemical action might be enough to put a hole in them. Acid solutions can corrode or etch stainless steel sinks and damage aluminum fixtures, countertops, or wood. They may heat porcelain enough to crack it, so they should not be used in toilets.

SAFETY

Despite their proven hazards, there are still a large number of chemical drain openers. The biggest sellers contain lye as their principal ingredient. The heating action and chemical attack that these products produce are supposed to loosen any blockage enough to let it ease down the pipe.

The labels of chemical drain openers contain multiple warnings and precautions. Some of their advice, however, could do more harm than good.

One label tells you to use a plunger if the product doesn't clear the blockage—an invitation to disaster. It would be all too easy to splash caustic water onto your hands or into your eyes. Still other containers may have a shrink-wrapped label that can easily come off, leaving behind an unlabeled container of dangerous chemical.

The first-aid advice on labels varies, partly because doctors themselves disagree on the proper course of action in cases of accidental ingestion. Some labels suggest you attempt to neutralize the chemical with baking soda (for acids) or citrus juice (for lyes) or dilute it with water. But those treatments can cause a chemical reaction that liberates more heat and gas, aggravating the injury. Most of these chemicals are so immediately and catastrophically damaging if swallowed that home remedies are apt to be dangerous, even fatal.

The best advice in the case of accidental poisoning is: Do not try to induce vomiting; rush the victim to the hospital immediately, being sure to bring a sample of the ingested substance with you. If drain cleaner splashes in someone's eye, flush it with cool water for at least 20 minutes, then get medical help as quickly as possible. Continue rinsing the eye on the way to the hospital.

FULL-SIZE VACUUM CLEANERS

The first question to ask in choosing an all-purpose vacuum cleaner is: What kind of surface will you be vacuuming most? If your floors are largely carpeted, you need a good upright or a good canister equipped with a power nozzle, which is a motorized brush. If you have bare floors or if you expect to vacuum upholstered furniture, you need the kind of attachments, and the suction, that a canister is more likely to provide. For a brief description of the types, see the following box.

CLEANING EFFECTIVENESS

The key to a vacuum cleaner's performance, of course, is how well it picks up dirt. A given machine may do that by brushing the carpet and sucking dirt up, or by suction alone.

Deep cleaning. Uprights, with their characteristically robust brush action, generally do a very good or excellent job of deep-cleaning rugs. Unless a canister has a power nozzle, which seems to help remove embedded dirt, it shouldn't be relied on for deep cleaning.

Suction. Suction tends to decrease as a cleaner's bag fills with dirt. Suction in an upright tends to be lower than in a canister.

ALLERGIES AND VACUUM CLEANING

Pet dander, pollen, molds, dust-mite feces, and other forms of household dirt can cause allergic reactions in some people. Vacuuming can launch those sneeze inducers into the air in several ways: A porous cleaner bag can allow them to escape; a rotating brush can kick them up as you move it across the rug; or an exhaust vent at the base of the cleaner can blow them around.

Some manufacturers claim that their machines control dust emissions.

Many models retain dust well. The Danish-made *Nilfisk,* a canister that promotes its ability to scoop up and hold onto allergens, proved to be the top dust trapper.

On the other hand, three bagless cleaners—the *Amway Clear Trak, Sears Kenmore Destiny,* and *Rainbow*—virtually spew tiny particles. The *Amway* and *Sears,* both uprights, trap dirt by swirling particles inside a plastic container. The *Rainbow,* a canister model whose maker, Rexair, boasts about its air-cleaning prowess, collects dirt by bubbling dusty air through a container of water. Even after Consumers Union testers installed a foam filter the manufacturer recommends for especially dusty jobs, the machine showed only a small drop in emissions.

Occasionally manufacturers use the presence of a filter behind the bag as a selling point, but such filters don't guarantee effective particle retention. And special double-layered dust bags that are supposed to minimize dirt dispersion don't do any better than the cheaper regular ones.

Using a vacuum cleaner that excels at retaining dust can help reduce irritants, but because allergenic substances are more at home in carpets than on bare floors, the best solution for people who are severely allergic to dust may be to use as little carpeting as practical.

CONVENIENCE

A vacuum cleaner gets a lot of use. It should be a convenient appliance. Even a standout performer will leave you fuming if it's awkward to use. Here are some of the traits you'll need to consider when buying a cleaner.

Putting the Pieces Together. With an upright, you may have the one-time task of attaching the handle, but that's about all the assembly required. Setting up the hose is easiest when one end can remain attached to the cleaner. Some inconvenient models make you snap an adapter over the carpet brush. Just as bad: having to unhook the drive belt to connect the hose.

To put together a canister vacuum, you typically insert the hose, then attach a metal or plastic wand, which may consist of several pieces. Latches or clicking buttons hold metal wands together; plastic wands are held in place by friction alone. Apply too little force and the fittings can fall apart; apply too much and they're difficult to separate. The power nozzle and its wiring must be detached and put aside if you want to attach other tools.

Turning it on. The On/Off switch should be high on an upright's handle. When it's lower, you have to stoop to reach it. On most canisters and a few uprights, the switch is on the base, where it's easily worked by foot. Most canisters have a separate switch to turn off the power nozzle. That's helpful when you're cleaning flat-weave rugs that can be damaged by heavy brushing.

Controlling suction. When vacuuming loose or billowy objects like throw rugs, slip covers, or curtains, you may not want a lot of suction lest the nozzle inhale the material. Most canisters and some uprights let you reduce suction by uncovering a hole near the handle. Models with more than one speed allow for varying degrees of suction.

Pushing and carrying it. An upright equipped with power-assisted wheels glides over carpeting with hardly a push; you just have to keep it going in the right direction. With models that require you to do the pushing, large wheels or rollers can make the job easier.

Uprights can usually be hoisted with one hand. Vacuum cleaners tend to be heavy, with uprights in the 10-to-24-pound range, and regular canisters weighing in at 20 to 27 pounds. That can be an argument for more than one cleaner in a multilevel home.

But what about between levels? Vacuuming stairs can be awkward. With most canister models, you use one hand to balance the tank on a step, use the other to hold the nozzle, and deal with the On/Off switch by using a free knee or foot. But a few canisters and uprights locate their switch conveniently on the nozzle handle. Some have a miniature power brush attachment that is helpful on stairs. (See next section on hand-held vacuum cleaners.)

Several canisters allow the hose to swivel. Nonswiveling hoses can form curlicues as you wend your way around a room.

Adjusting brush height. If a vacuum's brush is too high, it won't clean enough; if it's too low, it may be hard to push or hard on the carpet. The

Cleaner Types

The upright. Uprights come in two basic forms, those with the familiar vertically mounted soft bag and those whose exterior housing is rigid plastic. Both typically contain disposable inner bags. The types differ mainly in how dirt travels from floor to bag.

As a rule, uprights clean carpeting especially well. Much of their cleaning effectiveness derives from rotating brushes that loosen and sweep up dirt lodged in the carpet's pile. Their limited suction, used primarily to carry the loosened dirt into the dust bag, means that they're generally less effective on bare surfaces and upholstery.

Newer models tend to carry a hose on board, along with various tools: perhaps a thin attachment to poke into crevices, a soft-bristled brush to clean delicate surfaces without scuffing, and a nozzle with partitions to keep it from sucking up light fabrics. Having attachments ride on the cleaner is more convenient than having to rummage through the closet for them. On the other hand, uprights are awkward in close quarters—too bulky to slip under a wing chair, too gangly for stairs.

The canister. With a canister, you push only the nozzle assembly. The rest of the cleaner is a squat tank that follows along on a wheeled base—a setup that makes the unit more agile than an upright, especially on stairs. Usually, attachments are housed under a lid on the tank.

Canisters are designed to do things an upright may not do really well—clean upholstery and around furniture, say. They have more suction than most uprights. Many models have a power nozzle, a motorized brush designed to add carpet-cleaning ability to a canister's traditional floor-cleaning prowess.

The canister has several drawbacks: Its parts are cumbersome to store, its bag is usually small, and you have to give the hose a hearty yank every so often to keep the stubby body trailing behind you.

The compact canister. Compacts are promoted with an emphasis on light weight and easy storage. Their performance is often lackluster, and the emphasis on weight seems misplaced. At 12 and 16 pounds, a compact isn't appreciably lighter than many uprights.

Ratings of Full-Size Vacuum Cleaners

Excellent	Very Good	Good	Fair	Poor
⊙	◓	○	◒	●

Overall score: ■ Performance ▨ Convenience (scale 0–100)

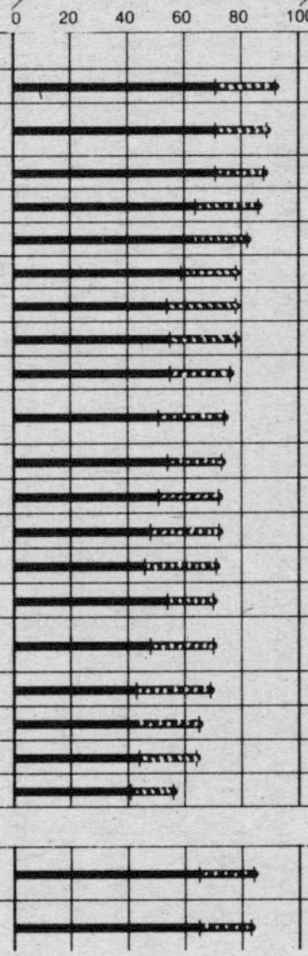

Brand and model	Price	Type	Weight	Deep cleaning	Suction	Filtration	Noise	Hose use	Dirt disposal	Pushing ease	Carrying ease	Dirt capacity	Cord reel	Tools stowed	Change-bag indicator	Advantages	Disadvantages	Comments
				Performance					Convenience				Features					
Uprights																		
Panasonic MC-6250	$170	H	15 lb.	⊙	◓	◓	○	○	◓	◒	○	◒	—	—	✓	A,D,I,K,S	h,o,u	—
Kirby Generation 3 G3D	1600	S,P	24	◓	⊙	⊙	◒	●	◓	⊙	●	⊙	—	—	—	C,K,M,O, Q,U,Y	g,n,r,u	*C,H*
Eureka The Boss Plus 2134AT	100	S	13	⊙	◒	⊙	◒	●	○	◓	○	⊙	—	—	—	—	b,c,g,r,u	*C*
Eureka Powerline Gold 9410	130	S	14	⊙	◒	⊙	●	◓	○	◓	○	⊙	—	✓	—	N	c,f	*C,E*
Eureka The Bravo Boss 9334AT	100	S	13	◓	◒	⊙	●	◓	○	◓	○	⊙	—	✓	—	N	c,f,p	*C,E*
Royal 994	420	S	16	⊙	◒	◓	●	●	◓	⊙	○	⊙	—	—	—	A,O,P,Q,S,V	g,u	—
Hoover Legacy 810	180	S	15	○	◒	⊙	●	⊙	○	◓	◒	⊙	—	✓	—	H,N,V	a,d	*K*
Hoover Elite II 640	140	S	14	◓	◒	⊙	●	◓	○	◓	◒	⊙	—	✓	—	—	a,d	*K*
Hoover Elite II 430	100	S	14	○	◒	⊙	●	○	○	◓	◒	⊙	—	✓	—	—	a,d	—
Sears Kenmore 39575	270	S,P	18	◓	◒	◓	●	○	◓	⊙	◒	⊙	✓	—	—	B,C,K,M,N, O,P,Q,R,W	u	*K*
Singer SST1900	240	S,P	17	◓	●	◓	●	●	○	◓	○	⊙	✓	—	—	B,C,N,X	d,g,r,t,u	—
Amway Clear Trak	625	H	22	◓	○	◒	○	⊙	◒	○	◒	◒	—	—	—	G,H,I,S	c,i,k,p,r,s	*A,C,D,H*
Hoover Power Max U3729-910	300	S,P	24	○	●	⊙	●	⊙	◓	⊙	◒	⊙	—	✓	—	A,H,N,Q	n,t	—
Royal Dirt Devil 7200	140	H	16	○	◒	◓	◒	⊙	⊙	◓	○	◓	—	✓	—	C,H,K,T	d,f	*K*
Singer SST460	80	S	12	◓	◒	◓	●	●	○	○	◓	⊙	—	—	—	B,C	c,g,n,r,u	*C*
Electrolux Genesis LX	430	H	17	○	◒	◓	◒	○	⊙	◓	○	◒	—	—	✓	A,C,D,I,K, L,S,T,U,V	d,h,u	*E,F,H,K*
Royal Pro Series 7470	200	H	16	●	○	○	○	⊙	⊙	◓	○	◓	—	✓	✓	C,H,I,K,T,V	d,f	*K*
Regina Housekeeper Plus H06307	140	H	15	◒	◒	◓	●	⊙	⊙	◓	○	◓	—	✓	✓	B,C,H,I,K,T	a,c,f	*K*
Sears Kenmore Destiny 31999	400	H	22	◓	○	●	◒	⊙	◒	○	◒	◒	—	✓	—	H,I,L,N	c,r,s	*A*
Oreck XL 9200	300	S	10	○	●	◓	●	—	◓	⊙	◓	⊙	—	—	—	Q	e,h,i,n,t	*C*
Canisters																		
Sears Kenmore 22551	300	PN	26	◓	⊙	○	◒	—	◓	○	○	◓	✓	✓	✓	A,B,E,I,J,K,L, N,O,P,S,W	q	*J*
Sears Kenmore 2143090	250	PN	25	◓	⊙	○	◒	—	◓	○	○	◓	✓	✓	—	E,J,K,L,N, O,P,W	q,v	*C,K*

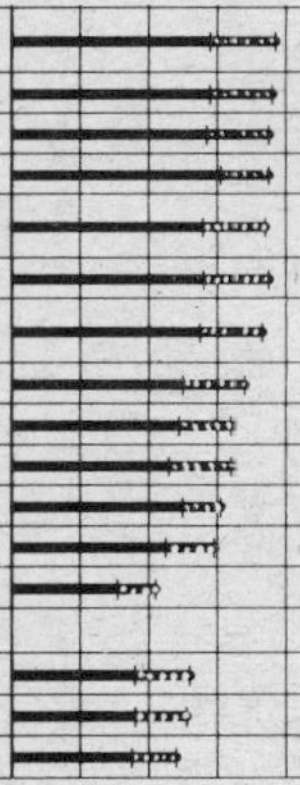

Sanyo SCP-92	500	PN	24	○	⊙	⊙	●	—	◓	○	○	○	✓	✓	✓	A,B,I,J,K,L, N,S,W	h,p,q	*C,G*
Miele S280i	540	SO	21	●	⊙	◓	◓	—	◓	◓	○	◓	✓	✓	✓	B,I,J,N,W	h,l,p	*C*
Eureka Rally 3987	240	PN	21	⊙	○	◒	◒	—	◓	◓	○	○	✓	✓	✓	E,I,N,W	h,q	*C,K*
Nilfisk GS 90	645	SO	20	◒	⊙	⊙	○	—	◓	◓	◒	◓	—	—	—	—	c,l,p,q	*C*
Panasonic MC-9530	300	PN	27	○	◓	○	◓	—	◓	○	○	○	✓	✓	✓	B,I,J,K,L, N,W	h	*C*
Singer System 90 SL1000	200	PN	27	○	◓	○	○	—	◓	◓	○	○	✓	✓	✓	I,K,N,W	h	*C*
Hoover Spectrum 900 S3595	280	PN	25	◓	○	○	●	—	○	⊙	○	○	✓	✓	✓	A,B,I,J,K,N, Q,R,S,W	h,q	*C,I*
Hoover Futura 650 S3555	190	PN	22	○	◒	○	○	—	○	◓	○	○	✓	✓	✓	I,J,N,Q,R,W	h,q,v	*C*
Oreck XL Celoc 2	400	PN	27	◒	◓	◓	◒	—	◒	○	◒	◓	✓	—	✓	F,I,K,W	h,p	*C,E*
Electrolux Diplomat LX	650	PN	22	○	○	◓	●	—	⊙	○	○	◒	✓	✓	✓	E,I,K,L,T,U,X	b,d,h	*B,D,F,H,K*
Princess III PN93	600	PN	26	◒	○	◓	◓	—	●	◓	◒	○	—	✓	—	F	c,i,j,m,n,p,v	*A,C,H,L*
Royal 4600	500	PN	27	◒	○	○	○	—	○	○	◒	◒	—	✓	—	A,B,E,L	j	—
Rainbow SE	1100	PN	26	◒	◒	●	◒	—	●	◓	◒	◒	—	✓	—	L,M,U,Z	c,h,n,p,v	*A,H*
Compact canisters																		
Royal Dirt Devil Power Pak 3113	170	PN	16	◒	◒	○	●	—	◓	⊙	⊙	◒	—	✓	—	L,Q,S	c,h,i,p	*C*
Hoover Tempo 320 S1331	80	SO	12	●	◒	◓	○	—	○	⊙	◓	●	—	✓	✓	I,M,N,Q,S	c,h,p,q	—
Eureka Mighty Mite 3140	100	SO	12	●	◒	○	○	—	⊙	●	◓	◒	—	✓	—	L,M,S,T	b,c,i,o,p	*C,K*

Key to Advantages
A–On/off switch located on handle.
B–Motor control with more than one speed.
C–Upright with suction control.
D–Upright with On/off switch for carpet brush.
E–Power-nozzle cord connects automatically at hand grip when reassembling.
F–Regular hose is extra-long: 10-11 ft.
G–Has second, extra-long hose.
H–Hose can remain attached, ready for use.
I–Full-bag indicator.
J–Swivel joint on canister makes it easy to maneuver hose.
K–Carpet brush wider than 12 in.
L–Motor shuts off automatically when overheated or overloaded.
M–Cleaning gap at front of nozzle is ½ in. or less.
N–At least one cleaning gap at side edge of nozzle is ½ in. or less.
O–Rug-pile-height adjustment especially convenient.
P–Headlight easy to replace.
Q–Easy to push when cleaning high-pile carpet.
R–Judged easiest to use on carpet by persons with limited hand or arm function.
S–Easier to use on stairs than others of its type.
T–Bag replacement easier than most.
U–Comes with extra, useful attachments.
V–Power cord more than 30 ft. long.
W–Pushbutton cord rewind.
X–Pull-and-release cord rewind.
Y–Upright that can be used as blower.
Z–Has hose for use on wet surfaces.

Key to Disadvantages
a–On/off switch low on body.
b–Power cord less than 20 ft. long.
c–Cord storage or release is awkward.
d–Headlight difficult to replace.
e–Lacks crevice tool and brush attachments.
f–Hose less than 5 ft. long.
g–Hose difficult to set up or attach.
h–Lacks adjustment for rug-pile height.
i–Carpet brush narrower than 11 in.
j–Cleaning gap at side of nozzle is over 1½ in.
k–Cleaning gap at front of nozzle is over 1 in.
l–Optional carpet nozzle failed to improve deep cleaning.
m–Canister that lacks suction control.
n–Inconvenient for use on stairs.
o–Hard to push on high-pile carpet.
p–Lacks headlight.
q–Canister that cannot be used as blower.
r–Clearance under furniture worse than most.
s–Cannot reach more than 2 ft. under furniture, even when clearance is 14 in.
t–Because of low suction, may clean poorly when fine dust clogs bag.
u–Upright with hose not on board.
v–Canister that lacks independent On/off switch for power nozzle.

Key to Comments
A–Uses container or transparent bin instead of disposable dust bags.
B–Motor shuts off when bag is full or clogged.
C–On/off is by foot switch.
D–Grounded 3-prong plug.
E–Polarized plug.
F–Has small motorized brush for stairs.
G–Claims to kill dust mites by heating bag.
H–Sold only or mainly by home demonstration.
I–Discontinued; replaced by **S3585,** $449.
J–Discontinued; replaced by **23651,** which lacks variable speed, $400.
K–Discontinued.
L–Available also as *Filter Queen*.

Listed by types; within types, listed in order of estimated quality. Closely ranked models differed little in quality. As published in a **February 1993** report.

Brand and model. Models are upright, canister, or compact canister cleaners. If you can't find a model, call the company.

Price. The average nationally advertised sale price.

Type. Uprights are soft-body (**S**) or hard-body (**H**). Soft-body uprights have the familiar vertical bag; hard-body uprights have a rigid plastic exterior. Four of the tested soft-bodies are self-propelled (**P**). All canisters are hard-bodies. Most have a power nozzle (**PN**), a revolving brush that beats the carpet. Suction-only (**SO**) models lack a power nozzle and are less effective at cleaning carpeting.

Overall score. A graphic representation of relative overall quality, made up of scores for performance and convenience.

Performance. The cleaners best at **deep cleaning** picked up four times as much dirt as the worst ones in a given time. High **suction,** usually more prevalent in canisters than in uprights, makes it easy to clean bare floors. Machines that scored well in **filtration** kept dust levels low. As for **noise,** the worst cleaners not only were raucous, they also whined or whistled.

Convenience. Many uprights try to approximate the versatility of a canister by providing an on-board hose and attachments. The most convenient in **hose use** let you keep the hose attached to the unit. **Dirt disposal** is easiest when you can replace a bag by sliding or dropping its cardboard collar into a slot. **Pushing ease** reflects how much effort it took to move the cleaner over a plush carpet. The best moved almost effortlessly. **Carrying ease** reflects judgments of a cleaner's balance as well as its weight. Soft uprights have the greatest **dirt capacity**—about four quarts. But vacuuming fine dusts, such as plaster, can clog any bag prematurely and make you replace it before it's full.

Features. A **cord reel** that rewinds when you press a button or tug on the cord is a big plus. It's more common on canisters; uprights tend to have hooks for manual coiling. If you don't mind the extra weight, having accessory **tools stowed** on the machine can be convenient. Many canisters and hard-body uprights have a **change-bag indicator** that tells you when the bag is full or air flow is reduced. An overfilled bag reduces a cleaner's efficiency.

Features in Common

Except as noted, all: • Have headlight. • Have rug-pile-height adjustment. • Have 20-to-30-ft. power cord. • Have powered carpet brush 11-12 in. wide. • Come with crevice tool and brushes for dusting and upholstery. • Use disposable dust bag. • Can be used on dry surfaces only.

Except as noted, all canisters: • Can be used as blower. • Have suction control. • Can reach at least 3 ft. under furniture that has 3-to-4-in. clearance. • Have separate On/off switch for power nozzle.

Except as noted, all uprights: • Have on-board hose at least 5 ft. long. • Cannot be used as blower. • Can reach at least 3 ft. under furniture that has 9-in. clearance. • Lack separate On/off switch for carpet brush. • Lack suction control.

nozzle of most uprights and a few canisters can be raised or lowered—by dial, sliding lever, or foot pedal—to suit a particular nap. Some models have an automatic height adjustment instead of, or in addition to, manual settings.

Cleaning edges. Run a vacuum cleaner along a baseboard and you'll notice a narrow swath of carpet left untouched because of space taken up by the brush's housing. Usually the untouched area measures one-half to three-quarters of an inch, but some models leave a gap of more than an inch and a half.

Noise. The loudest vacuum cleaners will drown out conversation or whine annoyingly. Uprights, especially the soft-bag models, tend to be noisiest.

Disposing of dirt. Most vacuum cleaners collect dirt in a disposable paper bag; some have an indicator that tells you when the bag is full or when air flow is blocked. Soft-body uprights have the largest bags; they hold about four quarts. Compact canisters' bags are smallest.

Replacing the bag is easiest when you can drop the bag's cardboard collar into a slot. Other models make you slide the bag's sleeve over a tube and secure it with a spring band.

Storing the cord. The most convenient machines have a spring-driven button or pedal that slurps up the 20-to-25-foot power cord automatically. Other cleaners have two hooks around which you wind the cord. If one hook swivels, you can loosen the cord quickly. With some canisters, you must wrap the cord around the tank.

Preventing a problem. If an object gets caught in a cleaner's power nozzle, its motor can overheat and burn out, leaving you with the prospect of a costly repair. Many canisters have a shutoff mechanism to avert burnout.

HAND-HELD VACUUM CLEANERS

The most popular hand-held vac operates on rechargeable batteries and can roam from room to room. But hand vacs with cords offer serious competition, since they can extend vacuuming beyond the 10 minutes or so that a typical rechargeable model allows.

There are extras such as revolving "power brushes" to beat dirt out of carpeting, as well as an assortment of attachments and extensions designed especially for nooks, crannies, drapes, and ceilings.

Cordless models come with a wall-mounted storage bracket that has a built-in battery charger. Car vacs, which plug into an automobile's cigarette-lighter socket, look much like the cordless models, but they come without a wall storage bracket.

CLEANING ABILITY

Most cordless models rely solely on suction to do the job. Their business end typically tapers to an oblong slot some three inches wide.

Plug-in models, on the other hand, generally provide wider coverage. They often come with a built-in five- or six-inch revolving brush well suited to cleaning rugs.

The plug-ins tend to be heavier than the cordless models and auto vacs, but they also tend to be better balanced.

We tested cleaning with a variety of soils spread across a smooth wood surface that simulated hardwood flooring. A hand vac should be able to deal with such things as granulated sugar, rice, and bread crumbs.

Low-pile carpeting littered with tougher material, however, highlighted the power advantage most plug-in models enjoy over their cordless cousins. To retrieve, say, potting soil from a carpet, most cordless vacs and car vacs need 20 to 30 passes; a good plug-in model, with its spinning brushes, may need just 5 to 10 passes. Results should be generally similar with dog hair ground into the carpet.

Hand vacs without revolving brushes have a tougher time with beach sand. And gravel can be a problem even with power-brush cleaners.

Gravel may also scrape particles of plastic from the innards of some plug-in models. Cordless or car vacs won't suffer similar damage, since their filter cup intercepts large debris before it reaches any moving parts.

CONVENIENCE

A revolving brush gives the plug-in vacuums an edge in cleaning carpeting, but it's a mixed blessing. The action of the brush is so vigorous in some models that it competes with their suction, flinging coarser soils about instead of helping to ingest them. Here are some other factors to consider:

Capacity, emptying. Tests with spilled barley showed that the models with the greatest capacity—plug-ins with an external dust bag made of cloth—can hold about six to eleven cups of soil. Most cordless models use an internal dust compartment that can hold only a cup or two of soil (or even less, should the filter clog before the cavity is full).

Models that hold the most soil often prove the messiest to empty. Some bags are held on by an elastic band; you have to stretch the bag's opening or turn the bag inside out to remove the debris, a messy business. Then you must coax the dusty bag back into place. Dust cups are easier to empty, as long as the vac's nose or housing unlatches easily. Some don't.

Dealing with Wet Spills

A few cordless vacs are wet/dry models. They're designed to sip up the proverbial spilled milk, or even the contents of a tipped goldfish bowl. Since they are cordless, there's no shock hazard.

You should clean the vac after every use (a messy job) lest the soggy contents turn stagnant. It might be easier to use a sponge in the first place.

Edge cleaning. The narrow nozzle of most cordless models can slip into tighter spots than can the broad brush heads of the plug-in models.

Fallout. Most vacs have a trap or a flap in the intake designed to prevent debris from dropping back onto the floor when the vac is switched off. None works perfectly.

Blowby. Sometimes the filters in these vacuums don't stop dust or grit from shooting out through vent holes. It's a good idea to wear eye protection when you vacuum coarse debris.

Noise. The noise these vacuums make—measured at arm's length with a sound-level meter—tended to track their cleaning prowess, especially with plug-in models.

FEATURES

Some of the vacuums include attachments that can change their basic character. There may be, for instance, a snap-on revolving brush to convert an ordinary vacuum snout of a cordless model into a vacuuming carpet sweeper, like that on most plug-in models. But the add-on places a heavy burden on the batteries, significantly reducing their ability to run the cleaner before an overnight charge is needed.

A few plug-in models work the opposite way: An accessory hose lets you convert their business end from the built-in revolving brush to a suction-only nozzle.

Here are some other noteworthy features to consider:

Dual speeds. Several vacuums offer two motor settings. Others let you reduce suction by opening an air intake. Less suction may be useful for vacuuming curtains, blinds, or loose-fitting upholstery.

Brushes, wands, nozzles. On a power-brush model, snap-on dust brushes let you gently rake upholstery. And on suction-only models, they improve carpet cleaning by stirring up the embedded litter. A wandlike crevice tool focuses suction powerfully in small areas, while a broad floor nozzle lets you cover more area more quickly. The Ratings note which machines come with such attachments.

When Batteries Go Bad

The rechargeable nickel-cadmium batteries in cordless hand vacs should accept hundreds of charges. But eventually, the clock runs out even on those batteries. Since the batteries are difficult to replace in many hand-vac models, Consumers Union testers called several authorized factory service centers to see how they handle the job.

Four of the five manufacturers whose cordless vacuums were included in the Ratings were willing to replace spent batteries. Only Sears maintained that the section of the vacuum containing the batteries is "not serviceable."

Black & Decker's local center offered to replace the batteries for $15. For the *Douglas* and *Hoover* models, the quote was $30 and $40, respectively. (Alternatively, the *Douglas* or *Hoover* battery pack could be purchased over the counter for about $21, a do-it-yourself job requiring the soldering of a couple of wires.)

A Sanyo service center refused to quote a price over the telephone, saying they would have to see the cleaner first.

Spending $15 to replace the batteries in, say, a $70 or $80 appliance makes sense. But hand vacs often cost much less than that, so in some cases it may pay to simply replace the entire vacuum.

A decision to throw away the vacuum poses an environmental problem. The nickel and cadmium in nicad batteries are toxic, and they can leach out of landfills to contaminate ground-water supplies. Incineration can release the metals into the air, an even greater hazard.

Some companies will accept their old cordless products for proper disposal. Check with the manufacturer before you trash an appliance.

A growing number of states, including Connecticut, Minnesota, New Jersey, and Vermont, require that the batteries in cordless appliances be easy to remove so they can be disposed of separately.

Ratings of hand-held vacuum cleaners

◉ ◓ ○ ◒ ●

Better ⟷ Worse

Brand and model	Price	Weight	Cleaning carpet	Cleaning smooth surfaces	Blowby	Noise	Emptying dirt	Running time	Dry capacity
Plug-in models									
Hoover Brush Vac II S1133	60	3¼	◓	◓	◓	○	◉	—	1½
Panasonic Jet Flo MC-1040	38	3	◓	◉	◉	○	◉	—	1¼
Eureka Step Saver 53A	35	3¼	◒	◉	◉	○	◉	—	2
Royal Dirt Devil 513	44-64	3	○	◉	◉	○	◒	—	6
Sears Klean'n Vac 60071	50+	3¼	◓	◉	◓	◒	●	—	11
Sanyo Dustie SC-181	40	1¾	○	○	◉	○	◓	—	2
Bissell Featherweight Vac 3103-1	30	2¼	○	○	◉	○	◒	—	4
Hoover Help-Mate S1059-6	45	2	○	◓	◉	○	◓	—	1¾
Oreck PowerBrush PB-250	89	3¼	◓	◉	◓	◒	●	—	11
Douglas ReadiVac R6744	55	3¼	◓	◉	◓	◒	●	—	11
Royal Dirt Devil Appliance 103	34-50	3	◓	◉	◓	○	◒	—	6
Black & Decker DirtVac AC7050	58	3¼	◓	◉	○	◒	◒	—	11½
Regina Dirt Magnet DM1800	49	3½	◉	○	●	●	◒	—	8
Cordless models									
Black & Decker Dustbuster Plus DB5400	78	2½	◒	○	◒	◒	◉	11 [1]	2¼
Black & Decker Dustbuster Plus 9338A	70	1¾	●	○	○	○	◉	15 [1]	1½
Hoover Dubl Duty S1103 (wet/dry)	50	2	◒	○	◓	○	◉	6½	2¾
Black & Decker PowerPro DB6000	72	2½	◒	○	○	◒	◉	13½	2¼
Sears Craftsman 17834 (wet/dry)	32+	2¼	●	○	●	○	◉	10	4¼
Black & Decker PowerPro DB2000 (wet/dry)	57	2¼	●	○	◒	○	◉	7½	1½
Black & Decker PowerPro DB3000	57	2¼	◒	○	○	○	◉	11½	2¼
Sanyo Porta Buttler PC-5 [3]	35	1½	●	○	◉	○	◓	7	2¼
Douglas ReadiVac Pow'r Pac R4030	35	1¼	●	○	◓	◓	○	9	1¾
Black & Decker Dustbuster 9330A	39	1½	●	○	○	○	◉	7½	1¼
12-volt car models									
Black & Decker CarVac Plus 9511	35	1	◒	○	◉	○	◉	—	1¼
Black & Decker CarVac 9509	26	1	●	○	◓	◒	◉	—	1¼
Douglas ReadiVac Autovac R4012	30	1	◒	○	◓	○	○	—	2

[1] *Power brush cuts battery running time to a minute or two.*
[2] *Attachment (included) snaps onto vacuum-only nozzle.*
[3] *Successor model, PC-5L.*

Features in Common
All have: • A plastic housing and washable filter/bag.
All cordless and car vacs have: • Suction-only nozzle about 3 in. wide (exclusive of attachments).
Except as noted, all have: • A single-speed motor.
Except as noted, all plug-in models: • Have revolving brushes 5 to 7 in. wide. • Cannot be used as suction-only vacuums.
Except as noted, all plug-in and car models have: • A power cord 15 to 20 ft. long.

Basic tools: Revolving brush	Crevice tool	Dust brush	Advantages	Disadvantages	Comments
✓	—	✓	A,L	—	—
✓	—	—	—	n	—
✓	—	—	B,E,F	h,n	—
✓	✓	✓	A,B	a,d,o	*A,B,H*
✓	—	✓	B,C,D	b,d,h,o	—
—	✓	✓	K	k	*D,J*
—	✓	—	—	a	*I,J*
—	✓	✓	—	i,k	*K*
✓	—	✓	B,D	b,d,h,o	—
✓	—	—	—	b,d,h,o	—
✓	—	—	—	a,d,o	—
✓	✓	✓	B	a,c,f,o	*A,B,E,F,H,L*
✓	✓	✓	K	a,c,d,e,g,i,j,o	*A,H*
[2]	✓	—	A,G	e	*C,E,H,K*
[2]	✓	—	G	e,k,m	*H*
—	—	—	E,J	k,m	—
—	—	—	A	e,i,k	*K*
—	—	—	E,I	e,k	*G*
—	—	—	E,I	k	*G*
—	—	—	A	e,i,k	—
—	✓	—	H	i,k,m	*M*
—	—	—	L	k,l,m	—
—	—	—	—	k,m	—
—	✓	✓	K,L	k	*E*
—	—	—	K,L	k	—
—	✓	✓	L	k,m	—

Key to Advantages

A–Has two motor speeds; gentler setting may be useful for curtains and such.
B–24- or 25-foot power cord, longer than most.
C–Has headlight.
D–Has air-control valve for reducing suction.
E–Has transparent dirt compartment so you can see when it's full. (The **Black & Decker's** tinted compartment is hard to see into.)
F–Opening for rotating brush can swivel upward for stair risers and other vertical surfaces.
G–Accessory power brush (included) was fairly effective and easy to attach.
H–Has charging-indicator light.
I–Wet capacity about 1½ cups.
J–Wet capacity about one cup.
K–Motor housing shaped so power cord winds neatly around it for storage.
L–Cleaned carpeting closer to wall than most.

Key to Disadvantages

a–External dirt bag, somewhat messy to clean.
b–External dirt bag, very messy to clean and difficult to reattach.
c–Test with gravel damaged internal plastic fan.
d–Test with gravel abraded internal parts.
e–May eject grit; wear eye protection.
f–Expelled fine dust through cloth dirt bag.
g–Two of three samples expelled dust through switch recess.
h–Power brush scattered coarse litter more than most.
i–Retaining catch for access to dirt compartment was difficult to release.
j–Handle felt uncomfortable.
k–Nozzle clogged easily in tests with cornflakes.
l–Connector plug disconnects from charging stand every time vacuum is removed, a nuisance.
m–Spring-loaded power switch must be held down to operate vac, a nuisance.
n–Replacing belt for revolving brush more difficult than most.
o–With granular soils, some debris fell out when vacuum was turned off.

Key to Comments

A–Has short (3½-foot) hose.
B–Comes with wand.
C–Comes with ceiling extension for crevice tool.
D–Comes with two wands.
E–Has upholstery brush.
F–Has extra filter cup.
G–Has squeegee for wet pickup.
H–Cleaner attachments can be stored on separate wall bracket (included) or charger cradle.
I–Converts to lightweight upright vacuum with extension handle and broad floor nozzle.
J–Regular nozzle about 3 in. wide, appreciably narrower than on most plug-in models.
K–Wet pick-up kit available for $13.
L–Model *AC7000* ($51) is essentially similar, but comes without accessories.
M–Discontinued. A later model, *PC-5L*, is essentially similar except for added headlight, according to mfr.

Listed by types; within types, listed in order of estimated overall quality. Except where separated by bold rules, closely ranked models differed little in overall quality. Models judged about equal in performance are bracketed and listed alphabetically. As published in a **July 1992** report.

Price is manufacturer's suggested retail price or range. + indicates that shipping is extra.

Weight. To the nearest 1/4 pound.

Cleaning carpet. How well a vacuum picked up debris, including potting soil, sand, dog hair, pins, and brads, from low-pile carpeting. The best needed far fewer passes than did the low-rated models.

Cleaning smooth surfaces. How well a vacuum picked up debris from a smooth, hard surface such as wood flooring or a countertop.

Blowby. Most models expelled some fine dust through vents or external dust bags. The worst also ejected sand grains, from which you might need eye protection.

Noise. The most raucous models rivaled a full-size vacuum in noisiness. The quietest sounded about one-quarter as loud.

Emptying dirt. Models with an internal dust cup were generally easiest to empty. The messiest use an external cloth bag, which must be detached and shaken out. Wet/dry models can be messy as well when loaded with soggy debris.

Running time. How long, to nearest 1/2 minute, the cordless models could vacuum effectively before they needed recharging. The longest ran about 15 minutes; the shortest, about seven minutes.

Dry capacity. How much dry soil, to the nearest 1/4 cup, a vacuum can hold in its dirt compartment or dust bag. The most capacious models, with an external cloth bag, held 6 to 11 1/2 cups; the skimpiest models, with an internal dust cup, held only one or two cups.

Basic tools. A built-in **revolving brush,** standard in most plug-ins, helps beat dirt out of a carpet's pile. A **crevice tool** is a slender accessory nozzle for reaching into tight spots. A **dust brush** fits over the nozzle opening or on the end of an accessory hose. In suction-only machines, it can help the cleaner pick up tenacious soils like pet hair or sand; in machines with a revolving brush, it can act as a spacer between the brush and loose or delicate fabrics.

RECOMMENDATIONS

A power cord would seem to compromise the main advantage of a hand-held vacuum. But an extra-long cord (some stretch 25 feet) may make a plug-in vac an attractive alternative to a cordless model.

Plug-in models are strong performers and some provide much greater dirt capacity than that available with a cordless vac. Most have a broad revolving brush, which helps them make quick work of a variety of soils ground into a rug. Plug-ins also should be at least as effective as cordless models on a smooth wood surface.

GARBAGE BAGS

The labels on some garbage bags boast that they're multi-ply or use a high-strength plastic. But even if you know how to select a strong garbage bag, you still have to sort through more choices. Manufacturers offer a huge variety of sizes, styles, closure gimmicks, colors, even scents.

Garbage bags go by many names, such as trash, rubbish, scrap, kitchen, wastebasket, or lawn and leaf. The name, along with some fine print on the box, is supposed to help you pick the right-size bag. But you've probably grabbed at least one box of "small garbage bags" instead of the "tall kitchen bags" you wanted. Or you may have bought a bag that "holds up to 26 gallons" that barely fits your 26-gallon can. This happens because some manufacturers measure capacities when the bags are filled to the brim; others measure them closed. Another reason may be the sizing of your can. Without industry-wide standards, some bags will not fit some garbage cans, even though the gallonage claimed is the same for both.

BAG STRENGTH

You might think that the thickness of the plastic or the number of plies, as given on the label, would be a good guide to the quality of a bag. Not so, judging from Consumers Union's tests. The thickest bags tested were labeled 2 mils, or 0.002-inch thick. (A mil is one-thousandth of an inch.) Those brands failed the test. But bags 1.3 mils thick passed.

You might also think that the more plies, the stronger the bag. Again, not so. Double- and triple-ply bags failed the test about as often as they passed. Many packages make no mention of plies, which may mean they contain single-ply bags. Or it may mean the number of plies changes whenever a distributor switches suppliers.

RECOMMENDATIONS

Plastic garbage bags are unpredictable. Tests show that paying more or buying the thickest bags you can find are no guarantees you'll get a strong bag. The fact is, you may not even need a strong bag. Unless you nearly always have very heavy garbage, you may be paying for unneeded extra strength. In that case, you might consider a cheaper bag of unknown strength. If the cheaper bag turns out to be strong enough most of the time, but not for the occasional heavy load, consider lining the garbage can with two bags when necessary. In the long run, this can be cheaper than buying stronger bags.

GLASS CLEANERS

Squeegee-wielding professionals know that plain water can clean lightly soiled windows. But if you put off washing your windows until they're really dirty, you'll need something more potent.

The best glass cleaner is one that works fast and removes grime with a minimum of help from you. Unfortunately, many of the glass cleaners on the market are mediocre products. Homemade recipes can equal or best many of the aerosols, sprays, and premoistened towels in the stores.

Consumers Union's laboratory tests showed that cleaners vary widely in their effectiveness.

The home-brew formulas did respectable work, cleaning the glass in about 25 strokes, putting many a store-bought cleaner to shame in the process.

The vinegar variant of high-rated *SOS Ammonia Plus* was one of the poorest performers. Other vinegar brands were generally inferior to their ammonia-based versions.

Both specialty products, *ClearVue* and *Seventh Generation,* offered disappointing performances. So did *Spiffits* and *Glass Mates* towels. *ClearVue* and *Spiffits* performed best among the four, but neither came close to plain tap water in the test.

To see how the cleaners could cope with greasy, dirty smudges, the testers concocted a mixture of artificial skin oils, mineral oil, lampblack, powdered clay, cornstarch, and water. A technician made handprints on hundreds of glass panes, let them dry overnight, then worked with paper towels, testing each cleaner up to eight times. A panel of staffers judged the results for spots, streaks, and smudges on a 10-point scale.

A lemon home brew was the best cleaner in this test, performing more consistently from one pane to the next than any of the commercial brands.

Most commercial products performed inconsistently in this test, cleaning one pane well, the next not so well.

CLEANING

The home-brew formulas are far cheaper than anything you can buy—no more than a penny an ounce, compared with five cents an ounce or more for the supermarket brands. Pump sprays generally carry a lower cost per ounce than do aerosols, and supermarket house brands are generally cheaper than national brands.

With most commercial products, an ounce of cleaner goes pretty far. It would cost only a few pennies to clean both sides of a window measuring 2 × 3 feet. With the home brews, the cost per window is insignificant. On the other hand, premoistened towels qualify as premium-priced cleaners.

THE ENVIRONMENT

Among the ingredients in any window cleaner, detergents, ammonia, and lemon break down and degrade readily. None of the brands tested pose any evident problems for the environment. None of the cleaners contain phosphorus, and none of the aerosols use ozone-depleting propellants.

Ratings of Glass Cleaners

◉ ◓ ○ ◒ ●
Better ⟷ Worse

Listed by types. Commercial products are listed in groups in order of ability to clean heavily soiled glass; within groups, listed in order of increasing cost per ounce. As published in a **January 1992** report.

Package. Cleaners come in plastic pump bottles (**P**), aerosol cans (**A**), metal pour-cans (**C**), and in packages of premoistened towel-wipes (**T**). People with hand or arm limitations will find some packages easier to use than others; the Ratings Comments give the specifics.

Price. For home brews, the price paid for ingredients. For commercial products, the estimated average price for the size tested, based on prices paid nationally. A * indicates the price paid (a national average price wasn't available). A + indicates an additional shipping charge.

Cleaning. How well products cleaned glass panels heavily soiled with a tough tobacco-smoke extract. Highest-scoring cleaners removed the extract completely and with the fewest strokes.

Product	Package	Size, oz. or fl. oz.	Price	Cost per oz. or fl. oz.	Cleaning	Advantages	Disadvantages	Comments
Home brews								
Plain tap water	—	—	—	—	◓	—	—	*D*
CU's lemon formula	—	128	$ .16	0.1¢	◓	A	b	*C*
CU's ammonia formula	—	128	1.01	0.8	◓	—	—	—
Commercial products								
K Mart With Ammonia	P	22	1.56	7	◉	—	b	*A,L*
SOS Extra Strength Ammonia Plus	P	22	2.05	9	◉	—	b	*A*
Savogran Dirtex	A	18	2.13*	12	◉	—	b	*B*
Walgreen's With Ammonia	P	32	1.69*	5	◓	—	—	—
A&P With Ammonia	P	22	1.62	7	◓	—	b	*A*
Albertson's With Ammonia	P	22	1.61	7	◓	—	—	*A*

Lady Lee With Ammonia (Lucky Stores)	P	22	1.49	7	◓	—	—	*A*
Glass Plus	P	22	2.05	9	◓	—	b	*A*
K Mart With Ammonia	A	19	1.67	9	◓	—	b	*B,F*
Windex With Ammonia-D	P	22	2.16	10	◓	—	—	*A*
Windex With Ammonia-D King Size	A	20	2.27	11	◓	—	—	*B*
Gold Seal Glass Wax	C	16	1.84	12	◓	—	a,b	*G*
Scott's Liquid Gold	A	14	1.73	12	◓	—	—	*E*
Easy Off "Lemonized" With Ammonia	P	22	2.96	13	◓	—	b	*A*
A&P With Vinegar	P	22	1.19	5	○	—	—	*B,H*
Kroger Bright With Ammonia +	P	22	1.58	7	○	—	—	*A*
ClearVue Professional	P	20	1.94	10	○	—	—	*B,I,M*
Spiffits One Step Towels	T	[1]	2.77	12	○	—	b	*A,I*
Windex Lemon Fresh with Ammonia-D	P	22	2.19	10	◒	—	—	*A,C*
Seventh Generation	P	22	4.50+*	20	◒	—	a,b	*B,I,M*
Sparkle	P	25	2.00	8	●	—	b	*A,K*
SOS Extra Strength Vinegar	P	22	1.96	9	●	—	—	*A,J*
Windex Fresh Scent With Vinegar-D	P	22	2.17	10	●	—	b	*A,J*
Glass Mates Wipes	T	[1]	2.75	14	●	—	b	*B,I*

[1] **Spiffits** *box holds 24 moist towels;* **Glass Mates** *canister holds 20 towels. Cost listed is per towel. One* **Spiffits** *or two* **Glass Mates** *towels can clean one heavily soiled window or more than one lightly soiled window.*

Features in Common
Except as noted, all smell of ammonia.

Key to Advantages
A–Somewhat better than most in cleaning greasy, sooty handprints.

Key to Disadvantages
a–Somewhat worse than most in cleaning greasy, sooty handprints.
b–May stain painted surfaces slightly if spills aren't wiped up quickly.

Key to Comments
A–Easier to use than most, especially for people with hand or arm limitations.
B–Harder to use than most, especially for people with hand or arm limitations.
C–Lemon scent.
D–Odorless.
E–Orange scent.
F–Floral scent.
G–Petroleum odor.
H–Vinegar odor.
I–Alcohol odor.
J–Fruity scent.
K–Solvent odor.
L–Only finger-pump bottle tested; other bottled products sold with trigger pump.
M–**ClearVue** sold mainly in East. **Seventh Generation** sold by mail (800-456-1177).

Newspaper vs. Paper Towels for Cleaning Glass

Over the years, there have been many opinions about which window-washing solutions and polishing techniques are best. People have sworn by fuller's earth, alcohol, soap, detergent, chalk dust (favored by stained-glass workers), vinegar, and, of course, copious amounts of water. Professionals do their wiping with natural-sponge applicators and rubber squeegees.

In England, purists feel the job is unfinished without the careful application of a good chamois leather. In this country, many people swear by yesterday's newspaper.

In a Consumers Union test, newspaper was found to be not very absorbent, and it took a fair amount of wiping and rubbing to clean and polish a window with it. Fresh newspaper also blackens hands and leaves ink smudges around window mullions. Ink smudges are much less pronounced with six-month-old paper.

Newspapers make a satisfying "squeak-squeak" as you rub; the stiffness of the paper itself might help when scrubbing a truly filthy, dirt-encrusted window; and cleaning windows is a way to recycle newspaper. In the end, however, you end up with an ungainly pile of soggy, crumpled newspaper. Paper towels are much better.

As for solid waste, most of the pump bottles are made of polyvinyl chloride, a type of plastic that's rarely recycled. Steel aerosol cans are increasingly being recycled, as recyclers start using more sophisticated ways to separate metals from plastics.

CARE IN USE

Any glass cleaner, even plain water, will soften latex paint on mullions and sills around a window. Most will soften semigloss latex paint as well. A few will also soften oil-based semigloss paint. The paint will reharden once it has dried. Still, you should use a cleaner sparingly and quickly, and wipe it off painted surfaces without hard rubbing.

HOME BREWS

Consumers Union's home-brew recipe proved quite effective. For lightly soiled windows, try a lemon cleaner—four tablespoons of lemon juice in a gallon of water. It's best for cleaning greasy handprints and costs only 0.1 cent an ounce. For heavier soil, try an ammonia recipe—one-half cup sudsy ammonia, one pint rubbing alcohol, and one teaspoon dishwashing liquid with enough water to make a gallon. This should clean up baked-on soil quite well, costing only about a penny an ounce. Even plain tap water can equal or better many store-bought brands.

OVEN CLEANERS

Many drain-cleaning products contain sodium hydroxide or lye, one of the most dangerous substances sold for household use—and so do most oven cleaners. Baked-on oven dirt is too tough for ordinary cleaners, which can only soften or dissolve grime. Lye causes a chemical reaction, decomposing the stuck-on fats and sugars into soapy compounds you can wash away. Lye-containing oven cleaners are corrosively alkaline, with a pH of about 13 on the 14-point pH scale. Any substance that far from the neutral pH of seven is reactive enough to cause serious burns, which is why most of the labels contain a long list of warnings.

The majority of the cleaners on the market are aerosol sprays, which are quick to apply but hard to aim neatly. Clouds of aerosol mist deposit cleaner not only on oven walls but also on heating elements, thermostats, light fixtures—and in your lungs. Most product labels warn you not to inhale the "fumes," by which they mean the aerosol droplets of lye.

As explained below, some application methods and container designs protect you more than others from exposure to caustic lye. Still, any product that contains lye must be used with extreme caution. Lye can burn skin and eyes. Inhaled droplets can actually burn the throat and lungs. Before using any cleaner containing lye, you should don safety goggles, a long-sleeved shirt, and rubber gloves. If you're using an aerosol, wear a paper dust mask (to keep from inhaling the droplets) and protective goggles.

Not only should you take steps to protect yourself from the corrosive effects of lye, you should also protect nearby floors, counters, and other surfaces. Spread newspaper on the floor in front of the oven. Take care not to splash any of the cleaner on aluminum, copper, or painted surfaces outside the oven, and keep it off the heating element, gaskets, and light fixture inside. Use oven cleaner only on shiny porcelain, coated metal surfaces, or glass. Never use it on continuous-cleaning (dull finish) or self-cleaning oven finishes or on bare metal.

Another way to avoid dangerous fumes and corrosive spatters is to use an aerosol cleaner without lye. For years, the only such product on the market was *Arm & Hammer* oven cleaner. The maker of *Easy-Off* bought *Arm & Hammer*'s cleaner and renamed it *Easy-Off Non-Caustic Formula* (according to the maker, a more recent designation is *Easy-Off Fume Free Oven Cleaner*). Instead of using lye to break down oven grime, the *Easy-Off* product uses a combination of organic salts that are activated by heat. The product doesn't have to carry a long list of warnings on its label. It won't damage kitchen surfaces. You don't have to arm yourself with rubber gloves and a face mask to use it because it isn't likely to irritate.

PACKAGING

An oven cleaner's packaging affects its convenience of use and safety. Oven-cleaning products come in four forms: pad, aerosol, brush-on jelly, and pump spray. All have drawbacks.

Because they don't create airborne lye particles, pads are a relatively safe way to apply oven cleaner, as long as you've covered your hands and forearms. Aerosols are easy to apply, but they're also easy to get on gaskets, heating elements, and sometimes your face by mistake. A broad, concave button makes it harder to misdirect the spray than a small button.

Not only is it tedious to paint an entire oven with brush-on jelly using a brush that's barely an inch wide, it's almost impossible to keep the jelly from spattering. Finally, a hand-pumped spray can be a real annoyance. The adjustable nozzle produces anything from a stream to a misty, broad spray. The stream doesn't cover much and splatters, and the spray is unnecessarily diffuse and easy to inhale.

RECOMMENDATIONS

Even if you lack a self-cleaning or continuous-cleaning oven, you aren't necessarily sentenced to the hard labor of cleaning your oven. An oven in continual use can reach a steady state at which grease and grime burn off at the same rate they accumulate. Serious spills, such as when a cake overflows its pan, can be scraped up after the oven cools. A little dirt in the oven never hurt anybody—a little oven cleaner might.

PAPER TOWELS

Some brands of paper towels are the same nationwide, but there are also many regional and store brands. In a few cases, towels of a nationally known brand name vary from region to region.

Manufacturers try to control a larger share of the market by selling a variety of brands, aiming a premium one, for example, at consumers who believe that a high price connotes high quality and aiming a moderately priced one at consumers who treat one roll of towels pretty much like any other. One supermarket executive termed premium-priced towels "overspecified," meaning they are thicker and heavier than they have to be. The overspecified towel gives the advertiser something to brag about and helps justify the generally higher price, which in turn pays for both the manufacturing costs and the heavy advertising and promotion expenses.

Paper towels lead a brief and unglamorous life. They're typically called upon to scour a dirty oven, sop up a kitchen spill, or wipe a window—and then within moments they're gone. And yet, to perform these seemingly unexacting tasks, paper towels need several disparate qualities. Even when wet, they should withstand scrubbing without falling apart.

For mopping up, a costly but highly absorbent towel can be as economical as a cheap but less absorbent towel. For spilled salad dressing or motor oil, a poor-quality towel tends to smear the spill rather than absorb it.

Towels should separate cleanly at their perforations; otherwise, you may be left holding either a torn sheet or more sheets than you need. Generally, the two-ply towels detach more evenly than the one-ply towels, although there are exceptions.

Paper towels with short, weakly anchored fibers tend to shed lint, a particular problem when you clean a mirror or windowpane.

Softness is relatively unimportant in a paper towel—at least according to an informal poll of more than 60 Consumers Union staffers. Even so, a panel of lab technicians judged relative softness for people who care about it. Soft towels are usually more absorbent, but they may not hold up as well during scouring.

RECOMMENDATIONS

The strongest, most absorbent towels are likely to be the premium-priced brands, which does not make such towels the best value. Use an economical one for everyday chores. For more demanding tasks, you might want to buy a roll of strong and absorbent, relatively expensive towels to keep around the house.

MICROWAVE OVENS

For modest microwaving chores—steaming fish or poultry, cooking vegetables or bacon, preparing hot sandwiches—it's wise to wrap or cover the food with white paper towels. They keep the oven clean by absorbing spattered grease and excess moisture and help to keep certain foods from drying out or becoming soggy. But are some paper towels better than others for microwaving?

Procter & Gamble states that its *Bounty Microwave* towels are "specially formulated for microwave tasks." However, *Bounty Microwave* and regular *Bounty* looked suspiciously similar to Consumers Union's technicians; the two were closely matched in strength and absorbency, so both were tested in a microwave oven.

The technicians wrapped bread and rolls (with and without cheese) in both types of towels and warmed them at the same oven settings. They also wrapped bacon slices and cooked them. There were no meaningful differences in the taste or appearance of any of the foods.

The tests were repeated, comparing *Bounty Microwave* with one-ply *Viva* and the two inexpensive towels, *A&P* and *Page*. It was necessary to use several extra *Page* towels to fully contain the bacon fat. But again, there was no meaningful difference in the appearance or taste of the food.

The conclusion: For simple microwaving, there's no need to pay extra for *Bounty Microwave*. Any plain white paper towel should do.

TOUGHER TOWELS FOR TOUGH JOBS

Shop towels are for cleaning up grime in the garage or workshop, scrubbing away rust, and other tasks too tough for ordinary paper towels. Shop towels made of paper are throwaways; cloth towels are meant to be washed and reused.

Scott *Shop Towels on a Roll* and *Scott Rags* come in 55-sheet rolls and cost about three cents per towel. They're fairly thick single-ply sheets measuring about 11 × 10½ inches. One is blue, the other is white.

J. C. Whitney (1917-19 Archer Avenue, P.O. Box 8410, Chicago, IL 60680) sells bundles of 72 hemmed plain-weave 14 × 16-inch cloth shop towels for about 28 cents a towel.

The two *Scott* shop towels were stronger than the best ordinary paper towel. The cloth shop towels were far stronger than any of the paper products.

Both paper and cloth shop towels cleaned greasy tools and scrubbed rust effectively. The paper towels tended to shred a bit but did the job nevertheless.

The paper shop towels took only one second to absorb a drop of water. After several washings to remove their sizing, the cloth shop towels still didn't absorb water as quickly, but were fine for oil.

Paper shop towels are certainly more convenient than cloth. But the cloth shop towels are cheaper if they're used at least 10 times. (Household rags, of course, are cheaper still.)

Ratings of Paper Towels

◉ Better ← ◓ ○ ◒ → ● Worse

Listed in order of estimated quality. Closely ranked models below *Job Squad* were judged similar in quality. As published in a **January 1992** report.

Product. The Comments note where performance varied widely within a brand from region to region.

Plies. A towel consists of one or two layers, or plies. (One-ply and two-ply *Viva* and *Pathmark* towels are different models and are rated separately.)

Price per roll. The average price, based on prices paid nationally for a single roll, according to a survey. * is average price paid by CU.

Sheets per roll. As stated on wrapper.

Cost per 100 sheets. A more meaningful measure of cost than price per roll.

Wet strength. Determined by how much lead shot a wet towel could support and how well it held up during scrubbing.

Absorbency. The best absorbed about four times as much water as the worst.

Absorption rate. The best towels absorbed water in a twinkling; the worst took about 16 seconds. Oil went more slowly—from three or four seconds to more than two minutes.

Tearing ease. Sheets should separate cleanly and easily from the roll.

Linting. Annoying if you clean windows or mirrors with paper towels. A high score means relatively few flecks left behind.

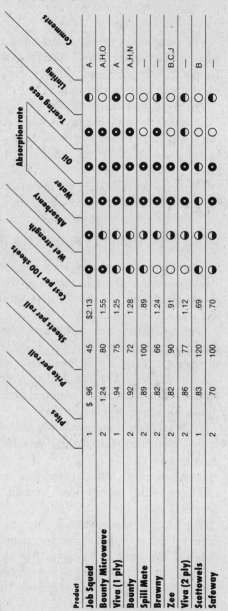

							Absorption rate				
Product	**Plies**	**Price per roll**	**Sheets per roll**	**Cost per 100 sheets**	**Wet strength**	**Absorbency**	**Water**	**Oil**	**Tearing ease**	**Linting**	**Comments**
Job Squad	1	$ .96	45	$2.13	◉	◉	◉	◉	◉	◓	A
Bounty Microwave	2	1.24	80	1.55	◉	◓	◉	◉	◉	○	A,H,O
Viva (1 ply)	1	.94	75	1.25	◓	◓	◉	◉	◉	◉	A
Bounty	2	.92	72	1.28	◓	◓	◉	◉	◉	○	A,H,N
Spill Mate	2	.89	100	.89	◓	◒	◉	◉	○	○	—
Brawny	2	.82	66	1.24	○	◓	◉	◉	◉	◒	—
Zee	2	.82	90	.91	○	◒	◉	◉	○	○	B,C,J
Viva (2 ply)	2	.86	77	1.12	○	◒	◉	◉	◓	◓	—
Scottowels	1	.83	120	.69	◓	◒	◓	◓	○	○	B
Safeway	2	.70	100	.70	◒	◒	◉	◉	○	◓	—

Start	2	.93	81	1.15	◒	◒	◉	◉	○	◒	B,C,D
Scottowels Junior	1	.61	95	.64	○	◒	○	◓	◓	◓	B,F
Gala	2	.77	90	.86	◒	◒	◉	◉	○	○	—
Sparkle	2	.75	90	.83	◒	◒	○	◉	○	○	—
Truly Fine (Safeway)	2	.99*	105	.94	●	◒	◉	◉	◒	○	—
Mardi Gras	2	.78	100	.78	●	◒	◉	◉	◓	○	H
Marcal	2	.67	100	.67	◒	◒	◓	◉	◒	◒	C,D,P
Hi-Dri	2	.67	96	.70	◒	◒	◓	◉	○	◓	B,C
Green Forest	2	.77	100	.77	●	◒	◉	◓	○	○	C
Pathmark (2-ply)	2	.69	100	.69	●	◒	◓	◉	○	◓	—
Kroger	2	.57	100	.57	●	◒	◉	◉	○	○	C
Big'N'Thirsty	1	.65	100	.65	◒	◒	◓	◒	◒	○	B,K
Seventh Generation	2	1.00*	90	1.11	●	◒	◉	◉	○	◓	C,E,G,I
So-Dri	2	.58	100	.58	●	◒	◉	◓	○	○	H,I
A&P	2	.67	100	.67	●	◒	◉	◉	◒	◒	C,I
Delta	1	.61	100	.61	◒	●	◒	●	◒	○	B
C.A.R.E.	2	.89*	88	1.01	●	◒	○	◉	◒	◒	D
Pathmark (1-ply)	1	.69	140	.49	◒	◒	●	◒	◒	◒	B
Marigold (Safeway)	1	.56	90	.62	◒	◒	●	●	●	○	B
Page	1	.44	75	.59	●	◒	●	●	○	○	B,L,M
Cost Cutter (Kroger)	1	.53	75	.71	●	◒	●	●	○	○	B,C

Features in Common

Except as noted, all: • Fit a standard dispenser.

Key to Comments

A–Judged softer than most.
B–Judged rougher than most.
C–Made of 100-percent recycled paper.
D–No chlorine bleach used in manufacturing, according to manufacturer.
E–Unbleached, according to manufacturer.
F–About 3 in. narrower than most; requires adapter (free from mfr.) for standard dispenser.
G–Sold by mail order, 30 rolls to a box. For ordering information, call 800-456-1177.
H–Wrapper perforated for easier opening.
I–First sheet forms easy-to-grasp pull tab.
J–Samples bought in Washington State judged much slower to absorb oil.
K–Samples bought in Texas judged much slower to absorb water.
L–Samples bought in Maryland judged much more difficult to tear cleanly.
M–Samples bought in Texas produced much more lint.
N–All current single-roll packs will now have 72 sheets, according to mfr.
O–All current single-roll packs will now have 108 sheets, according to mfr.
P–Samples bought in Maryland averaged 67¢ per roll in 3-roll package.

ENVIRONMENTAL CONCERNS

It's hard to say which is worse for the environment: dumping used paper towels into landfills and incinerators, or washing cloth towels that have absorbed used engine oil or solvents, sending such contaminants into the water system.

Most paper towels these days contain some recycled paper, but the exact amount is often undisclosed. Some paper towels, mostly small and private-label brands, mention their recycled content on the label, but most major manufacturers don't.

Towels made of 100-percent recycled paper may require some sacrifice on the part of consumers. They generally don't perform as well as those made of virgin fiber.

Bleaching, a manufacturing process that is supposed to make paper products more attractive, is another environmental concern. It can create pollution at the pulp plant, especially when chlorine bleach is used. A few towels on the market are unbleached, but you may not be able to determine this from reading the label.

Among the factors that discourage "recycled" labeling is the absence of a nationwide definition of "recycled content." Various states and the District of Columbia have different standards, and manufacturers are understandably reluctant to print 51 different labels for each product.

Another complicating factor is the classification of recycled paper as either "postconsumer" or "preconsumer" waste. The former is paper salvaged and turned in by consumers; the latter—paper such as print overruns, paper-mill trimmings, and the like—has never reached consumers.

Preconsumer waste is cheaper to process, so manufacturers don't need much encouragement to use it. Environmental groups are understandably eager to push manufacturers into using more postconsumer waste. But manufacturers complain that when recovered paper arrives at a recycling mill, some of it isn't easily identifiable as pre- or postconsumer waste.

Among the current labeling standards, one of the weakest is California's, where a product that is labeled as recycled may contain as little as 10 percent postconsumer waste.

Recycling alone can't solve the growing problem of solid waste. Paper towels, no matter how "green," cannot be recycled; eventually, most end up in landfills and incinerators. Most things that a paper towel can do, a cloth or sponge can do just as well, with less waste of resources.

TOILET BOWL CLEANERS

A common cause of persistent toilet-bowl staining is minerals that build up around the waterline and under the rim. The culprit is usually hard water, which has a high mineral content. As the water evaporates, mineral salts such as calcium or magnesium compounds and darker colored iron compounds are left behind, coating the upper part of the bowl and eventually hardening into a scale. Even with soft water, molds can form a brown coating in the bowl. If the ceramic surface is slick, such deposits hardly find a foothold. But if the surface has been scratched by abrasive cleaners or roughened with age, the buildup can grow rapidly.

Automatic, in-tank products are the easiest to use but generally only mask the dirt. The real cleaners are the liquid and granular in-bowl cleaners that are meant to be used with a brush.

IN-BOWL CLEANERS

Most in-bowl cleaners use acid to dissolve mineral scale and eradicate stains. Active agents include hydrochloric, phosphoric, and oxalic acids; some granular cleaners use sodium bisulfate, which when dissolved works like sulfuric acid. Brands with the highest total acidity have the greatest potential for cleaning. Products with lower acid content may require a bit more cleaner or a bit more muscle to do the job.

Nonacidic liquids won't be very effective at removing mineral stains. But they should work well on nonmineral stains, which are relatively easy to remove with a brush.

Ounce for ounce, the best bargain costs less than 20 cents a dose. You might try a dash of liquid all-purpose cleaner. Brushed on, it can clean a lightly soiled bowl quite satisfactorily for less.

Compared with liquids, powders are less convenient to apply around the bowl and under the rim. Most liquids come in a bottle with a flip-top spout. Unfortunately, even bottles with a recessed flip-top—supposedly child-resistant—can be opened easily by twisting off the entire cap.

The chemicals in these cleaners are powerful and should be handled carefully. Never mix an in-bowl cleaner with other household chemicals (including in-tank toilet cleaners). To do so could release toxic fumes.

IN-TANK CLEANERS

Most in-tank products rely heavily on blue dye to tint the water and hide the dirt that accumulates between real scrubbings. Although blue cleaners generally contain small amounts of detergent and other ingredients to curb stains, none actually claim to clean a dirty bowl. With an in-tank cleaner, then, the question is not how well it works but how long it lasts. Don't be too quick to change containers when the blue vanishes. Check to see if the dispensing valve has clogged or if the product is actually used up.

Some blue cleaners claim to deodorize. If you sniff packages on the store shelf, you may notice wintergreen, pine, or lemon scents. Indeed, the packages sometimes have a very strong smell. But once the cleaner dissolves in the tank, the scent is practically imperceptible.

BLEACH

Some in-tank cleaners slowly dispense chlorine bleach to lighten stains and give off a scent that many people associate with cleanliness. Products containing bleach are likely to last longer than blue cleaners.

Consumers Union tested some products packaged in weighty plastic dispensers containing solid, organic bleach and other products filled with pebbles or calcium hypochlorite bleach.

The amount of bleach such cleaners release can vary considerably from flush to flush. Typically, it's very little—much less than a thimbleful of regular laundry bleach. They release enough chlorine to bleach stains, however, since the water may stand in the bowl for hours. Normally, such water won't harm pets should they drink from the bowl, and neither will blue-colored water. But when a toilet isn't flushed at least once a day, the bleach can become more concentrated and may damage parts inside the tank. Some plumbing-fixture manufacturers recommend against using in-tank cleaners containing hypochlorite bleach.

Since chlorine is not as visible as blue dye, you might not know when to replace a bleach-based bowl cleaner. If your water is chlorinated, your nose may not tell you. You can use a drop of food coloring in the bowl to test. If the coloring lasts for more than a few minutes, it means that the cleaner is spent.

RECOMMENDATIONS

The best way to clean the toilet bowl is to brush it frequently with a liquid all-purpose cleaner. In-bowl toilet cleaners are for more serious stains. Scrubbing with an acidic powder or liquid is the one sure way to attack the mineral matter that causes most toilet bowl stains, particularly around the rim.

In-tank cleaners, blue-colored or bleaches, are easy to use, but don't expect miracles. If you start with a spotless toilet, they will only slow the buildup of new stains and keep the bowl presentable between more thorough scrubbings. In-tank bleach cleaners should not be used in a toilet that isn't flushed regularly. Enough chlorine can accumulate to damage parts inside the tank.

Finally, do not let any brand's claims to disinfect sway you. At best, a "disinfecting" cleaner can only temporarily cut the population of some germs.

LAUNDRY

You can save energy and time and still end up with laundry loads that look clean and smell fresh if you sort clothes following the guidelines described below.

As you sort wash loads, remember to empty pockets and close zippers to prevent snagging. Next, check for heavy or troublesome stains which may become set by the washing process. Many stains won't respond well to a presoak or laundry booster alone, and require special treatment *before* washing. Check the Stain Removal Chart at the end of this book for detailed instructions on removing a variety of typical, and not so typical, stains.

In general, try to separate heavily soiled clothes from lightly soiled ones. Heavy soils have a tendency to become transferred, making whites and light colors appear dingy. Wash intense colors (very dark or very bright) separately. They may bleed, especially when washing for the first time, and permanently tint white or light-colored clothes washed in the same load. A good guide is the maker's care label.

Most wash loads do quite well in cold or warm water. Heavy soils may respond better to a hot-water wash, although hot water may have an adverse effect on a garment's permanent-press properties. Again, check the garment's care label.

Try to avoid sorting into loads that are too small: A washing machine is most efficient in its use of water (especially hot water) and electricity if it is at its recommended full capacity, reducing the total number of loads you'll need to do on any given washday.

For the best ways to cope with a pile of dirty laundry, check the following reports on bleaches, detergents, boosters, softeners, and washing machines.

BLEACHES

Liquid chlorine bleach is the old standby, having earned its place in the laundry room as well as in the bathroom and kitchen for whitening and removing stains and mildew.

But chlorine bleach also has its problems. The telltale signs of misuse or overuse of chlorine bleach are splotches of faded color or white spots, where undiluted bleach has splashed, and fabrics that have faded from vivid to dim.

Nonchlorine, "all-fabric" bleaches promise the benefits of chlorine bleach without the risk, but the real story unfolds in the laundry room.

Both chlorine and nonchlorine bleaches use an oxidizing agent (usually sodium hypochlorite or sodium perborate) that reacts with and lifts out a stain, with the help of a detergent. Liquid chlorine bleaches all have about the same amount of active ingredient, and there is little difference from one brand to another.

PERFORMANCE

Chlorine bleaches have always been better than nonchlorine, all-fabric bleaches at whitening clothes.

All-fabric bleaches, especially the powdered products, do whiten, but not nearly as well as chlorine bleaches. In fact, all-fabric liquid bleaches are hardly better at whitening than detergent alone. If you wash the laundry load successive times with an all-fabric bleach, the whitening process continues, but even several applications won't match the whitening power of a single use of chlorine bleach.

HARD-TO-REMOVE STAINS

Some stains, such as spaghetti sauce, red wine, and blood, seem to have an affinity for clothing and, once entrenched, leave with great reluctance.

Neither chlorine nor nonchlorine bleach can completely remove spaghetti sauce. In general, chlorine or nonchlorine bleach should be used with a good laundry detergent to succeed at removing greasy stains.

See the Stain Removal Chart for Fabrics on page 208 for additional information.

FADING

Bleach, especially chlorine bleach, can cause colors to fade.

Initially, bleach may have no noticeable effect on the brightness of colors. Chlorine bleaches may not seem harsher than an all-fabric product. After a few washings, however, the chlorine begins taking its toll. Slight fading becomes evident and then, after more washings, objectionable. But an all-fabric bleach will continue being kind to colors.

RECOMMENDATIONS

Chlorine bleach, when used properly, is the most effective way to whiten fabrics, including some synthetics. It's ideal for the occasional whitening your wash may need, but knowing how to use chlorine bleach is essential: Improper and long-term use may take its toll on colors and fabric life. Using chlorine bleach may be tricky, but buying it is simple. The only real difference you are likely to find is price.

All-fabric powdered bleaches have the advantage of being safe with most fabrics and dyes, even over the long term. They're much more expensive to use than chlorine bleaches; however, they aren't as good at whitening.

A more reasonable and less costly approach might be the occasional and cautious use of chlorine bleach on chlorine-safe white fabrics to deliver the whitening you need. Use all-fabric bleach to brighten colors without fading and to whiten fabrics that are not safe for use with chlorine bleach.

When you use chlorine bleach, follow these guidelines:

- Bleach only when necessary.

- Before you bleach, read the garment's care label.
- Don't use chlorine bleach on wool, silk, mohair, or noncolorfast fabrics or dyes. If you're unsure about a garment's fabric content, experiment with a diluted solution of bleach on an inside seam. Any discoloration should appear in a minute or so.
- If your washer has a bleach dispenser, use it according to the manufacturer's directions. If there's no dispenser, follow the labeled directions on the bleach and on the laundry detergent.
- *Never* use chlorine bleach with ammonia or toilet cleaners. The combination can produce deadly fumes.

BOOSTERS

Many ordinary household stains are too stubborn for an ordinary detergent. Stain-fighting laundry boosters were created for times when the rag pile looks more inviting than the hamper. Sometimes boosters work; sometimes the clothes go to the rag pile after all.

Boosters are sold as powders, pump sprays, aerosols, liquids, and sticks.

They may contain many of the same ingredients as detergents: surfactants, or cleaning agents; enzymes; water-softening "builders"; fluorescent dyes; and so forth. The powders include all-fabric bleach. Common boosters don't contain phosphorus.

Consumers Union testers checked the effectiveness of boosters on a variety of stains: chocolate syrup, makeup, grape juice, spaghetti sauce, blood, mud, grass, tea, black ink, and used motor oil. Each stain was smeared onto a separate set of three large white cotton-polyester swatches, and then a booster was used according to label instructions (but without presoaking).

THE EFFECTIVENESS OF BOOSTERS

Here is a summary of the results.

Chocolate syrup. None of the boosters significantly improved upon the performance of the comparison product, a low-priced nonphosphorus laundry detergent powder. Many detergents, used alone, have no trouble removing chocolate stains.

Makeup. Stain removal was far from perfect even with the best boosters.

Grape juice. Several products eliminated most of the stain, but a bluish haze remained.

Spaghetti sauce. Only *Spray 'N Wash* stick could lift additional amounts of this stain, a tough one for all detergents.

Blood. Used alone, the comparison detergent had no effect on this protein-based stain. *Biz Bleach* was the only booster that removed any blood.

Mud. Only *Biz Bleach* improved on the fair job that the detergent had done.

Grass. The detergent couldn't touch this stain. When it was treated with *Spray 'N Wash* stick, however, barely a trace remained.

Tea. Several products were effective in removing this stain.

Used motor oil. A success story for boosters. Although none of the detergents could clean motor oil by themselves, the comparison detergent plus three boosters lifted some of the stain; and two aerosol boosters—*Spray 'N Wash* and *Shout*—wiped out most of it.

Ink. Ink from a black ballpoint pen proved too hard to remove for all the detergents, and it was beyond the capability of all the boosters.

Detergent alone. Applying part of a laundry dose of *Advanced Action Wisk* or *Tide* directly onto the stains before washing them was the most effective method of cleaning spaghetti sauce, mud, and grass.

CONVENIENCE

Launderers with a single stained garment might like the *Spray 'N Wash* stick, which works the way a lipstick tube does. (*Bleach Stick* also comes in a tube, but you must push the booster up with a finger or pencil.) There are situations in which a stick would be decidedly inconvenient, however. Imagine rubbing a washload's worth of grass-stained knees, oil-stained overalls, and T-shirts dotted with last week's spaghetti dinner. Liquids, likewise, must be rubbed in.

Ratings of Laundry Boosters

Better ⟵ ⟶ Worse

Listed in order of estimated quality, based on enhancement of stain removal. Products with identical overall performance are bracketed and listed alphabetically. As published in a **February 1991** report.

Product (type). Leading brands were tested in several forms: **Powders** are added to the washing machine along with detergent; **liquids, sticks, aerosols,** and **pump sprays** are applied directly to the stain before the wash is laundered.

Cost per use. The average paid to treat a 3-by-3¼-inch stain, based on the cost of the whole product and on label recommendations for the amount to use

Enhanced stain removal. How well each product improved the stain-fighting ability of a nonphosphorus powdered detergent (*Purex*). + means stain removal was better; ++ means stain removal was much better; — means improvement was negligible.

Product (type)	Cost per use	Chocolate syrup	Makeup	Grape juice	Spaghetti sauce	Blood	Mud	Grass	Tea	Ink	Used motor oil	Comments
		Enhanced stain removal										
✔ **Spray 'N Wash (stick)**	26¢	—	+	+	+	—	—	++	++	—	+	E
Biz Bleach (powder)	2	—	+	—	—	+	+	+	—	—	—	E,F,G,I
Spray 'N Wash (aerosol)	5	—	—	—	—	—	—	+	—	—	++	I
Easy Wash (liquid)	12	—	—	+	—	—	—	—	+	—	—	A,H
Shout (liquid)	9	—	—	—	—	—	—	—	+	—	+	A,B,I
Bleach Stick	30	—	—	+	—	—	—	—	+	—	—	D,G,I,J
Spray 'N Wash (pump)	4	—	—	—	—	—	—	—	+	—	—	C,H
Clorox 2 Bleach (powder)	2	—	—	+	—	—	—	—	—	—	—	E,G,I
Clorox (liquid)	9	—	—	+	—	—	—	—	—	—	+	A,H
Grease Relief (liquid)	6	—	—	—	—	—	—	—	—	—	—	A
Shout (aerosol)	5	—	—	—	—	—	—	—	—	—	++	I

Features in Common
All • Are phosphorus-free.
Except as noted, all: • Contain perfume. • Warn about contact with eyes or skin.

Key to Comments
A–Squeeze-bottle with convenient spout.
B–Ribbed cap effective for rubbing product on stain.
C–Trigger-pump bottle easy to use.
D–Dispensing tube inconvenient to use.
E–Contains enzymes.
F–Fails to warn about contact with eyes or skin.
G–Recommends pretesting to determine if fabric is colorfast.
H–Tested container easier to use than most by people with limited hand or arm function.
I–Tested container harder to use than others by people with limited hand or arm function.
J–No perfume.

Sprays are a bit easier; you douse stains, then toss the dirty clothes into the washing machine.

When stains are pervasive, you might prefer a powder that you pour into the machine along with a detergent. But presoaking with a powder is problematical. You can let the stained clothes soak in the water, but that ties up the machine. A messy alternative is to let the laundry soak in a tub, then transfer it to your washing machine.

RECOMMENDATIONS

You may not need a booster if you lead a low-soil life and use a good detergent. You can also use the detergent as a booster. To do this with a powder, mix it with a little water until it forms a paste, then rub it into the stain with an old toothbrush.

It may make sense, however, to keep a booster on hand for those inevitable spills that even the best detergent can't handle.

Choose a product based on its effectiveness and on your idea of convenience. Some boosters cope quite well with some stains, but most aren't any more effective than detergent alone. One standout, *Spray 'N Wash* stick, can improve detergent performance significantly.

A note of caution: Some boosters contain ingredients that may irritate eyes or, occasionally, skin. If you get one of these products in your eyes, rinse them immediately and thoroughly with water.

CLOTHES WASHERS

Automatic washing machine design has matured to the point that periodic model changes are mostly small refinements. A manufacturer may change the shape of the agitator, or restyle the control panel, or replace mechanical controls with electronic ones.

Machines at or near the top of each company's line come with such amenities as two agitation and spin speeds, variable water-level controls, and bleach and fabric-softener dispensers. Less expensive models may have somewhat smaller capacities, lack some of those features, or have less elaborate versions of them. Most of these rather deluxe washers have mechanical controls; several models have electronic controls. "Suds saver" models let users recycle the wash water.

Top-loaders dominate the market in the United States.

Just about any washing machine on the market will clean just fine, provided you use the right amount of detergent and the right amount of water. Other critical factors are convenience, efficiency (machines that use less water get higher marks), and load-size capacity.

For any machine to wash properly, clothes must swirl around the tub, move toward the agitator, then sink. If that doesn't happen, the clothes nearest the agitator will take a pounding while those around the side move only slightly.

Consumers Union testers made up loads of white or light-colored items plus six "flags"—brightly colored washcloths. The testers put each machine through its regular cycle with the lid up so they could count and time the appearance and disappearance of the flags. If the flags circulated well, the testers ran larger loads until two flags no longer circulated.

Consumers Union's tests showed considerable differences in capacity.

The size and shape of the tub and the design of the agitator contribute heavily to those differences.

ENERGY AND WATER

Water consumption is a critical factor, given the periodic drought in some parts of the country, the strain that a large load of wash water imposes on septic systems, and the cost of heating the wash water. (Providing hot water consumes far more energy than running the washing machine itself.)

To monitor water and energy consumption, tests were run using the warm wash/cold rinse settings that are suitable for most clothes.

Water use. On a regular cycle with an eight-pound load, water use ranged from about 38 to 44 gallons. On the permanent-press cycle, consumption ranged from about 39 to 53 gallons.

Washers are most efficient when run at full capacity, using the highest water level. You can adjust the water level for partial loads, but you shouldn't try to wash a full load on a partial water fill. That will hamper the machine's performance and may also damage the clothing.

Energy use. The energy-efficiency scores in the Ratings reflect hot-water consumption weighted against performance in the load-capacity test.

The range of hot-water use for the machines is striking. Here's how the scores might affect your hot-water bill for a year. Assume you do about 42 pounds of clothes per week, or 2,184 pounds per year. One of the more efficient machines would do that much laundry in 182 loads, using 2075 gallons of hot water per year. A relatively inefficient machine would need 273 loads and 2,812 gallons of hot water. That's 35 percent more. Actual differences would probably be less dramatic because you wouldn't fill a machine to capacity for every load.

The "suds saver." The *Maytag A9700W* "suds saver" should more accurately be termed a water saver. It spews wash water into a tub or sink next to the machine, then sucks it up again to be reused for one or more additional wash-water fills. Sediment from the first wash settles out in the sink or tub. The washer's intake hose is designed to leave about half an inch of water, so the sediment is not pumped back. That arrangement saved about 17 gallons of water and about half the detergent for each reuse. (The *Maytag* added about a gallon of fresh water to the next load of laundry to compensate for what was left in the sink.)

The more the wash water is reused, the less effective and the cooler it becomes; it is up to the user to decide when to stop recycling. Fresh detergent in each reuse, plus fresh-water rinses, keep cleaning performance up.

OTHER CHARACTERISTICS

Here are some aspects of performance other than capacity and efficiency.

Unbalanced loads. Ski jackets, mattress pads, blankets, and other bulky items strain a machine's suspension by making the tub oscillate as it spins. Consumers Union's testers gave each machine an increasingly unbalanced load and watched to see if the machine banged or "walked" across the floor.

A few machines do quite well. Others may bang loudly even with a moderately unbalanced load.

Still others have a switch that shuts the machine off if the load goes out of balance. But such a switch can work all too well, sometimes shutting off the machines even with a slightly unbalanced load.

To minimize rocking and vibration, the legs on a washer must be leveled, yet kept as close to the floor as possible. Many machines have self-leveling rear legs linked together, a design that makes the machine less apt to rock.

Sand disposal. To find out how well these machines could remove sand and other grit from the laundry, the testers deliberately spiked a load of wash with about half a cup of fine sea sand. After the washing, they carefully checked the clothes and the washer's tub to see if any sand stayed behind. Then, after tumble-drying the clothes and cleaning the tub, they washed the load again to see if any sand was redeposited.

Most machines do quite well in removing quite large amounts of sand in the first wash. Even the worst should remove all the sand in two washes.

Linting. Laundering inevitably produces lint, but a well-designed washing machine should filter it out. Most even have a self-cleaning lint filter that flushes lint away when spinning.

Noise. Noise becomes an important consideration if you live in an apartment or a small house, where the washer is near the main living area. As a rule, machines are quietest in the Spin cycle, noisiest when filling with water. Though the Fill cycle is short, it can be downright boisterous.

Safety. Most machines on the market are designed to minimize hazards. The majority have a brake that stops the spinning tub if you lift the lid. Some lock the lid during Spin, and make it impossible to lift the lid for about 45 seconds after the tub has stopped.

CONTROL

Most washers on the market let you choose a regular cycle, a permanent-press cycle (with an extra cold-water spray or a deep rinse to relax wrinkles), and a knits/delicates cycle (with slow agitation and spin). The *Maytags* with mechanical controls show only regular and permanent-press cycles, but they allow you to control agitation and spin speeds. Most other

Ratings of washing machines

◉ Better ← ◓ ○ ◒ → ● Worse

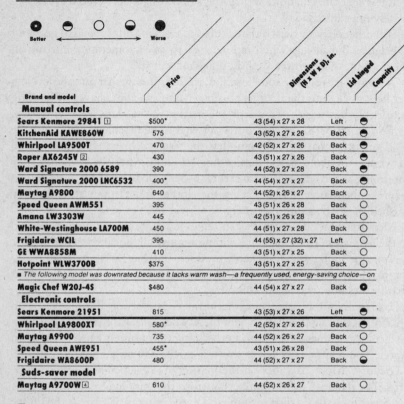

Brand and model	Price	Dimensions (H x W x D), in.	Lid hinged	Capacity
Manual controls				
Sears Kenmore 29841 [1]	$500*	43 (54) x 27 x 28	Left	◓
KitchenAid KAWE860W	575	43 (52) x 27 x 26	Back	◓
Whirlpool LA9500T	470	42 (52) x 27 x 26	Back	◓
Roper AX6245V [2]	430	43 (51) x 27 x 26	Back	◓
Ward Signature 2000 6589	390	44 (52) x 27 x 28	Back	◓
Ward Signature 2000 LNC6532	400*	44 (54) x 27 x 27	Back	◓
Maytag A9800	640	44 (52) x 26 x 27	Back	○
Speed Queen AWM551	395	43 (51) x 26 x 28	Back	○
Amana LW3303W	445	42 (51) x 26 x 28	Back	○
White-Westinghouse LA700M	450	44 (51) x 27 x 28	Back	○
Frigidaire WCIL	395	44 (55) x 27 (32) x 27	Left	○
GE WWA8858M	410	43 (51) x 27 x 25	Back	○
Hotpoint WLW3700B	$375	43 (51) x 27 x 25	Back	○
■ *The following model was downrated because it lacks warm wash—a frequently used, energy-saving choice—on*				
Magic Chef W20J-4S	$480	44 (54) x 27 x 27	Back	◉
Electronic controls				
Sears Kenmore 21951	815	43 (53) x 27 x 26	Left	◓
Whirlpool LA9800XT	580*	42 (52) x 27 x 26	Back	◓
Maytag A9900	735	44 (52) x 26 x 27	Back	○
Speed Queen AWE951	455*	43 (51) x 26 x 28	Back	○
Frigidaire WA8600P	480	44 (52) x 27 x 27	Back	◒
Suds-saver model				
Maytag A9700W [4]	610	44 (52) x 26 x 27	Back	○

[1] *Successor model, 22481.*
[2] *Successor model, RA57245A.*
[3] *Performance varied from ◒ to ○.*
[4] *Manual controls.*
[5] *Score when machine is in normal/suds-saver modes.*
[6] *Scored higher in suds-saver mode.*

Features in Common
All: • Have bleach dispenser. • Provide at least 2 agitation and spin speeds. • Have variable water-level controls. • Did about equally well extracting water from laundry in the tests.
Except as noted, all: • Have only hot, warm, or cold wash, cold rinse. • Have porcelain-coated steel tub, painted top. • Have softener dispensers. • Have instructions on lid. • Agitation and spin speeds chosen automatically when you select cycle or fabric type. • Have self-cleaning lint filter system. • Are limited to max. drain height of 48 or 60 in. • Have lip on top to contain minor spills.

Key to Advantages
A–Electronic temperature control to blend hot and cold water worked well.
B–Porcelain top and lid.
C–Self-adjusting legs at rear.
D–Timer shows remaining time for cycle.
E–Digital clock.
F–Delay start.

Water efficiency	Energy efficiency	Unbalanced loads	Sand disposal	Linting	Noise	Ease of use	Servicing	Advantages	Disadvantages	Comments
◓	◓	◉	◉	◓	○	○	◉	A,B,C,N	f	*E,G,I,K,L,N*
◓	◓	◓	◉	◓	◓	◒	◉	B,C,M,N	b	*E,G,K,L*
◓	◓	◉	◓	◓	○	◒	◉	C,M,N	b	*E,G,K,L*
◓	◓	◉	◓	◓	○	○	◉	C	a,b,d	*E,G,K*
◓	◓	◉	◒	○	○	◓	○	J,K,M,N	—	*B,D,G,I,K,L*
◓	◓	◓	○	◓	○	○	●	C	—	*A,K,N*
○	○	[3]	○	◓	○	◓	◉	B,J,K,M,N	b,c,d	*E,K,L,M*
○	○	[3]	◓	◓	○	◓	◓	J,K,N	c	*C,L*
○	○	[3]	◓	◓	○	◓	◓	J,K	c	*C,E,K*
○	◒	◉	○	○	◒	◓	○	C,J,K,N	—	*B,E,G,L,M*
◒	◒	◉	○	◓	◒	◓	○	J,K,M,N	f	*B,E,G,J,L,M*
◒	◒	◓	◓	◓	●	○	●	B,C,J,K,M	—	*F,H,K,M*
◒	◒	○	◓	◓	◒	◓	●	B,C,K	g	*E,F,M*
its permanent-press cycle.										
◓	◓	●	○	◓	○	◒	●	C	e	*A*
◓	◓	◉	◓	◓	○	◓	◒	B,C,D,F,G,I,J,K,L,M,N	f	*D,E,G,J,K,L*
◓	◓	◓	◓	◓	○	○	◓	C,D,L,M,N	b	*E,G,K,L*
○	○	[3]	○	◓	○	◓	◓	B,D,G,H,J,K,L,M,N	b,c,d	*E,K,L*
○	○	[3]	○	◓	○	○	○	D,F,G,J,K,L,M	c	*C,K,L*
●	●	◉	○	◓	◒	○	◒	C,D,E,F,G,H,J,K,L,M,N	d	*D,G,J,K,L*
○/◉ [5]	○/[6]	[3]	◓	◓	○	◓	◓	B,J,K,N	b,c,d	*E,H,K,M*

G–Programmable custom cycle settings.
H–Settings between Cold/Warm and Warm/Hot.
I–Dial light.
J–Softener dispenser easy to use and clean.
K–Large bleach dispenser, judged better than others. **Sears Kenmore** delays dispensing until late in the wash cycle.
L–Has end-of-cycle signal.
M–Has extra rinse setting.
N–Slow agitation available with warm wash/warm rinse; possible advantage for woolens.

Key to Disadvantages

a–No softener dispenser.
b–Top has no lip to help contain spills.
c–Moderately unbalanced load stopped Spin.
d–No instructions on lid.
e–Only hot or cold wash in permanent-press.
f–Lid doesn't open completely to lie flat.
g–Lacks soak/prewash settings.

Key to Comments

A–Painted steel tub with extended warranty.
B–Plastic tub with extended warranty.
C–Stainless-steel tub with extended warranty.
D–Lid locks during Spin cycle.
E–Readers complain that slots under agitator snag laundry; that didn't happen in our tests.
F–Can be installed to 96-in. drain height.
G–Can be installed to 72-in. drain height.
H–Lacks self-cleaning lint filter.
I–Controls judged better than others for visually impaired people.
J–Electronic temperature control didn't work.
K–Warm rinse available with hot wash.
L–Warm rinse available with warm wash.
M–Separate control for agitation and spin.
N–**Sears** replaced by identical **22841; Ward** discontinued.

Listed by type of controls; within types, listed in order of estimated quality. Except where separated by bold rule, closely ranked models differed little in quality. As published in an **August 1992** report.

Brand and model. Full-featured, "extra large capacity" models were tested. If you can't find a model, call the company.

Price. The estimated average, based on prices quoted. An * denotes the price CU paid (an average price wasn't available).

Dimensions. These machines differ only by an inch or two, but that may be critical if space is tight. The height includes the control panel. The figure in parentheses gives the height or width with the lid open. All machines need extra clearance in the rear for water hoses.

Lid hinged. Most flip up from the front.

Capacity. A judgment based on tests to determine how much laundry a machine can hold and still circulate it in the tub. The best machines could handle over 50 percent more clothes than the worst.

Water efficiency. Based on the gallons used in the Regular wash cycle for the amount of laundry each machine could accommodate. The worst use about 39 gallons of water to wash an eight-pound load. The better ones use a little more than 41 gallons to wash a 12-pound load.

Energy efficiency. Scores reflect a calculation, based on hot-water consumption in our water-efficiency test. The worst machines would use about 35 percent more hot water than the best to wash the same amount of clothes. A Regular cycle with a hot or warm wash and a cold rinse were used.

Unbalanced loads. How well the machine handled progressively unbalanced loads in the Spin cycle. The best were unfazed; the worst knocked and "walked" along the floor. Some machines have an automatic shutoff switch that works if an unbalanced load causes too much vibration. But it sometimes tripped with only a slightly unbalanced load.

Sand disposal. The best could eliminate a measured amount of sand after one cycle. The worst needed two cycles.

Linting. Most machines have an internal filter to trap lint when the wash is agitating, then wash it down the drain. Most did a very good job of keeping lint off clothes.

Noise. Important if the machine will be in or near the living space.

Ease of use. The score covers these points: How legible are the controls? How sensibly are they arranged? Are the bleach and softener dispensers easy to use?

Servicing. These scores reflect the advice of a retired washer repairman; he tended to favor machines with an easily removed cabinet and major components that can be reached from the front. Electronic controls, he believes, are usually more expensive to repair than mechanical controls.

machines set agitation and spin speeds automatically when you choose a cycle.

Most machines offer a setting for a second rinse, but any of these machines can be set by hand for an additional rinse and spin at the end of a cycle. An extra rinse is useful if you're using extra detergent to wash heavily soiled items or if you're sensitive to detergent and want to be sure it's removed from the clothes. Otherwise, the extra rinse just wastes water.

Most machines can be set for at least the basic wash and rinse temperatures: a hot wash/cold rinse for white or very soiled colorfast items; a warm wash/cold rinse for more lightly soiled or permanent-press wash; and a cold wash/cold rinse for delicates.

A few have additional water-temperature settings between hot and warm and warm and cold. They provide more flexibility in adapting choice to specific water temperatures. Other washing machines offer a warm wash/warm rinse and slow agitation, settings that are preferable for washable woolens.

A few models have an electronic temperature control. It's supposed to regulate the mix of hot and cold to produce warm water. Other machines mix a preset proportion of cold and hot.

Manual controls differ in their ease of use. Large, easy-to-read lettering, uncluttered areas, and color or other clear markers to illustrate the different cycles are best. No dial has it all. But some are straightforward and color-coded. Others have very large, easy-to-read dials that may be better suited for visually impaired persons.

An electronically controlled machine may seem formidable at first, but most prove simple to use. With the typical electronic machine, you choose a cycle, then press Start. The electronics handle all the choices for water temperature, agitation, and the like. You can use Up/Down buttons to change the preset water level, the water temperature, the washing time, and so on. Some machines display prompts to show you which button needs to be pressed next.

Electronically controlled units usually command a premium price. A retired independent repairman told Consumers Union that electronic controls are more expensive to repair than mechanical ones. But the manufacturers CU contacted maintained that electronic controls in washing machines are inherently more reliable than mechanical ones. Any problems that occur show up immediately and can be fixed under warranty, say the manufacturers.

RECOMMENDATIONS

Deluxe machines come with the added features and price tags that typify top-of-the-line equipment. Less-expensive machines should get your clothes just as clean, but they may have a smaller tub or more rudimentary controls. They may also lack such amenities as a bleach or fabric-softener dispenser.

Models with conventional manual controls seem to offer better value. The electronic machines perform no better overall, and they sell for $100 to $300 more than their mechanical counterparts.

REPAIR HISTORY

Washing machines from Hotpoint, Maytag, and General Electric have had a more reliable record than other brands, according to a 1991 reader survey. Front-loaders from White-Westinghouse have been the most trouble-prone.

The older the washer, of course, the more likely it has ever been repaired. Accordingly, age is taken into account when analyzing the repair data. Usage also affects a washer's reliability. Among machines used for one to four loads a week, only 15 percent ever needed repair. Some 20 percent of the machines used for five to seven loads a week have needed some repair. And 26 percent of the machines used for eight or more loads per week have needed repair. The reader survey showed the same pattern for all brands, so it didn't adjust for usage.

The bars in the graph indicate the percent of washers that have ever needed repair. A particular brand's repair index includes many models, not just the ones tested. And the analysis is necessarily historical. Even so, the findings have been consistent over the years. Choosing a brand that's been reliable in the past should improve your chances of getting a brand that will be reliable in the future.

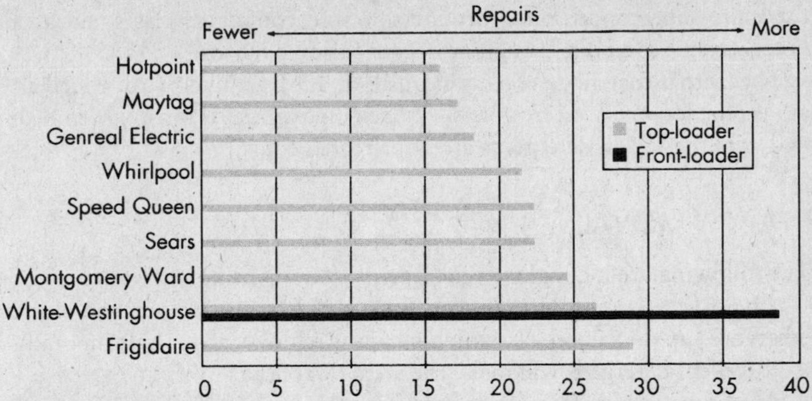

Washing-machine repairs are based on nearly 255,000 reader responses to Consumers Union's 1991 Annual Questionnaire. Readers were asked about any repairs to a full-size washer bought new between 1981 and 1991; machines with a service contract or an extended warranty were excluded. Data have been standardized to eliminate differences among brands due solely to age. Differences of less than three points aren't meaningful.

DETERGENTS

Detergent manufacturers try to attract buyers who have specific laundry problems. There are powders that resemble old-fashioned soap and liquids that ease pretreatment of tough soils. Some detergents come with color-safe bleach; others have fabric softener; still others include perfumes or stain-fighting enzymes. Some powders contain phosphates for added cleaning power; others are made without it to avoid possible harm to waterways (see page 101). Several brands suggest that they will give the user not only a cleaner clean but a healthier planet.

There are detergents in regular and concentrated strengths. And now there are superconcentrated products, whose container is as small as a lunchbox but can hold enough detergent for many loads.

The truth is that all detergents clean clothes. All are likely to be excellent at keeping loosened soil from settling back on clothes. As for stain removal and brightening, all detergents are also created equal.

STAIN REMOVAL

The following are highlights of detergents' stain-fighting abilities:

Chocolate syrup. No problem for most detergents. Even the worst detergent can do a good job, which means it removes about half the stain. An excellent detergent will make the stain disappear.

Makeup. Oil-based beige makeup contains iron oxide (rust), a very stubborn stain. Detergents with phosphorus are the most effective overall, but good nonphosphorus products can do quite well, too. The least effective detergents fade the stain slightly but fail to lift it.

Grape juice. This is a tough stain. Few detergents will remove all of it. The poorest ones will leave bluish blotches.

Spaghetti sauce. No detergent is likely to lift more than about half of the greasy stain left by tomato sauce with olive oil.

Blood. Products with enzymes are generally the most effective at removing blood.

Mud. Phosphorus detergents tend to clean mud a lot better than nonphosphorus products.

Grass. This stain is hard to remove. In Consumers Union tests, more than half of the nonphosphorus detergents had no effect.

Tea. Phosphorus tends to improve results.

Ink, motor oil. Dirty motor oil and black ink from a ballpoint pen are too tough for a laundry detergent. However, results improve remarkably if you use certain detergent boosters before laundering (see page 83).

BRIGHTENERS

Most laundry detergents contain optical brighteners that convert part of the invisible ultraviolet rays that come from the sun or fluorescent bulbs into visible light, thereby giving fabrics a little glow. (Because the effect does not show up in incandescent light, it's likely to be more evident in an office or outdoors than it is at home.)

PRICES

You don't have to pay extra for performance. Indeed, there is little correlation between price and cleaning ability. You will pay more for the convenience of liquids or premeasured packets. The addition of bleach will add a few pennies per wash. Detergents containing fabric softener don't cost any more than the detergent products alone. They also don't work very well, either as detergents or as softeners.

You can save the most money by forgetting brand loyalty: Clip coupons and stock up on whatever satisfactory product is on sale.

RECOMMENDATIONS

Consumers have become so used to hearing manufacturers tout "new and improved" products, it's easy to forget how much better the state of laundering is today than it was in the soap age. On a load of laundry grayed with everyday dirt, the range of performance with today's products would be clean to cleanest, not dirty to clean. Of course, some detergents do work better than others. But unless your clothes are very soiled, these differences may not matter all that much.

When faced with badly soiled laundry, opt for a high-quality detergent. If you live in an area that permits the sale of phosphorus detergents, you have your pick of phosphorus or nonphosphorus products. Obviously, where phosphorus is banned you must choose a nonphosphorus detergent.

Some liquids can clean nearly as well as the leading powders.

You'd do well to stay away from detergent–fabric softener combinations, which are only moderately successful at either task. The optimal softener is a liquid you add during the rinse cycle (see "Fabric Softeners," page 109).

If you suffer from allergies or sensitive skin, consider a detergent without enzymes or perfumes, the most likely sources of irritation.

For all detergents, an ideal package is light in weight, easy to open, and easy to handle once it's opened.

Ratings of Laundry Detergents

◉ Better ◓ ○ ◒ ● Worse

Listed by types; within types, listed in order of overall laundering score, based on laboratory tests in warm, soft water. Products with identical scores are bracketed and listed alphabetically. As published in a **February 1991** report.

Product. Powdered detergents often come in phosphorus and nonphosphorus versions. All liquids are phosphorus-free.

Type. Liquid (**L**), powder (**P**), packet (**PK**).

Phosphorus content. Phosphates—compounds including the element phosphorus—enhance cleaning but can spur the growth of algae in waterways. The phosphorus detergents had approximate phosphorus concentrations of between 5 and 17.5 percent by weight.

Cost per use. Based on the manufacturer's recommended dosage for laundering our heavily soiled load and on prices paid for containers that were medium-sized—64 ounces for liquids and about 40 ounces for powders—or the next-closest size.

Laundering. How close each product came to the test criteria for excellence in stain removal, brightening, and ability to keep loosened soil from settling back on fabrics. Performance varied greatly on the first two counts; all detergents were excellent on the third. Products whose scores differed by less than 20 points did not differ meaningfully in performance on most stains.

Brightening. Most detergents contain colorless dyes that give laundry a glow in sunlight and fluorescent light. Brightening was assessed by viewing laundered white cotton swatches under ultraviolet light.

Stain removal. No detergent got test swatches spotless, and none could lift used motor oil or black ink at all.

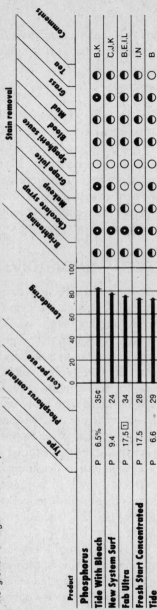

Product	Type	Phosphorus content	Cost per use	Laundering (0–100)	Brightening	Stain removal: Chocolate syrup	Makeup	Grape juice	Spaghetti sauce	Blood	Mud	Grass	Tea	Comments
Phosphorus														
Tide With Bleach	P	6.5%	35¢		◓	◉	◓	◉	○	◓	◓	◉	◓	B,K
New System Surf	P	9.4	24		◓	◉	◓	◓	○	◓	◓	◓	◓	C,J,K
Fab Ultra	P	17.5 [1]	34		◓	◉	◓	○	○	◓	◓	◓	◓	B,E,I,L
Fresh Start Concentrated	P	17.5	28		◓	◉	○	○	○	◓	◓	◓	◓	I,N
Tide	P	6.6	29		◓	◓	◓	◓	○	◓	◓	◓	○	B

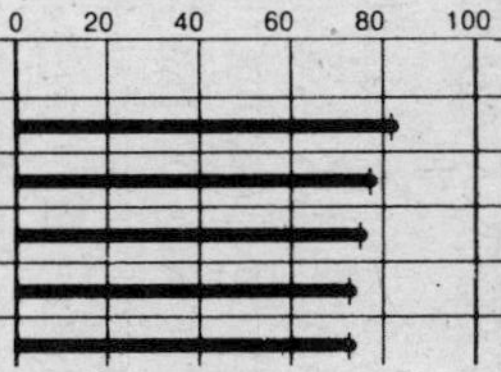

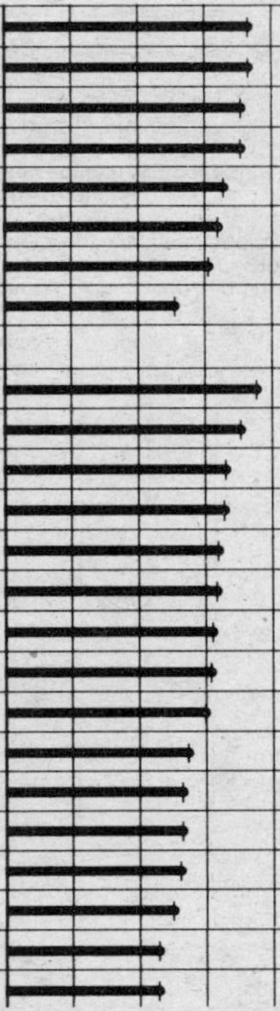

Unscented Tide	P	6.6	28	○	⦿	◓	◓	○	◓	◓	◓	◓	B,H
Wisk Power Scoop	P	12.1	36	○	⦿	◓	◓	○	◓	◓	◓	◓	B,E,I,K,L
Cheer w. Color Guard	P	6.4	27	○	◓	◓	◓	○	◓	◓	⦿	○	C,J
Ultra Tide	P	8.7	38	○	⦿	◓	◓	○	◓	◓	◓	○	B,E,J,L
Clorox w. Bleach	P	5.0	42	◓	◓	◓	◓	○	○	◓	◓	●	B,G,I,K
Fab w. Softener	P	6.3	22	○	⦿	◓	○	○	◓	○	◒	◓	C,G,J
Oxydol w. Bleach	P	5.8	45	◓	○	○	◓	○	○	○	◒	◓	C,G,J
Fab 1 Shot w. Softener	PK	15.5 [1]	64	●	◓	◓	○	○	◓	◓	●	○	I
Nonphosphorus													
Tide w. Bleach	P	—	35	○	⦿	◓	⦿	○	◓	◓	⦿	○	B,K,M
Tide	P	—	29	○	⦿	◓	◓	○	◓	◓	◓	○	B,M
New System Surf	L	—	43	○	⦿	◓	○	○	◓	○	◓	○	I,K
Advanced Action Wisk	L	—	42	◓	⦿	○	◒	○	◓	○	◓	○	I
Tide	L	—	47	○	⦿	◓	◒	○	○	○	◓	◓	I
Fresh Start Concentrated	P	—	31	◓	⦿	◓	○	○	◓	◓	◒	●	I,M,N
Unscented Tide	P	—	28	◒	⦿	◓	◓	○	◓	◓	◒	○	B,H,M
Oxydol w. Bleach	P	—	34	○	⦿	◓	◓	○	◓	◓	◒	●	C,G,J,M
Cheer w. Color Guard	L	—	51	◒	⦿	◓	◒	○	○	○	◓	◓	I
Shaklee Basic L	P	—	38	○	◓	◓	○	○	◓	◓	●	●	C,G,H,J
Bold w. Softener	P	—	30	◒	⦿	◓	○	○	◓	○	◒	●	C,J,M
Cheer w. Color Guard	P	—	27	◒	○	○	◓	○	◓	○	◓	●	C,J,M
Era	L	—	50	○	⦿	○	◒	○	○	◒	◒	○	G,H,I
Fab w. Softener	P	—	24	○	◓	◓	◓	○	○	◒	●	●	C,G,J,M
All	L	—	30	◒	⦿	○	○	○	○	○	●	●	G,I,K
Cheerfree	L	—	53	◒	◓	○	◒	○	○	◒	●	◓	G,H,I

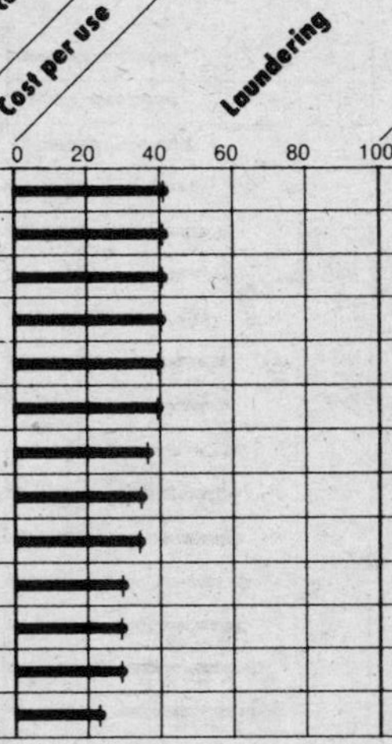

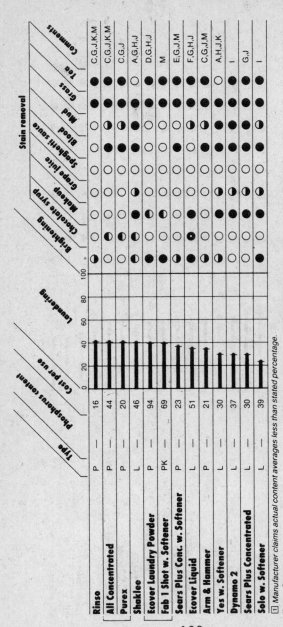

	Type	Phosphorus content	Cost per use	Brightening	Chocolate syrup	Makeup	Grape juice	Spaghetti sauce	Blood	Mud	Grass	Tea	Comments
					Stain removal								
Rinso	P	—	16	◒	○	○	○	○	○	○	●	●	C,G,J,K,M
All Concentrated	P	—	44	○	◓	○	○	○	●	◒	●	●	C,G,J,K,M
Purex	P	—	20	○	◓	○	○	○	●	◒	●	●	C,G,J
Shaklee	L	—	46	◓	◓	●	◒	○	●	●	●	○	A,G,H,J
Ecover Laundry Powder	P	—	94	●	○	◓	○	○	○	○	●	●	D,G,H,J
Fab 1 Shot w. Softener	PK	—	69	●	○	◓	○	○	○	○	●	●	M
Sears Plus Conc. w. Softener	P	—	23	◒	○	○	○	○	●	○	●	●	E,G,J,M
Ecover Liquid	L	—	51	●	◉	●	○	○	○	◒	●	●	F,G,H,J
Arm & Hammer	P	—	21	◒	○	○	○	○	●	◒	●	●	C,G,J,M
Yes w. Softener	L	—	30	◒	○	●	◒	○	●	●	●	○	A,H,J,K
Dynamo 2	L	—	37	○	○	●	◒	○	●	●	●	●	I
Sears Plus Concentrated	L	—	30	○	○	●	◒	○	●	●	●	●	G,J
Solo w. Softener	L	—	39	●	○	●	◒	○	●	◒	●	●	I

[1] *Manufacturer claims actual content averages less than stated percentage.*

Key to Comments

A–Small cap can't be used for measuring.
B–Has convenient lid or spout for pouring.
C–Has inconvenient push-in tab.
D–Box must be cut or torn open.
E–Comes with handy plastic measuring scoop.
F–Measuring cap inconvenient to use.
G–No enzymes.
H–No perfume.
I–Tested container easier to use than most for people with limited hand or arm function.
J–Tested container harder to use than most for people with limited hand or arm function.
K–Recommends testing for colorfastness.
L–Superconcentrated.
M–May contain slight amount of phosphorus, according to label, but considered a nonphosphorus product by law.
N–Powder packaged in plastic bottle.

Features in Common

Except as noted, all: • Contain perfume. • Contain enzymes.
Except as noted, all powders: • Come in cardboard boxes.
Except as noted, all liquids: • Come in plastic bottles whose caps double as measuring cups.

DETERGENTS AND THE ENVIRONMENT

The washing machine completes its cycle. You pull out clean clothes; the wash water drains away—somewhere. After you've finished using a laundry product, you throw away the empty carton, box, bottle, or can. It goes into a garbage truck and is driven away—somewhere.

What happens, though, to that water and those containers? Here is a primer on the environmental ramifications of doing the wash.

A CLEAN-WATER PROBLEM

Phosphates enhance the performance of cleaning agents in detergents by softening water, dispersing dirt, and emulsifying greasy soils. They're especially useful in hard water because they prevent minerals from resettling on clothing in the form of a grimy curd. No alternative cleaning agents are as versatile, effective, and inexpensive.

Detergent phosphates, however, are one class of chemicals that contribute to accelerating the growth of algae, which can eventually transform a lake into a bog in a process known as eutrophication. Excessive growth of algae is not simply an eyesore; in great enough amounts, algae can make water unsuitable for swimming, boating, fishing, and drinking.

Phosphorus is the element in the phosphate compound that causes problems, and detergents aren't the only source of phosphorus in surface water. Runoff from roads and fertilized land, human and animal wastes, phosphate mining, and soil erosion also contribute. Characteristics of the surface water itself—depth, temperature, flow rate, and the amount of sunshine it receives—can affect algal growth.

With so many sources of phosphorus pollution, it makes sense to control those that are controllable. So, since the early 1970s, various parts of the United States have banned or restricted detergents that contain phosphorus.

Today, such detergents are unavailable in some 30 percent of the country.

To market their products all over the map, manufacturers often make phosphorus and nonphosphorus versions of the same powder brand (phosphates aren't soluble or stable enough to be used in liquid detergents). Then they sell each version where it's allowed. You can learn the phosphorus content of the detergents on your supermarket's shelves by reading the phosphorus statement on the label. It will tell you the content or display a tiny code that will reveal the information.

Phosphorus detergents typically contain from 5 to 17.5 percent phosphorus by weight. When Consumers Union tested phosphorus and nonphosphorus versions of the same brand, the phosphorus versions matched or outperformed their partners in overall laundering. Phosphorus products excel in brightening ability and removal of tea, grape juice, and grass stains.

On other stains, though, the two types are about equal. Many nonphosphorus products work almost as well as the best phosphorus ones and significantly better than the worst.

Even in areas that haven't banned phosphorus detergents, choosing a nonphosphorus product may benefit the environment. You can determine whether this is true where you live by contacting your state water-quality agency (usually a division of the state department of environmental protection). Find out if eutrophication is a local problem and whether your household's waste water empties into a body of water that is considered at risk.

BIODEGRADABLE?

Most detergents claim—in small print—that their cleaning agents (surfactants and enzymes) are biodegradable. Some so-called green brands, however, make biodegradability and natural ingredients key selling points.

But all surfactants now used in U.S. detergents are readily decomposed by bacteria in water, soil, and septic systems. This has been true since the mid-1960s, when foaming waters prompted a reformulation of detergents.

As of early 1991, there were no convincing studies to suggest that the surfactants in major-brand detergents contain toxic or environmentally harmful ingredients. Consequently, there is no reason to conclude that the so-called natural brands are better. In fact, some of their ingredients are essentially the same as those found in regular nonphosphorus detergents.

As a rule, the so-called green detergents tested by Consumers Union were not only more expensive than average (in some cases much more) but they did not clean nearly as well as the top-rated detergents.

PACKAGING

As landfills, the final resting place for most of America's garbage, fill up and close down, packaging becomes a reason for selecting or rejecting a product. The laundry packages lining store shelves often contain a percentage of recycled materials. With boxes, this is nothing new; with plastic bottles, it is. In 1991, Lever Brothers and Procter & Gamble, the nation's largest household-products companies, started using recycled plastic in their laundry bottles. The companies hope that their actions will help spark a market for used plastic.

A larger market would be welcome. As it stands, however, although plastic bottles and paperboard boxes may be *recyclable,* they aren't often *recycled.* Some bottle and box materials are not easily separated or marketable, and many communities don't have recycling programs. The consumer may not be in the mood to sort trash and haul a bin outside, so laundry empties are often just thrown away with the rest of the garbage.

A few years ago, plastic containers seemed an environmental evil; the package of choice was made of paper or cardboard. Paper is "biodegradable," the thinking went, and eventually returns to the soil. But when it's in a landfill devoid of light and air, paper has staying power. In 1989, garbage archaeologists unearthed readable newspapers from 1942. It's clear that once trash (or at least nontoxic trash) lands in a landfill, its composition matters less than its volume.

The package that surrounds 10 pounds of powdered or liquid detergent weighs about half a pound—a product-to-package weight ratio of roughly 20 to one. Some smaller packages have a ratio of 10 to one. From the landfill's perspective, then, a small package can be twice as wasteful as a large one. Usually, the large size is cheaper, too.

Happily, for launderers who don't relish lifting bulky containers, there's now an exception to the bigger-is-better guideline: superconcentrates.

Detergent Ingredients

When soap and hard water mix, an ugly scum forms on both the fabric and the washing machine. By taking the soap (and, therefore, the scum) out of washing, today's synthetic detergents have practically made laundry soap obsolete. Their components are a far cry from soap's fat and alkali. Here's a rundown of five key ingredients you might find on a package of synthetic detergent.

Surfactants, or surface active agents, are dirt dissolvers. They act the way soap does, emulsifying oil and grease and the dirt that sticks to them and allowing all of that to be washed away. There are hundreds of such chemicals, and detergents may contain more than one kind. *Anionic* surfactants, which have a negative electrical charge, work best in warm, soft water. They are very effective on oily stains and in removing clay and mud. *Nonionic* surfactants, which lack an electrical charge, are less sensitive to water hardness. They excel at removing oily soils from synthetics at cool wash temperatures. Many liquids contain this type. Some powders contain both anionic and nonionic surfactants. *Cationic* surfactants, which carry a positive charge, are more common in fabric softeners and detergent-softener combinations.

Builders enhance the cleaning efficiency of surfactants by softening the water. They also maintain a desirable level of alkalinity, which boosts cleaning. Phosphates are basic builders. Because they aren't soluble or stable enough to be used in liquid detergents, they're used only in powders. For environmental reasons, they are also restricted or banned in about a third of the country.

Nonphosphorus powders use old-fashioned washing soda with extra ingredients to make up for the lack of phosphorus. Liquids may contain other water-softening chemicals such as sodium citrate.

Whitening agents, also known as optical brighteners, are colorless dyes that give laundry an added glow in sunlight and fluorescent light, making garments appear brighter than they normally would.

Enzymes help break down complex soils—especially proteins, such as those in blood—so they can be more easily removed. They digest stains much the way stomach enzymes digest your food. Two common types of enzymes are protease and amylase. A protease breaks down protein, as in egg or blood stains. An amylase digests carbohydrates, as in honey or maple syrup.

Years ago enzymes caused skin rashes and respiratory problems in some of the workers who handled them. Today's granular enzymes essentially eliminate these hazards. Still, some people may notice skin irritation after using a detergent with enzymes. In such cases, it's wise to use rubber gloves when doing the laundry. Better yet, try a non-enzyme product.

All-fabric bleach, a popular addition to powders, is not as good as chlorine bleach at whitening. But chlorine bleach has its problems. Overuse or misuse can cause colors to fade and fabric to weaken. All-fabric bleaches (the most common one is sodium perborate tetrahydrate) are safe on most materials and dyes, even over the long term. If you're worried about harming a garment, check the label to see if it's colorfast, or experiment with a diluted solution of the bleach or detergent-plus-bleach on an inside seam.

With some, you just use less: a quarter to a half cup per washload. With others, you mix the concentrate with water before use and store it in a previously purchased bottle. Either way, there's less packaging to throw out.

Boosters come wrapped in paperboard, plastic, or metal. The obvious way to keep from tossing all that packaging is to try to get along without a booster: See if a high-rated detergent will do the trick.

If you need a softener, it might seem logical to cut back on trash by using a combination detergent-softener. But think twice: Even the best detergent-softener does only a middling job at either task.

HAND-LAUNDRY DETERGENTS

Your best guide on how to clean a fabric is the care label, which by law must be sewn into all articles of clothing. If the label says a garment must be dry-cleaned, take the advice, or you will have no recourse with the manufacturer or retailer should something go wrong. If the label permits hand-washing, you have to decide how to wash it.

On supermarket shelves, next to the regular detergents, stand many products that make special claims for cleaning wool, cotton, and silk. But if a detergent seems *too* specialized, shoppers may pass it up for one that can tackle a wider variety of garments. These cleaners may claim to work on other "fine washables," too. Increasingly, dishwashing liquids say they can double as detergents for fine washables.

WASHING WITH DETERGENT

A detergent is a big improvement over old-fashioned soap. In hard water, soaps leave behind a gray scum. Not so with detergents; they have synthetic ingredients to lift off soil and keep it suspended in the wash water. Detergents generally include other ingredients to help remove grease and improve sudsing. Some have optical brighteners to make whites look whiter and enzymes to help attack stains.

Think twice before using regular detergent on fine washables. Most regular detergents are alkaline, which could damage natural fibers like wool and silk. The specialized products are supposedly gentler.

EFFECTIVENESS

In its tests, Consumers Union used a special machine to simulate very gentle hand-washing and always washed fabric test swatches in water at 70°F, a temperature warm enough to be comfortable to hands but cool enough to prevent shrinkage. Wash and rinse times were kept to four minutes each because the less time delicate fabrics are left soaking, the better.

Cleaning. Although no test swatch was quite as white after laundering as it had been when brand new, some products cleaned appreciably better than others—a difference even untrained eyes could appreciate. The product's type had little bearing on how well it cleaned. Special detergents, regular detergents, and dishwashing liquids were all represented among the best cleaners.

Brightening. The optical brighteners found in regular detergents and most hand-laundering products adhere to fabric and give off a bluish color in sunlight or under fluorescents, which makes white cloth appear whiter than it really is. Dishwashing liquids do not have optical brighteners. Brighteners tend to work best on silk and cotton and show little effect on wool and synthetics.

Removing stains. Generally, a detergent's stain-removal ability corresponds to its overall cleaning ability. But no product leaves every stained garment looking like new. Some stains on some fabrics are a real challenge. Silk is hardest to clean. Spaghetti sauce doesn't come out; wine stains are almost as difficult. Stains on rayon likewise prove difficult. The easiest fibers to clean are nylon and wool.

HANDLE WITH CARE

Heat causes shrinkage, which is why fine fabrics are typically labeled for cold or cool wash, with no drying in the dryer. Even with lukewarm water you can expect some shrinkage with natural fibers.

Silk crepe tends to pucker and requires ironing after washing. Rayon washes poorly; it wrinkles badly unless pressed while quite damp. Wool crepe, its weave tighter in one direction, can lose shape. If, before washing, a fabric has more "give" in one direction as you gently stretch it, you may have shrinkage problems.

All the hand-wash products give directions for machine washing on the Gentle cycle. A garment's care label is your best guide to whether you should machine-wash it. A garment is the most vulnerable when it's being agitated, but a washer's Gentle cycle typically keeps that as brief as possible. Spinning, in which the garments are flattened and held in place by centrifugal force, won't hurt. In fact, it's less damaging than wringing the clothes

Washing Conditions

People don't wash laundry under the same conditions. Mineral-laden hard water is common, with hardness varying considerably, depending on where you live. Another variable that can affect a detergent's effectiveness is the temperature of the wash water.

A washing machine's cold-water setting is often used when washing dark colors or bright ones that tend to bleed.

Hard water. Minerals weaken a detergent's ability to fight stains. The problem is least prevalent with detergents that contain phosphates, which soften water effectively and protect a detergent against a loss of stain-cleaning ability.

Cold water. Detergents generally contain cleaning agents intended for cold-water use. Washing performance for most laundry loads shouldn't be noticeably poorer after a cold-water wash than when warm or hot water is used for the wash cycle.

Different dose. If you've wondered whether you can get away with using a lot less detergent in hot or soft water, the answer is no: Halving the recommended dose generally depressed cleaning scores in Consumers Union tests. On the other hand, raising the amount of detergent by as much as 50 percent didn't improve the wash's appearance very much.

Presoaking. Allowing clothes to soak for 15 minutes in a detergent-and-water solution can give washing performance a big boost.

by hand. When you hand-wash garments, roll them between towels and let them dry flat, away from heat and sunlight; do not wring them.

If you wash delicate fabrics in the machine, you may want to be careful about what detergent you use. Regular detergents tend to be alkaline, as are some special products. Soaking wool or silk repeatedly in any detergent that's too alkaline could eventually cause fibers to shrink or stretch.

It's prudent not to launder wool or silk in any enzyme-containing detergent unless the product's label says it's safe for hand-washables.

RECOMMENDATIONS

There is no reason to buy one of the specialized brands. Use a dishwashing liquid. All it lacks is the optical brightener that regular detergents and most hand-wash products contain to give whites extra dazzle. At about a penny a wash, dishwashing liquids are bargains.

If you have stains to clean, you'll have some luck depending on the fiber and type of stain.

FABRIC SOFTENERS

Detergents rinse out of fibers so thoroughly that they can leave clothes feeling scratchy, and dryers cause a static charge to build up, especially in synthetics.

Fabric softeners are waxy materials distantly related to soap. They perform much the same function on your laundry that hair conditioners do on your hair—they make it nicer to the touch.

Fabric softeners work by coating your laundry with lubricant and humectant chemicals. The lubricants let fibers slide past each other, reducing wrinkling. They also separate a napped fabric's fibers and stand them on end, which makes a towel, for instance, feel fluffy. The humectants help the fabric retain moisture to dissipate the static charges that would otherwise cause socks to cling to underwear and sparks to fly when you pull on a shirt.

There are three basic types of fabric softener. *Rinse liquids* are added to the wash during the rinse cycle; many washing machines add them automatically from a dispenser atop the agitator. *Dryer sheets* of fiber or foam are impregnated with softener. When you throw a sheet into the dryer along with the laundry, heat releases the softener. *Detergent-softeners* contain both products. The softener is present during the wash cycle, and the manufacturer has to use chemical tricks to make sure that it sticks around for the rinse cycle. A variation of the detergent-softener is the single-use packet. It looks like a big teabag. The bag contains detergent, which dissolves during the wash; the fibers of the bag hold the softener. When the washing machine has done its work, you transfer the empty bag to the dryer along with the laundry.

EFFECTIVENESS

Add combination detergent-softeners to the laundry load at the start of the wash cycle, add rinse liquids at the beginning of the final rinse (after a wash with a no-extras detergent), and toss the dryer sheets into the dryer with the wet laundry. (As recommended, place the sheets on top of the laundry, not under it. This is supposed to prevent spotting.)

For cleaning, soft water is better than hard; for softening, the reverse is true.

The most effective softeners are rinse liquids. But the least effective rinse liquids are much worse than the best.

All dryer sheets soften to roughly the same degree; they are about as good as a middle-of-the-road rinse liquid.

Detergent-softeners show that there's still a price to be paid for convenience. In tests conducted by Consumers Union, none was better than mediocre at softening. (It was much the same story in laundering tests—most of the combination products proved no match for other detergents.) The worst products left towels feeling as if a softener hadn't been used—oily, slimy, or rough in the testers' words.

STATIC CLING

Many people use a fabric softener to cut static cling caused by the dryer's tumbling. Untreated fabric can accumulate a 12,000-volt static charge. Because of its tiny amperage, the jolt isn't dangerous; nevertheless, it's enough to make the hair on your arms stand up.

The friction-reducing chemicals in softeners prevent a static charge from accumulating. Synthetic materials are more prone to static than is cotton.

Brightening. The waxy coating left by fabric softeners may eventually make clothes look dingy. Whites can turn ashen or jaundiced; colors can lose their punch. To counteract this tendency, some fabric softeners, and most detergents, have optical brighteners that give fabrics a slight glow.

With a few exceptions, only the detergent-softeners brighten effectively. The lion's share of the brightening, no doubt, is done by the detergent.

Our recommendation: If whiter whites and brighter brights are important to you, use a detergent with good brightening ability before you use a softener.

Absorbency. In the past, the waxy coating in softeners made towels less thirsty. Nowadays, any softener should leave clothes nearly as absorbent as if they hadn't been treated; apparently, manufacturers have licked the absorbency problem.

Fragrance. Makers of laundry products include fragrances partly because someone at the company thinks consumers like them and partly to hide the smell of other chemical ingredients. You may find the aroma of some dryer sheets reminiscent of cheap perfume. The liquids have fragrances, too, but they're less powerful.

No matter how potent it seems in the package, the fragrance is muted considerably by the time the wash is done. If you like a fabric softener for its other qualities but dislike the smell, let your laundry air out for a while before you put it away.

Some people can't tolerate *any* fragrance, whether for aesthetic or allergic reasons. Several fabric softeners and detergents that promote their lack of additives—and typically sport names that end in "free"—are available.

PRICING

The better rinse liquids cost between 11 and 16 cents per use. The price of a dryer sheet ranges from 4 to 8 cents. The most effective detergent-softener costs between 13 and 23 cents per use. If you consider that you also get your laundry cleaned for that price, combination products look like the best deal, but they're not; they neither clean nor soften as well as single-purpose products.

You can save money by buying whatever is on sale or using cents-off coupons. You might also try using a little less than the recommended amount of a softener—cutting a dryer sheet in half, for example.

If you look at unit-pricing labels on your supermarket shelves, you may not get the whole story. Some stores list price per quart or per pound,

Ratings of Fabric Softeners

◉ Better ◓ ○ ◒ ● Worse

Listed by types; within types, listed in order of estimated quality. As published in a **February 1991** report.

Cost per use. Based on the recommended dosage for an average-sized load and on prices paid for 64-ounce bottles of liquid, medium- or large-sized boxes of powder, and boxes containing 36 or 40 dryer sheets.

Softening. The main Ratings factor. Panelists made this judgment by touching

Product	Cost per use	Softening (0–100)	Static reduction	Comments
Rinse liquids				
Downy Refill April Fresh Scent	14¢		◓	A,D
Snuggle Morning Fresh Scent	11		◉	C
Snuggle Cuddle-Up Fresh Scent	11		◉	C
Downy Sun Rinse Fresh Scent	16		◓	C
Downy April Fresh Scent	16		◓	C
Final Touch	11		◉	C,E
Pathmark	7		◒	C
Kroger Fresh 'N' Soft	9		◒	E
Purex Sta-Puf	9		◉	—
Ecover	13		○	B,D
Safeway White Magic	9		◉	—
Lavender Sachet	11		○	D
A & P	5		◉	C
Dryer sheets				
Downy April Fresh Scent	8		◓	C
Pathmark Scented	4		◓	C
Kroger Bright	5		◓	—
A & P	4		◉	C

Features in Common

All detergent-softeners: Brighten fabric somewhat. *Except as noted,* rinse liquids and dryer sheets do not brighten fabric.

Key to Comments

A–Concentrated refill; dilutes to 64 ounces.
B–No perfume.

cotton-terry washcloths treated with the softeners. The worst performers scored no better than water alone. Products whose scores differed by less than 20 points did not differ meaningfully in performance.

Static reduction. Static charge was measured in fabric just removed from the dryer.

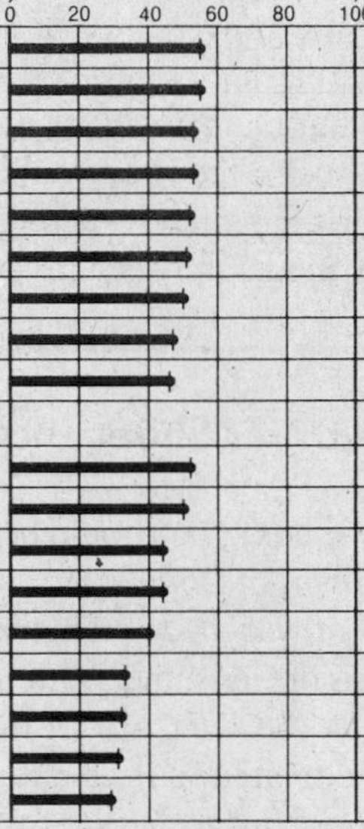

	Cost per use	Static reduction	Comments
Bounce StainGard	8	◓	C
Safeway White Magic	5	◓	E
Bounce Outdoor Fresh	7	◉	C
Snuggle Morning Fresh Scent	7	◉	—
Bounce Unscented	7	◉	B,C
Purex Toss 'N' Soft	5	○	—
Snuggle Cuddle-Up Fresh Scent	7	◓	—
Cling Free	7	◉	C
Pathmark Unscented	4	◓	B,C
Detergent-softeners			
Sears Plus Concentrated Liquid	13	◒	D
Fab Nonphosphorus Powder	16	○	—
Fab Phosphorus Powder	16	○	—
Solo Liquid	23	○	C
Fab 1 Shot Nonphosphorus Packet	31	◉	C
Fab 1 Shot Phosphorus Packet	31	◉	C
Kroger Bright Liquid	22	◓	—
Sears Plus Concentrated Powder	16	◓	D
Yes Liquid	19	◒	—

C–Tested container easier to use than most for people with limited hand or arm function.
D–Tested container harder to use than most for people with limited hand or arm function.
E–Brightens fabric somewhat.

regardless of whether the product is a concentrate. What counts, of course, is price per use.

RECOMMENDATIONS

For most people, fabric softeners are meant to do double duty, reducing static cling while they soften the wash. Since just about any softener is effective against static, choose one that's best at doing what its name implies, which means buying a liquid to add during the rinse cycle.

If you prefer the convenience of a dryer sheet, base your selection on price. Some supermarket brands cost half as much per sheet as the priciest national brands but perform about the same.

The ideal product, of course, would be a detergent-softener that did both of its jobs well. Unfortunately, detergents that moonlight as softeners are likely to be only moderately effective in either role.

A Dryer Sheet That Prevents Stains?

"After just one box, you should begin to see fewer permanent stains . . ." said the box of *Bounce StainGard* dryer sheets. Curiously, the same statement was made on boxes of 18, 36, and 54 sheets.

On the basis of Consumers Union's test results, there was little difference among the swatches treated with the *StainGard* version of *Bounce,* those treated with its brandmate, and those left untreated. The *StainGard* strips were slightly freer of mud and oil than the others, but the greatest differences in stain resistance seemed to be a result of the number of prewashings and not the product used.

At about eight cents per sheet, *Bounce StainGard* was one of the most expensive dryer-sheet softeners. It cost about a penny more per use than the other varieties of *Bounce.* Some sheets that softened equally well cost only half as much, so there seems little reason to spend the extra money. If you have tough stains, try one of the detergents or boosters that proved effective in the tests.

METAL MAINTENANCE

METAL POLISHES

Although many metal polishes make broad claims, no one product is likely to be outstanding for use on brass, copper, stainless steel, aluminum, and chrome.

COPPER AND BRASS

When used on copper and brass, some polishes must be washed off thoroughly because they can stain or etch metals if left in contact with them. Others, however, may be wiped or rubbed off. It's a good idea, therefore, to restrict your choice to a wipe-off polish for objects that can't be readily rinsed or submersed.

Some wipe-off brands may produce a better shine. Wash-off products, however, require less elbow grease to remove tarnish than do those of the wipe-off variety—a difference that you might consider important if you have to clean a heavily tarnished surface.

For things that may be only thinly coated with brass or copper, you should use the mildest cleaning method possible. This means a cloth with detergent or a wipe-off brand that's low in abrasion.

Before any polish can work, the metal surface must be free of any lacquer. It may or may not have a lacquer. If it does, you'll have to use a special cleaner to remove it. Apply the cleaner cautiously and sparingly.

COPPER-BOTTOMED COOKWARE

Wash-off products are particularly well suited to cookware, which can be washed easily and isn't necessarily required to have a high gloss. These products should be able to remove light tarnish with little or no rubbing, and heavy tarnish with less effort than a wipe-off material. Yet even with the most efficient product, you still must use considerable elbow grease to clean a heavily coated blackened pan bottom, and here a metal polish may not work. Steel wool will do the job more easily than polish but may leave the copper lightly scratched and with its mirrorlike finish diminished. If your pans are in bad shape but you are display conscious, you might first scour off the worst of the dirt with bronze wool and then finish the job with a wipe-off polish. This will reduce the scratch marks and rub up a good gloss.

If you are looking for an excuse to avoid cleaning the tarnish off copper-bottomed cookware, you can find one in the fact that the darkened surface is more efficient for cooking than a shiny one; it absorbs heat better.

SAFETY

Polishes, like other household chemicals, should be kept out of the reach of children. Some brands carry appropriate warnings.

This doesn't mean, however, that you can depend on a polish without warnings to be safe.

HOW TO POLISH STAINLESS STEEL, ALUMINUM, AND CHROME

Stainless steel may stain with heat; aluminum becomes discolored with use, and its polished surface may dull; chrome doesn't tarnish, but it can become dirty and splotched.

Stainless steel. Ordinary cleaning in the sink will suffice for stainless-steel cookware except for an occasional stain from heat. To remove heat stains from the matte finish inside of a saucepan or fry pan, a wash-off polish can do a competent job, at least as good as and maybe better than soapy steel wool. If the pan's polished exterior is also stained, use a polishing product cautiously. Work as quickly as possible to avoid leaving chemicals in contact with the metal for any length of time.

Aluminum. You shouldn't expect to be able to restore a polished aluminum finish to its original glossiness. Soapy steel wool, besides being better overall in cleaning and polishing, will probably do a better job of restoring at least some of the luster than will a special aluminum cleaner. Rubbing the metal with straight, back and forth motions, rather than in circles, helps to maintain a uniform appearance.

Chrome. The chrome plating on a metal product may be so thin that it is best not to use any abrasive polish on it at all. The mildest cleaning method possible should be used for chrome-plated appliances and utensils.

SILVER CARE

One type of silver-care product (three-way) removes tarnish, polishes, and treats silver with chemicals that retard further tarnishing. Another variety (two-way) cleans and polishes but doesn't claim to retard tarnishing. Both types of products include a mild abrasive. You rub on the polish, wipe it off, and then buff the finish to the shine you want.

There are also one-way products that come in liquid form and clean only. They don't require tedious rubbing to remove tarnish. You just dip the silver in them or spread them onto silver surfaces. Because of the acid in the liquids, you have to handle them carefully to prevent skin irritation, rinse cleaned silver thoroughly, and tolerate a disagreeable odor as you work.

USING JEWELER'S ROUGE

Cleaning and polishing heavily tarnished silver with a stick of jeweler's rouge entails coating a piece of flannel with rouge, rubbing silver surfaces with the flannel until they are tarnish-free, then buffing the silver with a piece of clean flannel. The result will be silver just about as clean and bright as you can get with the best silver polish. This method has two drawbacks: You have to rub a lot more, and the process is messy, producing quantities of red particles that can smudge clothes and furnishings. Rouge, however, is much cheaper than regular polish, and cleaning cloths are reusable until they start to come apart. You can get rouge from hobby shops or firms that supply professional jewelers. Look in the Yellow Pages under "Jewelers' Supplies" and "Craft Supplies."

SPECIAL PROBLEMS

Antique finishes. Dark-looking silver with an antique or oxidized finish is often deeply patterned. Silver polish is almost certain to remove some of the finish. Dip cleansers damage antique finishes, too, even when you wipe the liquids carefully onto the silver.

Satin finishes. Dips are the only cleaners that remove tarnish from satin, or low-luster, finishes without making them shinier to some degree.

Staining. If you accidentally allow drops of polish to fall on silver pieces, dip cleaners are likely to leave pale stains, and some other products may leave dark stains. You have to repolish to remove the stains. Many silver table knives are made with stainless-steel blades, and—just as the label warns—drops from dip cleaners can permanently spot or even pit stainless steel if allowed to dry on the surface. To avoid damage, rinse such knives off promptly after using a dip cleaner on their silver handles.

Acidic dip cleaners, as a class, have some inherent hazards: You should wear plastic or rubber gloves to protect your hands while cleaning because contact with the cleaner may irritate skin. Be careful not to get any cleaner in your eyes. Because excessive inhalation of their sulfide fumes may cause headaches, these cleaners should be used only where there is good ventilation.

RECOMMENDATIONS

As a class, three-way products are higher priced than other products. Nonetheless, a good three-way product is preferred. It also does the job of polishing—and does it well. What's more, because of its tarnish retardance, you won't have to clean the silver again quite as soon.

Dip cleaners work fast but you still may need to use a polish afterward, and polishing, after all, is like cleaning all over again.

MISCELLANEOUS

AIR CLEANERS

In the average American house, outdoor air replaces the indoor air at the rate of only about one air change an hour. A "tight" house, with well-sealed windows and doors, may have an air exchange only once every four or five hours. And it can harbor a wide variety of pollutants—radon gas, cigarette smoke, cooking fumes, gases and smoke from furnaces and gas ranges, solvents from dry-cleaned clothing, chemicals from paints, household cleaners, bug sprays, and the like.

Obviously, you can ventilate the house by opening the windows, especially when cooking or painting. But you wouldn't want to do that when the weather is very hot or cold. Obviously, too, the more pollutants and irritants you can eliminate or control, the better. (You can keep dust mites at bay, for example, if you wash bedding in hot water. And a kitchen exhaust fan can control cooking odors and smoke.)

Using an appliance to clear the air can be less effective, and much more expensive, than opening a window. Most air cleaners are designed to remove smoke and dust but not gases, tobacco odors, or viruses and bacteria. And an air cleaner can never completely eliminate pollution; new contaminants constantly enter the house.

A typical tabletop air cleaner can move only small amounts of air each minute; it would suffice for a small room or part of a large room. Bigger models are designed to move several hundred cubic feet of air a minute; they are meant for a large room.

HOW AIR CLEANERS OPERATE

Smoke particles, microbes, and many other solid contaminants are far smaller than the hair and dust you see floating in the air, narrower than the 10-micron threshold of visibility (a micron is about one twenty-five-thousandth of an inch). The gas molecules from smoke are many times smaller still. To remove such small objects, air cleaners typically use filters, electrical attraction, or ozone. Here are the basics of how the principal types work.

Filters. The finer a filter's sieve, the smaller the particles it traps. "High-efficiency particulate air" filters (HEPA, for short) snare 99.97 percent of particles larger than 0.3 microns. These filters were originally developed to trap radioactive dust in atomic plants. A variant, the pleated filter, traps up to 95 percent of the same particles. By comparison, a room air conditioner's foam filter traps particles only 10 microns or larger, and no more than 30 percent of them at that. But even the best HEPA filter can't catch something as small as a gas molecule. Activated carbon or charcoal filters, found on many HEPA or pleated-filter air cleaners, are needed for that task.

Electrical Attraction. There are three main types. In an electrostatic precipitating cleaner, a high-voltage wire charges particles drawn in by a fan, which are then attracted to a precipitating cell carrying the opposite electrical charge. An "electret" filter uses fibers with a static charge to trap particles. A negative-ion generator uses fine, electrically charged needles or wires to ionize particles, which collect in a filter or, more typically, on your walls and furnishings. None of the electrical-attraction cleaners remove gas molecules; they tend to diffuse back into the air.

Ozonation. An ozone generator uses a high-voltage electric charge to convert oxygen in the air to ozone, a pungent, powerful oxidant. At sufficiently high concentrations, ozone attacks and destroys gas molecules and microorganisms. Ozone has no effect on dust and other particulates, however. And, as explained on pages 123–24, ozone generators sold for home use can actually foul the air.

There is no universally accepted performance standard for comparing air cleaners. The closest thing to one is the clean air delivery rate (CADR), which expresses the number of cubic feet of clean air a unit delivers each minute. The CADR, developed and certified by the Association of Home Appliance Manufacturers, is used by some air-cleaner manufacturers on their products.

For rooms of various sizes, the CADR is based on both the percentage of particles removed and how quickly they are removed. Tests performed to the appliance association's specifications provide CADR numbers for dust, smoke, and pollen.

Consumers Union believes that CADR numbers alone don't provide a complete picture of an air cleaner's effectiveness. It's also necessary to know the unit's total air-flow rate to properly assess efficiency. Two cleaners may have the same CADR, but the one with the lower total air flow will be the more efficient.

DUST, SMOKE, ODORS

Pollen removal is a simple task for these devices. Pollen grains are relatively large and heavy; those not caught by an air cleaner will settle out of the air fairly quickly. (See "Dealing with Allergy," page 125.)

Air flow. Room units move more air than tabletop models do. Air flows, in Consumers Union's tests, were 10 percent lower than what manufacturers claim.

Dust removal. Consumers Union testers checked for dust-removing ability in a sealed, 9½-by-20½-by-8-foot chamber, using very fine laboratory dust dispersed evenly in the air. They monitored the dust concentration in the air with a laser spectrometer, a device that counts microscopic particles, which was set to look for particles 0.5 to 3 microns wide.

Smoke removal. Tobacco smoke tests were similar to the dust tests. So were the results. It did take the cleaners longer to remove smoke particles, which are typically less than 1 micron in diameter.

Odors. A telltale odor will linger long after you clear a room of tobacco smoke. That's because most air cleaners won't capture gases from the smoke, which stick to walls, furniture, and clothing, and which seep back into the air over time.

Ozone Generators

Ozone can purify drinking water, disinfect mildewed boats, and deodorize fire-ravaged buildings. But ozone is also a toxic gas, a component of smog, with no known beneficial health effects.

The U.S. Occupational Safety and Health Administration limits ozone exposure in industrial settings to 100 parts per billion (ppb) over an eight-hour day, six days per week. At that level, ozone irritates the eyes, makes the throat feel dry, and stresses the lungs. The U.S. Food and Drug Administration has set a limit of 50 ppb for the ozone from electronic air cleaners. That's a sensible limit for the home.

Given those facts, an ozone-generating air cleaner would seem a contradiction in terms. But the makers of the *Alpine 150* and the *Quantum Panda Plus Q11* would like you to believe otherwise.

Neither unit allows users to measure ozone output or to control ozone levels in a meaningful way. (The *Alpine* comes with a "regular" and a larger "power" generating plate.) *Alpine* promotional materials say you can tell if ozone levels are too high when the distinctive odor becomes apparent. But research has shown that odor isn't a reliable yardstick.

When Consumers Union tested the *Alpine* and *Quantum* under a variety of conditions, they almost always produced ozone levels well above the FDA's limit of 50 ppb.

In a sealed test chamber, the *Quantum* generated 150 ppb of ozone on its Low setting, 2700 ppb on High after 15 hours of operation. The *Alpine* generated less than 10 ppb on Low but 100 to 2600 ppb on High, depending on the plate used.

The testers also ran each unit at its high ozone setting for at least 24 hours in a chamber set for one complete air change an hour. The *Quantum* produced 700 ppb; the *Alpine,* 90 to 180 ppb with its regular plate and 625 ppb with its power plate.

Additional tests were done on a *Living Air XL15,* distributed by a company that uses the same address and phone number as Alpine Air

Products. The *Living Air* has a dial that lets users adjust ozone output according to room size. In that regard, it's a minor improvement over the *Alpine* and the *Quantum.*

The *Living Air* was tested in chambers corresponding to rooms 9½ by 20½ feet, 17 by 17 feet, and 37 by 37 feet, following instructions for the proper ozone setting. The chambers were sealed for some tests and had one air exchange an hour for others. Ozone levels dropped below 50 ppb only in the smaller chambers with one air exchange an hour.

Ozone generators have limited value in unoccupied spaces. But it's highly questionable whether they belong where people breathe.

Even the best air cleaners remove smoke particles far more effectively than they do smoke odors. The cleaners would have to run at least ten times as long to remove odors as to remove smoke particles.

NOISE

Few models are objectionably loud at their lowest fan speed, but many can be annoying at their highest speed. The lowest setting is generally preferable for continuous use.

Because an air cleaner is often used in a bedroom at night, it is a good idea to listen to the machine you are planning to buy. If you can't try it in a quiet location in the store, be sure the air cleaner is returnable if it turns out to be too noisy at home.

MAINTENANCE AND OPERATING COSTS

A few air cleaners consume a minimal amount of electricity over the course of a year—less than $20 at the national average electricity rate. Energy costs more typically range from about $20 to $40.

The cost of replacement filters can be quite high, however, particularly for units using a HEPA filter. Based on the manufacturers' recommended filter replacement intervals, HEPA filters may cost $50 to $140; other types, $20 to $80 a year.

Most air cleaners require little maintenance beyond filter changes and cleanings. If you choose an electrostatic precipitator, you'll need to wash its electronic cell every few months.

RECOMMENDATIONS

You may be able to improve the air quality inside your house without spending hundreds of dollars on an air cleaner. Just opening a few windows may do the job. In addition, you should do what you can to minimize or eliminate sources of air pollution. Even in winter, cracking open a window a couple of inches won't raise your heating bill by more than a few pennies an hour. In addition, a kitchen exhaust fan should effectively dispose of smoke and fumes from cooking.

But if you can't open a window—because the outside air is polluted or the temperature outside is bitter cold—or if you need to ventilate a windowless space, an air cleaner may be the only way to reduce smoke and airborne dust.

DEALING WITH ALLERGY

Simply setting up an air cleaner in the middle of the room will not reduce or prevent asthmatic attacks or offer relief from allergic and respiratory problems, according to Harold S. Nelson, M.D., of the National Jewish Center in Denver, who chaired a committee organized by the American Academy of Allergy and Immunology to study allergens in indoor air and air-cleaning devices.

"Most household dust is inert," he told Consumers Union. "Removing it from the air with [an air cleaner] won't help much. As for pollen, an air conditioner may be sufficient."

Dr. Nelson blames the fecal pellets of house dust mites (microscopic creatures that feed on human skin cells that are sloughed off) for many allergic reactions. The pellets are too large to remain airborne for long; they settle within minutes, so an air cleaner is rather ineffective against them.

Ratings of Household Air Cleaners

Excellent ⊙ · Very Good ◓ · Good ○ · Fair ◒ · Poor ●

Brand and model	Price	Type	Annual cost: Energy	Annual cost: Filter	Smoke removal	Dust removal	Noise: High	Noise: Low	Dimensions (HxWxD), in.	Weight, lb.	Advantages	Disadvantages	Comments	Mfr. phone numbers
Room models														
✓ **Friedrich C90**	$399	EP	$25	$34	Excellent	Excellent	Fair	Very Good	19x15x22	27	A,D	i	*F*	512-225-2000
Honeywell F59A	600	EP	21	80	Very Good	Very Good	Fair	Very Good	20x14x17	38	D,F	—	*L,M*	800-345-6770
Smokemaster P-600	649+	EP	27	40	Very Good	Very Good	Fair	Very Good	20x14x17	39	D,E	i,d	*L*	800-328-0787
Enviracaire EV-35A [1]	300	H	57	73	Very Good	Very Good	Poor	Fair	12x16x17	15	A	e,j	*F*	800-332-1110
Austin Air Sierra HEPA PFA-80-AC [2]	395+	H	30	52	Very Good	Very Good	Fair	Very Good	23x15x15	39	B	a,g,k	*F,H*	800-724-8403
Trion Console 250	279	EP	47	60	Good	Very Good	Fair	Very Good	27x12x12	35	D	—	*F,J*	800-227-3917
Vitaire H200	299	H	24	69	Good	Good	Fair	Good	20x14x15	30	A	a,d,g,k	*E,G,H, K,L,M*	800-447-4344
Hepanaire HP50	495	H	26	145	Good	Good	Fair	Good	15x21x20	39	—	e,g,k	*I,M*	908-291-3600
Cloud 9 Sterilaire 150	325+	H	32	139	Good	Good	Fair	Good	13x24x12	27	A	e,g,k	*K,O*	708-595-5000
Micronaire P-500	495	EP	34	98	Fair	Good	Poor	Very Good	16x12x15	23	D	f,l	*I,J,O*	908-291-3600
NSA 7100A	489	H	19	138	Fair	Fair	Good	Good	28x18x16	33	A,B,C,F,K	i	*D,F*	407-333-9225
Space-Gard 2275	180	PF	12	26	Poor	Fair	Fair	Very Good	14x12x12	12	—	a	*E,F,G*	800-545-2219

Tabletop models

Pollenex 1850	60	I,EF	20	60	○	○	○	◓	11x13x10	8	H,I	a,b,i	*D,F*	800-767-6020
Bionaire F-150	180	I,EF	20	68	○	○	◒	⊙	10x14x8	7	C,F,H	a,b,j	*C*	201-934-0755
Trion Super Clean II	129	I,EP	12	40	◒	◒	◒	◓	5x16x11	9	D,J	i	*F,J*	800-227-3917
Norelco CAM880	147	I,EF	16	120	◒	○	◒	◓	9x17x7	8	F,H,I,J	—	*D,F,H*	800-243-7884
Amcor Air Processor 2135 NI	119	I,EP	4	—	◒	●	○	◓	9x9x14	4	H	a,b	*A,F,I,J,K*	718-361-2700
Ecologizer Series 8000	140	H	19	108	●	●	●	◓	11x14x10	9	—	a	*B*	203-597-1812
NSA 1200A	179	EF	8	78	●	●	○	○	12x11x8	6	—	—	*B,F*	407-333-9225

Not Acceptable

■ *The following tabletop models can produce harmful levels of ozone and do not have an automatic control to limit ozone output. Listed alphabetically.*

Alpine 150	449	OZ	5	—	●	●	●	⊙	8x12x10	15	—	h,l	*F,G,H*	816-524-7200
Quantum Panda Plus Q11	499+	OZ	3	—	◒	●	○	⊙	6x12x10	9	A,G	c,h	*A,F,G*	800-966-5575

[1] *Successor model, EV-35B*
[2] *Successor model, Healthmate*

Features in Common
Except as noted, all have: • 2 or more fan speeds. • Conveniently located controls. • Rubber or cork pads or legs. • Grounded or polarized plug. • Washable prefilter and/or postfilter. • Activated-carbon or charcoal filter to remove gaseous odors. • On/off light. • Easily accessible cell or filter. *Except as noted, all lack:* • Handle, wheels, or casters. • Adjustable louvers. • Filter-replacement indicator.

Key to Advantages
A–Has handle.
B–Has wheels.
C–Adjustable louvers direct air flow.
D–Can't be operated if cover is removed.
E–Malfunction indicator light and test button.
F–Has filter-replacement indicator or schedule.
G–Self-clean switch cleans ozone power plate.
H–Separate On/off ionizer switch.
I–Separate indicator light for ionizer.
J–Can't run ionizer without fan on.
K–Has indicator light for both speeds.

Key to Disadvantages
a–No indicator light for normal operation.
b–Ionizer runs without fan on.
c–Has only 1 speed.
d–Inconveniently placed control knob.
e–No pads or legs.
f–Made annoying crackling sound.
g–Slight humming sound on Low.
h–High-pitched buzz at high ozone setting.
i–Made humming, vibrating sound on High.
j–High-pitched whine on High.
k–Tools needed to replace filter; a difficult task.
l–Internal electrical and moving parts can be easily reached from outside by a small finger.

Key to Comments
A–Has spare prefilter.
B–Chemically treated filter system.
C–Has 4-stage filter cartridge.
D–Electret and charcoal filters in 1 cartridge.
E–No prefilter.
F–No postfilter.
G–No activated carbon or charcoal filter.
H–No grounded or polarized plug.
I–Front grille acts as a postfilter.
J–Switch lets user dry cell after washing.
K–Separate tester shows ion production.
L–Optional casters.
M–Fan motor must be periodically lubricated.

Listed by size; within sizes, listed in order of estimated quality, based primarily on effectiveness in removing dust and smoke. Bracketed models, judged approximately equal in quality, are listed alphabetically. As published in an **October 1992** report.

Brand and model. Models with overall dimensions (height, width, depth) greater than 35 inches were considered room models. If you can't find a model, call the company.

Price. The manufacturer's suggested retail. A + indicates that shipping is extra.

Type. The method each unit uses to clean air. Electrostatic precipitators (**EP**) charge particles with high voltage, then attract them to collector plates. HEPA, or high-efficiency particulate air filters (**H**), have densely packed glass fibers that trap airborne particles. Pleated filters (**PF**) trap particles in much the same way HEPA filters do, though less efficiently. Ionizers (**I**) apply a high voltage to the air, generating negative ions. These attach to airborne particles, which can then be trapped by a filter or settle on walls, furniture, and floors. Electret filters (**EF**) trap particles in electrically charged polyester fibers. Ozone generators (**OZ**) aren't meant to remove particles. They convert oxygen to ozone, a powerful oxidant capable of reacting with many gases. In our tests, the two models listed easily produced more than 50 parts per billion of ozone, exceeding the level set by the U.S. Food and Drug Administration.

Annual cost. Energy shows an estimate of the cost to run each unit eight hours each day on High, at the national average electricity rate of 8¼ cents per kilowatt-hour. **Filter** is a benchmark figure, based on the suggested retail price of filters and the shortest replacement interval recommended by the manufacturer. The actual replacement interval will depend on pollutant levels and hours of use.

Smoke removal. How well each cleaner, running at high speed, removed cigarette-smoke particles, particularly those from 0.1 to 1 micron in diameter, from a 9½-by-20½-by 8-foot test chamber. The scores reflect two factors: the unit's clean air delivery rate, or CADR, a measure of performance that shows how many cubic feet of air a unit can clean per minute; and efficiency, which we define as the CADR divided by the cleaner's air flow. Units judged ◉ had a CADR of 230 to 300 cfm; those judged ◓, a CADR of 160 to 230 cfm; those judged ○, a CADR of 100 to 160 cfm; those judged ◒, a CADR of 40 to 100 cfm; and those judged ●, a CADR of 0 to 40 cfm. All but the lowest-rated units were at least 60 percent efficient.

Dust removal. How effectively and efficiently each model, operating at high speed, removed dust particles, particularly those from 0.5 to 3 microns, from the test chamber. Scores reflect both the units' CADR and their efficiency. Units judged ◉ had a CADR of 250 to 330 cfm; those judged ◓, a CADR of 170 to 250 cfm; those judged ○, a CADR of 100 to 170 cfm; those judged ◒, a CADR of 50 to 100 cfm; and those judged ●, a CADR of 0 to 50 cfm. Units judged ○ or better were at least 80 percent efficient. Any of these units would remove pollen more effectively than they would dust.

Noise. The scores combine instrument readings of decibel levels at High and Low fan speeds with scores from a panel that rated noise while listening with their backs to the cleaners.

Dimensions. To the nearest inch.

Weight. To the nearest pound.

Whole-House Air Cleaners

There are air cleaners designed to fit the ductwork for central heating or air-conditioning.

The simplest type is a filter that replaces the system's existing one. It should be possible for you to install and replace them yourself.

More complex—and more expensive—are electrostatic precipitators that should be installed by a contractor.

You can buy these filters through heating and air-conditioning dealers, or at home centers. It can cost as much as $300 to have a professional install one of the electrostatic precipitators.

In tests that mimicked air flow through air ducts, *Trion Max 5 1400* ($350) and a *Honeywell F-50E* ($500) electrostatic precipitators removed dust and smoke particles within a room about as effectively as the better room-sized portable cleaners. The *3M Filtrete,* a disposable electret filter ($15), was only a notch less effective. A *Newtron 1-1620* self-charging electrostatic filter ($195) was in the same league as a small tabletop air cleaner.

Any of these in-duct air cleaners may affect the overall performance of the heating and cooling system. The *Trion* and *Honeywell* precipitators have no fan of their own, relying on the furnace or air conditioner to move air through the system. So when the thermostat shuts down the system, it will also shut down the air cleaner unless the system has a switch to keep the fan going continuously. In addition, the *Newtron* and *3M Filtrete* filters will slow air flow through the ducts. That will make the system run longer to heat or cool, increasing your energy bill.

If you have air-quality problems throughout the house that can't be controlled in any other way—and if duct work is already in place—then the *Honeywell* or *Trion* could be useful. But if you just need to clean the air in a couple of rooms, a portable air cleaner would be a better choice.

The problem is that the mites thrive in mattresses, pillows, and blankets. An allergy sufferer buries his or her face in the bedding, breathes in the pellets, and suffers an allergic reaction.

The best relief comes from separating the patient from the allergen. The pillows and mattress should be sealed in special allergen-proof casings, available from surgical supply houses. Blankets and sheets should be washed often.

For the same reason, allergy sufferers should avoid lying on an upholstered couch.

Some manufacturers promote humidifiers as beneficial for allergies. Dr. Nelson believes a humidifier can do more harm than good, because house dust mites proliferate in humid conditions. He advises keeping indoor humidity relatively low, at about 20 to 30 percent. If you use a humidifier, clean it frequently and in accordance with the manufacturer's instructions.

Animal dander is lighter than most dust and tends to remain airborne longer, creating a serious problem for allergy sufferers. If you have a pet, at least keep the bedroom off-limits. Here, an air cleaner might help, since the particles of animal dander are of a size that these machines can collect.

AUTO POLISHES

One of the attractions of a new car is its showroom shine. Recent models have an additional clear coating that adds even more luster to the finish. But eventually sunlight, water, and air pollution age and erode the paint until the gloss fades, and the finish is no longer able to repel water and dirt. At this point, auto polish can make a dramatic improvement.

You'll find auto polish in liquid, paste, and spray versions. Many of the products are called "creams," "sealants," "glazes," or "protectors" by their makers, but they're basically just polishes. Some contain abrasives to remove stubborn stains or chalky, weathered paint from a car's finish. Most also contain waxes or silicones that can fill tiny cracks and renew the water-repellency of the finish.

EFFECTIVENESS

On car surfaces that are relatively new, some polishes will shine a little better than others. Yet even the better ones won't add dramatically to the gleam.

A major part of the sales appeal of auto polishes is the protection they're supposed to provide against the elements. But a polish can't protect anything once it has worn away. People who polish their cars tend to do it twice a year, spring and fall, which may not be often enough with most polishes.

If you want to see whether a polish is holding up, look at what happens to water on the car's surface. The beads of water that form on a well-sealed surface are relatively small, rounded, and sit high on the surface. As the polish wears away, the beads spread and flatten. Eventually, when the polish is completely gone, water doesn't bead at all; it lies in a sheet on the surface.

Liquids are somewhat easier to apply and spread better than pastes, but all products should go on easily. Spray-on products are especially easy to apply uniformly. But be careful not to get the spray—or any polish, for that matter—on vinyl surfaces or on the windshield. The polish may affect the appearance of the vinyl, and it will streak and smear the glass. (Be sure to shake a spray container before you begin; some of the ingredients may have settled to the bottom.)

Instructions on the labels of nonspray polishes call for spreading them on with an applicator (which is provided with some products), then removing the excess and buffing with a dry polishing cloth. Buffing is likely to be fairly easy with most. But a few products dry into a rather stiff coating that needs more effort to buff. Also, polish that has been left to dry on the surface too long might be hard to buff. On a dry, hot day, a polish can dry very quickly, so you should tackle small sections at a time.

ABRASIVENESS

The paint, not the polish, protects a car's metal from rust. So it makes sense to polish away no more paint than is necessary to restore a smooth finish.

You can see how much paint you're removing simply by looking at the buffing cloth. If it picks up much of the finish color, the polish contains an abrasive that is grinding away paint. (This test won't work on very new cars, because of the clear topcoat over the colored paint.)

A fine abrasive is useful for removing stubborn stains or a microlayer of chalky, weathered paint. For an extremely weathered finish, however, even the most abrasive polishes may not be adequate. Special, highly abrasive polishing or rubbing compounds are available for such challenging jobs. They are usually found right next to the auto polishes in the store. But do not rub too long or too hard with them, or you may rub right through the paint to the primer.

RECOMMENDATIONS

Whichever polish you use, be sure to wash the car thoroughly beforehand. Most road dirt is a good deal harder than a car's finish. If you polish a dirty car, you'll only grind the dirt into the paint, scratching the finish as you rub.

You may not need to polish a new car, but you should wash it often. Bird and tree droppings, salt, tar, and even plain dirt can eventually mar the finish. Frequent washing is especially important in the summer, when high temperatures increase the damaging effects of contaminants.

FABRIC PILLING REMOVERS

Pilling commonly occurs when fabric fibers that are worked loose by rubbing form little balls. Fibers that still hold firm in the fabric keep the pills from falling off. Loosely woven and knitted fabrics made from synthetic fibers and blends are the typical candidates for pilling. Usually, the stronger synthetic fibers hold the pill to the surface. Pilling can happen to clothes, blankets, and upholstery fabrics, but sweaters seem especially vulnerable.

Some pill-removing gadgets work like miniature electric shavers. A battery-powered motor drives a fan-shaped cutting blade. The blade sweeps behind a screen with holes large enough for most pills to stick through and, in effect, beheads the pill. Other pill removers are lightweight stones, like pumice.

In tests conducted by Consumers Union, the gadgets removed pills, but the effort and the results weren't always the same. They depended mostly on the type of fabric and the density of the pilling.

The shavers worked best on smaller pills, especially those on fabric that didn't have a nap. The shavers also worked better than the stones on stretchy knits, which tended to be pulled and distorted by the snaggers.

The stones worked best on large pills, especially those on firmly constructed materials such as overcoating or other heavy weaves. They also restored a nap on fabrics that had one. The tested stone emitted an unpleasant smell each time it was used, although the smell didn't linger.

Both gadgets removed pills, but the device you need depends on the fabrics that are pilling. If you have sweaters with light pilling and an overcoat with heavy pilling, you need both a shaver and a stone. However, one dry cleaner advised Consumers Union: "We in the dry-cleaning business have found that the fastest and most reliable way to remove pills (or slubs, as they are formally called) is to use a common twin-blade safety razor. You simply shave the pilled area as you would skin. The pills come right off."

PAINT REMOVAL

When you have to deal with paint in really poor condition, you may have to go beyond just stripping away the flaking and peeling paint. If you don't, the surface—whether that of furniture, walls, or the side of a house—may continue to deteriorate. You'd probably have far better results if you stripped off *all* the old paint.

The dozens of products that remove paint all work in one of three ways: with chemicals, heat, or mechanical force.

Chemical strippers soften and dissolve the old finish so you can scrape it off. They are sold as liquids, gels, or pastes; some are more toxic than others.

Heat is delivered via heat guns. Some people use a propane torch, but the open flame can char wood or even start a fire. By spewing air that can be hotter than 800°F, these hairdryerlike devices cause paint to blister and bubble; then you scrape.

Mechanical stripping relies on such tools as rasps, power sanders, and gadgets that attach to drills. Because they can scratch, these tools shouldn't be used on smooth or delicate surfaces.

Rather than try to strip the paint yourself, you can farm out the work to professionals. A pro is likely to do a more thorough job than you could have done, and the price is usually reasonable.

For this project, we tested eight chemicals and five heat guns. Most do-it-yourselfers use chemicals and/or heat guns for all kinds of interior woodwork: furniture, doors, moldings, and the like.

PAINT REMOVERS

Some chemical paint removers are made with volatile solvents—methanol (wood alcohol), toluene, and acetone. Although they're cheaper and faster than some less toxic types, they leave a sticky film you may need to remove with mineral spirits. But this is the least of their problems. Most are highly flammable, and their vapors can cause headaches and, after continued and prolonged exposure, nerve damage.

In the world of solvent strippers, however, those made with methylene chloride stand alone. A mainstay of paint-removal products for years, methylene chloride can dissolve a variety of tough finishes, including polyurethanes and epoxies, and isn't flammable.

But exposure to its fumes can lead to kidney disease, an irregular heartbeat, even heart attack. The Consumer Product Safety Commission has branded the solvent a possible human carcinogen, based on persuasive animal studies.

Any solvent-based paint remover, whether it uses volatile solvents or methylene chloride, can be dangerous to use indoors, even with a window open. Protective garb is essential—neoprene gloves (dishwashing gloves will dissolve), goggles, and a respirator to keep you from inhaling fumes.

LESS HAZARDOUS CHEMICALS

The past few years have seen the introduction of chemical strippers that pose fewer risks than the solvent products. Almost odor-free as well as safer to breathe, they are less likely to irritate skin. Cleanup is easy, too: Once the softened paint has been scraped, light scrubbing with a wet sponge or rag will clear away any remaining residue.

The safer products, however, are slow. A solvent stripper might remove several coats of paint in two or three hours. A nonsolvent stripper would have to sit from six hours to overnight. To make matters worse, some nonsolvent varieties dry out, which means you have to brush additional remover over the slightly moist paint. *Peel Away* 6 is an exception. It comes with a plastic-coated paper that's applied over the substance to keep it moist.

Nonsolvent chemicals can carry a higher price tag—anywhere from $20 to $43 a gallon, versus $20 to $24 for the solvent-based removers. At practical application rates, a gallon of nonsolvent product should cover 32 square feet, roughly both sides of a door.

HEAT GUNS

Using a heat gun is intense work, but it's faster than any chemical method. Unlike chemicals, heat guns rarely have to go over the same area twice. Once the hot paint separates from the underlying surface, you can peel it off easily.

After the initial expense—from about $30 to $70—heat guns are cheap to use, costing about 12 cents in electricity to strip one side of a door, at average utility rates. But they do have limitations: They're frustrating to use when the paint film is very thin (they work best when bubbling up several layers); they won't remove varnish or other clear coatings; and they're ineffective on painted metal. (Metal conducts heat too rapidly.)

Heat guns also have hazards. The expelled-air temperature may be as

Ratings of Paint Removers: Chemical Paint Strippers

● ◓ ○ ◒ ⊙

Better ←→ Worse

Listed in order of overall quality, based on safety, speed, results, and effort needed. Products judged approximately equal are bracketed and listed alphabetically. As published in a **May 1991** report.

Price. Manufacturer's average or suggested retail to nearest dollar, per gallon—the amount you're likely to need for even a modest job.

Cost/sq. ft. So you can determine the cost of an actual job. Based on the cost per ounce, with a coating about one-eighth-inch thick for the nonsolvent products, less for solvent types. You may use more or less, depending on how careful you are, how viscous the stripper is, and how many layers of paint you need to remove.

Ingredients. The chemicals containing nonvolatile esters (**E**) are least hazardous to use. Products using methanol, toluene, and acetone solvents (**MTA**) are flammable, produce toxic vapors, and can irritate skin. Methylene chloride solvent (**MC**) is a possible human carcinogen and may cause heart and kidney damage. We tested one typical product of this kind.

Safety. Products judged less than ⊙ can threaten health. The lower the score, the more serious or numerous the risks.

Speed. The total time it took to strip a 16-square-foot door of five coats of paint. The less hazardous products took more than 10 hours; the solvent-based products, two or three.

Results. Judged by a panel of staffers. How thoroughly the products removed paint from cracks, molding, and wood grain. Most left some paint residue.

Effort. Removing paint by chemical means is messy at best. Some products, however, require repeated application, are difficult to scrape, leave the softened paint quite sloppy, and provide no visual clue as to when the stuff is ready to be lifted off.

Brand and model	Price	Cost/sq. ft.	Ingredients	Safety	Speed	Results	Effort	Advantages	Disadvantages	Comments
Peel Away 6	$43	$2.50	E	⊙	●	⊙	○	A,B,C	g	*A*
3M Safest Stripper	20	1.20	E	⊙	●	⊙	◒	A,B,C	d,g	*B*
Easy Off Paint Stripper	25	1.50	E	⊙	●	◓	●	A,C	g	*B*
Savogran StrypSafer	33	1.90	E	⊙	●	◓	●	A,C	d,g	*B*
Parks No Drip Strip	20	.40	MTA	◒	◓	◓	◒	—	a,b	—

Savogran FinishOff	20	.50	MTA	◒	○	◓	◒	—	a,b	—
Bix Stripper	20	.50	MTA	●	◓	◓	◒	—	a,b,c,e,f	—
Rock Miracle Paint and Varnish Remover	24	1.10	MC	●	◓	◓	◒	—	a	—

Features in Common
All: • Can be applied with brush. • Are sufficiently viscous for use on vertical surfaces. • May require more than 1 application depending on finish type, condition, and thickness. • Have adequate instructions and warning labels.
All solvent-based strippers: • Come in metal container with childproof closure.
Except as noted, all: • Did not rust steel or discolor aluminum or wood.

Key to Advantages
A–Less likely to cause skin irritation or respiratory problems than solvent types.
B–Remained moister than most overnight.
C–Nonflammable.

Key to Disadvantages
a–Solvent vapors pose neurological and respiratory problems.
b–Flammable.
c–Highly alkaline; skin contact hazardous.
d–Rusted steel.
e–Stained aluminum.
f–Discolored pine and cherry wood.
g–May take overnight to soften several coats.

Key to Comments
A–Comes with plastic-coated paper to be applied over chemical; product works well even when uncovered.
B–Performance improved when covered overnight with plastic food wrap.

Ratings of Heat Guns

⊙ Better ◓ ○ ◒ ● Worse

Listed in order of estimated quality, based on safety, comfort, and number of heat settings. Products judged approximately equal are bracketed and listed alphabetically. As published in a **May 1991** report.

Price. Manufacturer's suggested retail.

Watts. As drawn in tests at the lowest and highest heat settings. Higher-wattage models consume more power but don't necessarily perform more vigorously. All models can be used with a common 15-amp household electrical circuit. If you need an extension cord, use one rated for the wattage the gun can draw.

Heat settings. Guns with a continuous **(Cont.)** setting allow a wide range of adjustments. But some models have only an On/Off switch; others offer two settings, High and Low.

Maximum air temperature. In degrees Fahrenheit, measured one inch from nozzle tip after running for several minutes. Machines that blow out hotter air don't necessarily remove paint faster. Stripping speed also depends on fan speed and air flow.

Safety. Heat guns are inherently hazardous. They can start a fire and burn skin. In addition, they can leave scrapings that can dry out and find their way into the air as dust. That's a serious danger if the paint contains lead. Some models lost points because they lack a rapid cool-down setting.

Speed. Based on stripping tests on old paint. The models were about equally fast, and all were much faster than any chemical paint remover.

Handling. How comfortable each model was to use and how balanced it felt in testers' hands.

Results. Judged by a panel. All guns removed paint thoroughly from cracks, moldings, and wood grain.

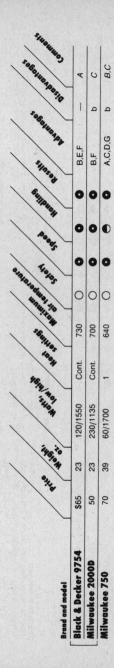

Brand and model	Price	Weight, oz.	Watts, low/high	Heat settings	Maximum air temperature	Safety	Speed	Handling	Results	Advantages	Disadvantages	Comments
Black & Decker 9754	$65	23	120/1550	Cont.	730	○	⊙	⊙	⊙	B,E,F	—	*A*
Milwaukee 2000D	50	23	230/1135	Cont.	700	○	⊙	⊙	⊙	B,F	b	*C*
Milwaukee 750	70	39	60/1700	1	640	○	⊙	◓	⊙	A,C,D,G	b	*B,C*

Black & Decker 9756	45	22	630/1240	2	650	◒	⊙	⊙	⊙	—	a	*A*
Wagner Power Stripper	29	24	715/1440	2	875	◒	⊙	⊙	⊙	E	a	*A*

Features in Common

All: • Reach dangerously high temperature at nozzle tip. • Can be rested without tipping over. • Can be hung on a hook when not in use. • Have 6-ft., heat-resistant cord. • Have convenient, lockable On/Off switch in "trigger" position on handle.
Except as noted, all: • Have plastic body.

Key to Advantages

A–Has fan-only setting for rapid cool-down.
B–Has very low setting for cool-down.
C–Fan air volume adjusted with louvered inlet.
D–Switch guard prevents accidental start-up.
E–Comes with shaped auxiliary nozzle tips.
F–Has continuous rotary heat adjustment.
G–Bracket keeps gun upright when not in use.

Key to Disadvantages

a–Lacks setting for accelerated cool-down.
b–Slightly noisier than others.

Key to Comments

A–Has double-insulated housing and 2-pronged plug.
B–Has metal housing.
C–Has 3-pronged grounded plug.

high as 875°F—high enough to cause a severe burn or even start a fire. Also, it's easy to ignore where you're pointing the gun as you dig out a persistent bit of paint. Always keep a wet rag and a bucket of water handy.

Even if you're never blasted by the gun's hot air, you can get burned by touching the metal nozzle. This is a serious concern, especially if you put down the gun near a child or curious pet. A few models have an essential feature: They allow the fan to run at a Low or Cold setting to hasten cooling.

Heat guns and mechanical strippers pose another, less obvious threat. If you're stripping lead paint, they can increase your exposure to lead by whipping paint dust into the air, where you can inhale it. When the dust settles, it can still be hazardous to young children.

Lead paint isn't found in just old, crumbling buildings. Lead paints were used in the United States as recently as 1970, and the remodeling of relatively new houses has caused lead poisoning in children. There are reliable test kits for detecting lead in dried paint. If you opt to remove lead-based paint yourself instead of hiring a professional, don't use a heat gun or any mechanical method that creates dust.

RECOMMENDATIONS

Any chemical or heat gun will remove paint, which makes the safety factor paramount.

Solvent-based strippers, particularly those containing methylene chloride, pose serious health hazards when used indoors. "Adequate" ventilation may not be enough. Protect your eyes and hands, and wear a respirator. If you choose a solvent product, try to use it outdoors. Better yet, consider going to a professional paint remover, who is likely to do a better job.

For immovable items, such as banisters, moldings, and door jambs, try a heat gun or one of the less toxic chemicals. Although the nonsolvent products are slow and expensive, they're safer than the others.

Heat guns are faster than chemicals but require precautions to minimize the risk of burns and fire.

Heat guns aren't effective on metal and won't strip clear finishes. They shouldn't be used to remove lead-based paint. Don't succumb to the seemingly attractive idea of a scraping blade mounted on the nozzle of a heat gun. It doesn't take long for the softened paint to pile up. When it does, you have to remove it. Steer clear of any device that encourages probing around the tip of a hot heat gun.

PROFESSIONAL STRIPPING

Professional paint removers have one big advantage over do-it-yourselfers: the tank. By immersing items in a cavernous vat of potent chemicals, professionals can get the last traces of paint out of nooks and crannies.

"Dip" stripping systems differ significantly. Some rely on corrosive lye; others on solvents. When you approach a firm, it's a good idea to ask about the method used.

A stripper using lye will dunk the painted object in a lye and water solution. The softened paint is scraped off, and the item is neutralized and rinsed with water. It's an inexpensive and effective treatment—too effective, in fact, if the dealer isn't careful.

Lye not only dissolves paint; it can also stain wood fibers, raise their grain (it feels "fuzzy"), and extract natural resins. In addition, immersion can dissolve glues and swell wood so badly that it warps or falls apart. This won't happen if the operator snatches an item from the tank as soon as the paint is softened. In practice, however, such care is not always possible.

For professionals, whose workplaces are regulated by the Occupational Safety and Health Administration, the solvent method is better. Oversoaking is less likely to produce ruinous results. Still, because some dealers who use solvents rinse the articles in water, wood grain can rise and iron parts can rust. Fortunately, there are solvent systems that avoid the use of water.

Consumers Union testers took old chairs and shutters to two professionals. Both stripped with solvents: one used methylene chloride, hand scraping, and a water washdown; the other, a *Chem-Clean* franchise, used xylol and dimethylformamide (DMF), first as a bath and then in a spray that dislodged the softened paint.

DMF worked very well. The methylene chloride cleaning was a bit less satisfactory: The shutter had some raised grain and mild rust on its fittings; the chair retained patches of paint and showed signs of too much scraping.

Both firms charged $75 for two items: a large, flat shutter and a kitchen chair. Stripping the shutter yourself with the cheapest chemical would cost $12 and a lot of effort; with top-rated *Peel Away* 6, the job could cost you $40.

MECHANICAL PAINT REMOVERS

Scrapers, rasps, and sandpaper substitutes are available. Each type has its uses, however specialized. Since none is really expensive, it's a good idea to keep more than one type in your tool kit.

Hook scrapers. A hook scraper is best suited for removing loose paint from flat surfaces. It looks something like an extra-large razor with a stiff, fairly dull blade. Also like a razor, it's pulled along the work surface so the edge of the blade scrapes away the paint.

Push scrapers. These resemble the familiar putty knife, although they vary in details. Some have a long handle, others a short one. Some have a blunt edge, others are sharpened. You have your choice of stiff or flexible blades in several widths. The differences are of minor importance. You should try to match the shape and size of the scraper to the job at hand—a narrow-bladed scraper, for example, will be best for working in and around window frames.

Push scrapers are useful on flat surfaces and for digging paint out of corners, but they are not meant to be used on curves. In general, they are less effective than hook scrapers on all but the loosest paint. It's harder to push a scraper than to pull it.

Rasps and abrasive blocks. These devices can scrape and sand and are generally available in a variety of sizes and abrasive grades. Rasps and blocks can also be used for sanding wood. Their shape, however, limits their use primarily to flat surfaces.

Sandpaper substitutes. Unlike rasps and sanding blocks, sandpaper substitutes are fairly flexible, so they can get into places that the others can't. They may be rectangles of tough cloth coated on both sides with sheets of abrasive-coated nylon mesh, or possibly a thin sheet of metal punched with ragged holes.

The substitutes are durable and fast-cutting and can be wrapped around a dowel to sand a concave surface or can be used with a sanding block. Some may leave the surface rather rough, making it necessary to do some sanding before painting.

Sponges and glass blocks. To sand moldings and other complex shapes, woodworkers often wrap sandpaper around a sponge. Sanding sponges come essentially prewrapped, with an abrasive coating that covers four sides. They are springy and flexible, as you'd expect sponges to be. They can also be rinsed out to unclog the abrasive.

Foamed glass blocks resemble chunks of hardened plastic foam. They wear away quite rapidly as they're used, leaving a residue of glass dust in the work area.

SAFETY

Paint removal, especially with power tools, requires certain safety precautions. To guard against the obvious hazard—flying chips of paint or grit—you should wear safety goggles or a face shield, work gloves, and a heavy jacket. Hearing protectors are also advisable.

You should guard against health hazards that may not be immediately apparent, such as the problem of lead. Removing paint with a hand tool or a drill attachment will disperse small particles into the air, where they can be inhaled. Likewise, "antifouling" paints are often used on boats and contain toxic ingredients that also might be hazardous if inhaled. In either case, you should wear a fitted respirator with a suitable filtration cartridge. If the paint is new and presents no toxicity hazard, a simple dust mask should suffice.

POWER BLOWERS

A power blower's roar may not endear you to your neighbors, but a blower can spare you a lot of time and sore muscles when whisking leaves from a lawn or blowing debris down the driveway.

There are hand-held electric or gasoline-powered blowers as well as machines meant to be worn like a backpack. Several blowers can accept accessories and attachments. The most common is a kit that converts the blower into an outdoor vacuum cleaner. Another common accessory lets you use a blower to flush the leaves out of rain gutters.

CLEANUP WITH A BLOWER

Backpack blowers are the most effective. They can easily slice through large piles, moving them where you wish. The more powerful ones move more than leaves. They can denude graveled areas and push fallen branches along the ground.

A hand-held blower is less effective than a backpack model, but a gasoline-powered machine can work very well. A good electric blower can also handle leaves capably. A weaker electric blower can pile up leaves, albeit slowly.

A gutter-cleaning attachment consists of several tubes that stack together to reach up to a first-story gutter, about 13 feet. It's best to keep the length as short as possible, because the longer extensions are harder to control. The handiest type of kit lets you swivel the nozzle from the ground. But with others, you can rotate the nozzle only by lowering the entire tube to the ground. Cleaning gutters is invariably sloppy. No amount of care will control the flying mess.

A BLOWER AS A VACUUM CLEANER

Vacuum attachments, like the gutter-cleaning kits, add to a hand-held power blower's versatility. With a suction tube and vacuum bag in place, these machines can handle more than dry leaves or grass clippings on a lawn. They can clean leaves out of ground cover or a flower bed, or pick up pine needles and small pieces of other kinds of lightweight debris.

The vacuuming attachments are not meant for large-scale leaf removal, though. The bags hold about two cubic feet of debris, which is a little less than two bushels. The more powerful models fill their bags in less than five minutes. Emptying the bag is easy enough, but it's not something you'd want to do many times.

The vacuums are not designed to pick up stones and other hard material, because they can damage the fan blade that draws material into the suction tube.

CONVENIENCE

Power blowers are so notoriously noisy that a number of municipalities restrict their use or ban them outright. The large backpack models produce the most racket, comparable to a chain saw. Most hand-held gasoline models generate a little more noise than a gasoline-powered lawn mower. Electric blowers by far produce the least noise. It's a good idea to protect your ears (with earplugs or sound deadeners worn like headphones) when using a gasoline model.

The more comfortable the blower, the longer you can use it before you tire out. A machine's low weight, good balance, and freedom from vibration contribute to comfort. As a class, backpack blowers are comfortable because most of their weight rides on your back. Many hand-held gasoline blowers come with a shoulder strap that makes them easier to handle, but not if a blower vibrates a lot.

The distance from where you grip the handle to the end of the nozzle is not critical with backpack models because you can swivel the tube as needed to direct the airflow. With a hand-held model, your height and the length of your arms and legs will determine the length that's most suitable for you. To get the right size, try models in the store before you buy one. A tube that's too short or too long makes the blower more tiring to use and diminishes its effectiveness.

The operating controls on a blower should be easy to reach and, on gas models, should vary the engine speed smoothly. The controls shouldn't be out of the way on the rear of the unit or be difficult to operate.

GASOLINE ENGINES

One tank of fuel should keep a blower running from about half an hour to an hour and three-quarters. Running time is especially important for a backpack-style blower that's being used for an extended period. You won't want to have to slide in and out of the shoulder harness any more than necessary.

Whether an engine continues to start easily depends on how well it's maintained and tuned. The basic care is similar to that required by power lawn mowers and chain saws:

1. Keep the air filter clean and check the fuel filter regularly.
2. Drain the fuel if the blower won't be used for a long time.
3. Change the spark plug once a year or whenever the manufacturer recommends.

Carburetor adjustments are best left to a mechanic unless you are experienced with small engines.

RECORDING AND PLAYBACK EQUIPMENT

COMPACT DISCS

The most serious damage to a CD is a scratch in the direction the disc spins. Small scratches in the *radial* direction, across the "grooves," are completely ignored by the CD player; therefore, always wipe a CD in the radial direction. Light dust will not harm play; heavier dust can be removed by gentle strokes with a soft cloth. Smudges or deposits should be washed off under running water, with a little liquid dishwashing detergent if needed; then rinse the CD and allow the excess water to run off and *carefully* wipe it dry with a soft cloth.

If the scratches on a compact disc are wide enough, the laser beam in a CD player, which "reads" the disc, won't be able to do its job properly. The result: music punctuated with clicks and pops, or possibly a CD that cannot be played at all. There are specialty products intended to rejuvenate scratched CDs. These probably won't work on severe scratches, but they could dramatically reduce the number of playing errors caused by light scratches. You might even be able to restore an unplayable CD to playable condition.

LONG-PLAYING RECORDS

Keeping an LP dust-free is the best way to make it last longer. Records can be cleaned with a cloth-pile brush before you play them; electronics stores sell such brushes. Keep the turntable's dust cover closed except when changing records, and handle records only by the edges to prevent perspiration and skin oils from attaching dust to the record's surfaces.

When putting a record away, make sure that the opening in the inner sleeve doesn't coincide with the opening in the outer cover, thus leaving the record case wide open for dust to enter. Always store records vertically to reduce the likelihood of warping and keep records away from any direct sources of heat.

STYLUS

Cleaning a stylus is neither difficult nor time-consuming. It's important to keep the stylus free from accumulated dust and dirt, which accelerate record wear and can cause mistracking and distortion.

Clean the stylus with a fine camel's hair or artist's sable brush lightly moistened with a little rubbing alcohol. Brush lightly from the rear to the front of the cartridge; brushing backward or sideways could bend the delicate stylus.

AUDIOTAPE RECORDING AND PLAYBACK HEADS

For best sound quality from an audiotape recorder, clean recording and playback heads periodically. Use a small cotton swab or, even better, a lint-free piece of cotton cloth wrapped around the swab; lint-free cloth has less tendency to release tiny fibers that might get into the moving parts of the machine. The swab or cloth should be lightly moistened with a cleaning agent. You can use isopropyl alcohol (rubbing alcohol), but it is probably safer and better to buy tapehead cleaner with a formulation developed specifically for this purpose from an electronics supply store. Tapehead cleaner is most likely to contain solvents that are safe for use on the heads as well as the materials around the heads. Clean everything in the tape path, not just the heads: the capstan (the rotating metal shaft that moves the tape past the heads), the pinch roller (the rubberlike roller that contacts the capstan), and the tape guides.

If the deck or tape player is built so that the heads are not accessible for cleaning, you might try a special head-cleaning tape. Follow the instructions explicitly. Never use any kind of abrasive material to clean the heads.

Clean as frequently as necessary, based on how often you play tapes, the quality of the tapes, and any evidence of dirt accumulation. Once a month is probably a reasonable interval between cleanings.

VCR RECORDING AND PLAYBACK HEADS

A video head is the device that picks up the video signal from the tape. Video heads are abraded and attract iron particles as they rub against the tape; eventually they wear out.

In tests of a VHS model and a Beta model running continuously for an extended period, with tapes changed every 200 hours, Consumers Union engineers found that the picture began to deteriorate after about 2,500 hours of play.

Replacing the heads can be expensive, running to a considerable fraction of the cost of the entire machine. There's not much you can do about normal wear resulting from the head spinning at high speed against the tape, and the tape moving past the head. You can try to keep the machine as free of dust as possible by covering it when the VCR is not in use and by storing tapes where they aren't likely to gather a lot of dust or other debris.

Sooner or later, however, the heads will get dirty and the picture will become "noisier" and/or fuzzier than it was when the machine was new. Cleaning the heads directly is not a do-it-yourself job. The heads are often accessible only through a maze of delicate wiring and mechanical components.

When the picture seems to need it, you might try a special VCR cleaning tape, using it cautiously and strictly in accordance with the manufacturer's instructions. Use a cleaning tape only when the picture becomes annoyingly deficient. If cleaning restores the picture, fine. If not, try the tape *once* more. If a second cleaning doesn't help, professional servicing may be necessary.

VIDEOTAPES

There isn't much you can do about keeping videotapes clean other than protecting them from smoke, dust, and dirt by keeping them in their cardboard sleeves. Properly cared for, videotapes can last a long time, perhaps 20 years. Store them upright—not flat on their sides, a position that puts pressure on the edges. Don't store tapes near a TV set, loudspeakers, or other devices that generate strong magnetic fields. Never expose tapes to sunlight or leave them in a car in hot weather. Run videotapes at least once a year in Fast Forward or Rewind to keep the layers from sticking together, and limit your use of a VCR's Pause or Freeze-frame feature; both increase wear on the tape and VCR heads.

STEAM IRONS

You can buy a steam iron that beeps, lights up, works without a cord, or shuts itself off if you accidentally leave it on. At the expensive end of the market are the so-called professional irons, with a large water chamber separate from the iron itself. At the other end are a few old-fashioned dry irons, plus the compact irons and travel irons and steamers (see page 153). The largest share of the marketplace is occupied by the full-size steam iron.

FEATURES

Irons with fancy features won't necessarily iron your clothes any better than a plain iron will, but they can often make a dreary task seem less like work.

Spray and burst of steam. These basic additions have been around for a long time. A built-in spray wets down a little patch in front of the iron; a burst of steam at the press of a button lets you set creases or smooth stubborn wrinkles. Both features are particularly useful for dealing with the wrinkles in clothing made of natural fibers.

Controls. The best temperature controls are located on the top of the handle, where you can set them with the hand that is holding the iron. Fabric guides give you an idea of which setting is best for different fabrics.

The best steam-dry controls are on the front of the iron. Many irons have the button awkwardly placed on the side.

Weight. Balance is probably more important than actual weight. Before you buy, pick up the iron and pretend to use it. It should feel well balanced and comfortable in your hand.

Water gauge and capacity. Look for a see-through plastic water chamber. Very dark plastic tanks, found on some models, are nearly impossible to see through. In general, a big tank lets an iron steam longer.

Ease of filling. Most irons are filled through an opening near the handle. Some have a removable water tank, which is easy to snap in and out.

Button groove. Look for a groove that extends along each side near the front of the soleplate.

Cord (while ironing). Try the iron to see if the cord hits your wrist. Some cords stick straight up; designs that send the cord off to the side are better. If you are left-handed, buy an iron with a straight-up cord or with a cord that can be switched from one side to the other.

Automatic shutoff. The shutoff function is typically connected with indicator lights. Some irons even signal audibly for you to turn them off.

All the automatic shutoffs should work pretty much as claimed. But if you accidentally knock an iron over onto your favorite shirt, soleplate down, it may leave a slight scorch mark. Chances are the shirt might be ruined, but there probably wouldn't be a fire.

Cordless irons. Cordless irons heat up in a separate base that is plugged into the electrical outlet. Their supposed advantage is that there's no cord to get in the way.

Cordless irons all share the same problem: An iron without a steady supply of electricity holds heat for only so long. To keep the iron hot, cordless irons must be set back into their bases often. You can get used to this routine, but it's a nuisance, and it slows down your ironing.

TEMPERATURE AND STEAM

Ironing reshapes wrinkled fibers. Steam (or sprinkled water) makes a fabric more pliable, the pressure of the iron sets it straight, and the heat dries it out.

Because some fabrics require more heat than others to set straight, an iron needs a range of temperatures. Stiff, woody fibers derived from plants (cotton and linen) need more heat than fibers from animal sources (silk and wool) and a lot more heat than synthetics. A synthetic's molecules can be custom-made for resilience, but they are often sensitive to high heat. Blends, including permanent-press cotton-polyester, usually take a medium temperature. (When in doubt, set the iron for the fiber that requires the lower temperature.)

Heating tests show irons to be more alike than different. The range provided by a typical iron is about 170° to 370°F. At their lowest setting, some irons are too cool even for acetate, a problem remedied by simply turning up the temperature control a bit. At its highest setting, an iron is unlikely to get hot enough to press linen totally flat, even if you use steam. Badly wrinkled linen, apparently, will respond to nothing less than dampening before ironing. A temperature of 400°F or so is best for linens.

An iron usually overshoots the mark when first set for a particular temperature. The temperature stabilizes after a few minutes. Irons take much longer than that to cool down—as much as 20 minutes. Therefore, iron delicate fabrics before the linens and cottons.

Within limits, the more steam an iron produces, the better. A filled iron usually steams better than a half-filled one. Most irons steam at a slower rate as they run out of water.

WATER FOR STEAM

Past experience may have taught you to use distilled water to avoid clogging your iron's steam vents with minerals. Most manufacturers say that unless you have extremely hard water—more than 180 parts per million of dissolved minerals—tap water is fine. (Note: Many manufacturers warn against using water passed through a water softener, since the minerals in such water can damage the iron.) If you use distilled water, many manufacturers suggest that you switch to tap water once in a while, as water with some minerals in it produces more steam than pure water.

Minerals often end up as off-white grit that stains clothes and dirties the bottom of the iron. To cope with the grit, some irons have a removable panel in the soleplate so you can clean the inside of the iron. Some models have a special self-cleaning feature that flushes the vents with steam and hot water. On a model with a burst-of-steam feature, you can use the burst to dislodge debris and mineral residue from the steam vents. To keep from inadvertently soiling your clothes with grit, shoot a spurt or two of steam into the air each time before you iron. With irons that lack either of these features, the best you can do is to fill the iron, set it on High, and iron over an old all-cotton towel for several minutes.

Many manufacturers, apparently to protect their products from outdated iron-cleaning tips, warn against using vinegar or a special iron-cleaning product. One safe way to help prevent a buildup of minerals is to empty your iron as soon as you are finished ironing, while it's still hot. Store the empty iron on its heel.

Nonstick soleplates ease another cleaning problem, the accumulation of spray starch or other residues on the bottom of the iron. Take care not to scrape over metal zippers or snaps, lest you abrade the nonstick coating.

Irons draw a lot of current. To avoid blowing a fuse or tripping a circuit breaker, you shouldn't plug one into the same circuit where another heating appliance is operating. If you can't set up your ironing board next to an outlet, use a heavy-duty extension cord (*not* the 18-gauge variety commonly used for lamp cords).

RECOMMENDATIONS

Before you rush out to get a fancy, modern iron, consider what kind of fabrics you iron. If you use an iron now and then to touch up permanent press, perhaps all you need is a plain steam iron. If you iron everything from cotton to acetate, if you are as apt to press in wrinkles as press them out, or if you find the idea of a steam iron that shuts off automatically appeals to your sense of safety, you should consider buying an iron with extra features.

TRAVEL IRONS AND STEAMERS

If a travel iron or steamer won't fit unobtrusively in a corner of the suitcase or slide into the pocket of a garment bag, it's likely to be left behind. A typical travel iron or steamer is small and lightweight (ranging from just under a pound to slightly more than a pound and a half) and comes with either a drawstring pouch or a zippered bag. On most, the handle folds down or comes off, but even those with a fixed handle aren't ungainly.

The controls on travel irons have been miniaturized more or less successfully. Travel irons have a narrower range of temperatures than full-size irons. Without the high heat and heft of a full-size iron, they're not as good at eliminating wrinkles in linen and cotton. Heat alone may be enough to smooth delicates, but for most other fabrics you also need some moisture, either steam or a spray of water, to make the fabric more pliable.

Steamers have no controls. They turn on when they are plugged in, off when unplugged.

As you'd expect, most irons and steamers make some provision for switching over to the 220-volt electricity you will encounter abroad. For those that don't, you'll need a small voltage converter intended for use with a high-wattage appliance.

Travel irons and steamers are much smaller than full-size irons, so it's harder to keep your hands away from the areas that get hot. You must be careful.

RECOMMENDATIONS

If you select your travel wardrobe carefully, pack judiciously, and unpack promptly, you might avoid wrinkled clothes altogether. In a pinch, you can always try hanging creased clothes in the bathroom (door closed, hot shower turned on), thereby creating a humid environment conducive to the relaxation of wrinkles.

Travel irons and steamers are make-do appliances. Travelers faced with a badly wrinkled suit and an important meeting would probably do better with the hotel's valet service or a nearby dry cleaner. But a steamer may be just what you need to touch up a suit or knock the wrinkles out of a drip-dried shirt.

DENTAL CARE

People in all age groups are losing fewer teeth and suffering less tooth decay and gum disease than they did a generation ago. Half the nation's schoolchildren have no cavities at all; in the early 1970s, only about one-fourth were cavity-free.

Although people are seeing their dentists more often for regular checkups, there's less drilling and filling for the dentist to do. Several factors can account for the nation's improving oral health. Americans not only see the dentist more but get better care when they go. Most communities have fluoridated drinking water, and most toothpastes contain fluoride as well. There has also been a flood of new consumer dental products, which has helped raise awareness of the benefits good home care can bring. Millions of Americans are now taking steps to fight plaque, the sticky film that can damage teeth and gums; tartar, the calcified, hardened form of plaque; and gingivitis, the gum inflammation that is a common, relatively mild form of gum disease.

The old primary goal of personal oral hygiene—to prevent cavities—is also as important as ever. Fortunately, many of the same steps that prevent tooth decay will help keep your gums healthy as well.

PRODUCT VARIETIES

Matching the burgeoning array of toothpastes in stores is an equally wide array of toothbrushes.

Various mouthwashes now claim to fight plaque, fight tooth decay, or control tartar, with varying degrees of accuracy. Electric toothbrushes and oral irrigators promote a technological approach to dental hygiene at a high price—$100 or more for some.

You certainly don't need every new product that comes along to keep your teeth and gums in shape. But some specialized products can help.

ELECTRIC TOOTHBRUSHES

Can an electric brush help teeth and gums in ways that an ordinary brush cannot? Some dental researchers believe it can, but others believe it can't.

The American Dental Association used to hold that any toothbrush can potentially clean teeth well. But now the ADA has been convinced that, for most people, an electric brush does in fact take off more plaque than a regular toothbrush. The ADA seal on most electric brushes calls them an "effective cleansing device." But the ADA says it hasn't seen research proving that any electric brush covered by its acceptance program is superior to any other.

Consumers Union's dental consultants believe that ordinary people can be trained to use a manual toothbrush with excellent results. But most people don't brush well enough or long enough. (People tend to brush for less than a minute. You need two or three minutes of manual brushing to do the job right.) An electric brush covers more area faster, and so can make it easier to brush effectively.

The key issue is whether someone who buys an electric toothbrush actually *uses* it. A survey of *Consumer Reports* readers painted a pessimistic picture. The problem readers mentioned most: the time and effort involved in using or maintaining the device.

In panel tests conducted by Consumers Union, enough consistent preferences emerged to make the *Braun Oral-B* the clear winner. The dental professionals consulted also thought the *Braun* superior; they pointed out that the small brush head was exceptionally easy to maneuver around the mouth and even made it easy to reach the back parts of the rearmost teeth, an area sometimes neglected.

USING AN ELECTRIC BRUSH

A little bleeding from gums can be expected when you first use an electric brush; the bleeding typically stops as your gums become healthier and as you learn how to control the device. If you continue to brush too vigorously, however, you can injure your gums or eventually cause them to recede. Children should be supervised as they brush, and those younger than 10 should probably not be using an electric brush at all.

The potential for bleeding, which can spread oral bacteria to the bloodstream, poses a special risk for people with impaired immunity and those with certain heart conditions, since oral bacteria can infect the heart valves. Before dental work, such people are routinely given antibiotics as a safeguard against the risk of infection from oral bleeding. They should check with a physician or dentist before starting to use an electric brush.

FEATURES

Extra heads. Brush heads wear out—some in as little as two or three months—so the price of replacements should be considered. You may also want to consider one of the models that includes extra brush heads for different family members.

Charge capacity. Will a brush run long enough between chargings to take on a trip?

The "run-down" times vary from nearly an hour for the *Sunbeam* to about six minutes for the *Interplaks,* a time so short it makes the *Interplaks* useless for travel unless you lug the charging stand. The *DentiBrush,* which uses a flashlight cell, will give four hours of brushing with an alkaline battery; with a typical rechargeable cell, it will brush for about 1½ hours.

Controls. The cheaper *Interplak*s have you turn a small, hard-to-twist button to set their speed. The company will supply a larger control on request. The *Interplak Plus* features a soft-touch button that starts the brush, bumps the speed up a notch with each succeeding press, then turns

Ratings of electric toothbrushes

⊙ Better ◓ ○ ◒ ● Worse

Brand and model	Price	Price, extra brushes	Dimensions (WxDxH), in.	Handset weight, oz.	Speeds	Brushes, supplied/stored on base	Overall performance	Instructions	Ease of use	Setup	Changing brushes	Cleaning brushes	Charge capacity	Advantages	Disadvantages	Comments
							Panel judgments									
✓ Braun Oral-B Plaque Remover D5545	$ 99	$10 (1)	1¾x3¾x8	6	1	4/4	⊙	⊙	⊙	⊙	⊙	⊙	◓	A	—	A,B,D
Interplak Family PB-2	99	13 (1)	2¾x3x8½	9	3	2/0	◓	⊙	⊙	⊙	○	◓	●	—	—	C,D,H,I,P
Water Pik Automatic Toothbrush AT-10W	45	5 (4)	3¾x2¾x8¾	6	1	4/4	○	⊙	⊙	⊙	⊙	⊙	◒	—	—	—
Teledyne Water Pik Plaque Control PC-2000W	50	5 (4)	3¾x2¾x8¾	6	1	4/4	○	⊙	◓	⊙	⊙	⊙	◒	—	a	—
Interplak Voyager TK-2	99	13 (1)	3¼x2¼x10	5	3	1/2	○	⊙	◓	◓	○	○	[1]	B	b	C,D,E,F,J
EpiDent C2500 [2]	79	17 (2)	5¾x2¼x8	7	2	2/2	◒	◓	◓	⊙	⊙	○	◓	D	c,d	F,K
DentiBrush BT-691-10	35	7 (4)	1¼x1¼x6¼	3	1	2/—	◒	⊙	◓	⊙	⊙	⊙	⊙ [3]	D	a,e	B,G,L,O
Interplak Plus PB-6	119	13 (1)	4x4¼x8¼	7	3	4/4	◒	◓	◓	⊙	○	◓	●	C	—	D,H,I
Conditionally Acceptable																
■ The following model was judged Conditionally Acceptable due to excessive electrical leakage in immersion test; it should be used only with its wall mount.																
Sunbeam Automatic Angle Toothbrush 4205	66	5 (2)	6¼x3¼x8½	5	2	4/4	○	⊙	⊙	⊙	○	◓	◓	B	—	A,M,N,O
Not Acceptable																
■ The following model was judged Not Acceptable due to excessive electrical leakage in immersion test; a wall mount is not available.																
Plak Trac PT-100	30	[4]	3¾x3x6¾	3	1	2/4	○	⊙	◓	⊙	○	◓	○	—	—	—

[1] *Plug-in model, powered on house current—no batteries.*
[2] *Product has been sold to another company and renamed* **OralGiene** *but otherwise unchanged, according to company.*
[3] *Based on tests with a typical rechargeable nickel-cadmium "C" cell; a regular alkaline cell would perform even better.*
[4] *Brush head holds 2 multitufted disks ("pods"), which may be replaced independently of the head; 1 head and 4 pods lists for $6; a set of 8 pods lists for $5.*

Listed in order of overall performance, based on judgments of CU's user panel. As published in a **September 1992** report.

Price. Manufacturer's suggested retail for the basic unit and for extra brushes (number of extra brushes shown in parentheses). Discounts are often available.

Dimensions. To the nearest quarter inch. The width (**W**) and depth (**D**) tell you how much shelf space the charging stand needs. The height (**H**) measures the device standing upright without the brush head in place; the brush adds two to three inches. Dimensions for the *Interplak Voyager* are for the unit in its travel case; for the *Denti-Brush*, for the hand unit (there is no charging stand—it runs on a flashlight battery).

Panel judgments. Staffers tried each model at home for one week and judged key aspects.

Charge capacity. An estimate of how long each brush will run after its batteries have been fully charged. The longest-running should give at least 45 minutes of tooth-brushing; the shortest, less than 10 minutes.

Features in Common

Except as noted, all: • Carry American Dental Association seal as effective cleansing devices. • Run on built-in rechargeable batteries, not replaceable by user, and include charging stand (base unit), which is connected to house current. • Use 120-volt AC only. • Have adequately long power cord. • Do not include wall mount.

Key to Advantages

A–Timer light flashes after about 2 min. to signal adequate brushing time.
B–Built-in voltage converter for foreign travel.
C–Automatically shuts off if excess pressure is exerted on teeth or gums.
D–Battery can be replaced by user.

Key to Disadvantages

a–Panelists noted excessive vibration when brushing.
b–Coiled power cord judged inconveniently short—only 4 feet.
c–Brush head is bulky, judged hard to maneuver inside mouth.
d–Push-button switch must be held down to operate—judged inconvenient.
e–Some samples had defective battery contacts and didn't work.

Key to Comments

A–Wall mount included.
B–Judged easier to use for people with limited dexterity or ability to grip.
C–Oversized control button available at no cost from manufacturer; makes it easier to change speeds.
D–The American Dental Association has allowed brush to claim significant dental plaque and gingivitis reduction.
E–Foreign plug adapters not available from mfr.; must be obtained elsewhere.
F–Judged harder to use for people with limited dexterity or ability to grip.
G–90-day warranty limited to defective material or workmanship; $5 service charge.
H–Wall mount not supplied but available from mfr. at no charge.
I–Storage clips for additional brush heads available from mfr. at no charge.
J–Travel case has room to store 2 brush heads.
K–Battery charger is completely separate unit, not a charging stand; the design eliminates the possibility that the charger will be accidentally immersed when plugged in.
L–Has no charger; runs on 1 "C" flashlight battery.
M–Wall mount holds 4 brush heads as well as charger.
N–Travel kit with foreign plug adapters available from mfr.
O–Lacks American Dental Association seal.
P–Discontinued, but may still be available.

it off when you're done. The two *Water Pik* models have a regular slider switch but also offer "touchtronic" starting: Pressing the brush against the teeth gets it moving.

Timer. The *Braun Oral-B* has a light to let you know it's charging. The light also works as a timer.

RECOMMENDATIONS

While any electric toothbrush can theoretically improve your oral health, it's crucial to find a brush you'll keep using once the novelty fades.

MANUAL TOOTHBRUSHES

The modern toothbrush was born in 1938, when Dr. West's Miracle Tuft Toothbrush came out with nylon bristles (other brushes then used hog hair). Since then, toothbrush design has evolved in curiouser and curiouser ways. The goal: Stand out on the crowded drugstore shelf, sell more product, and—maybe—help people clean teeth better. Consumers Union's dental consultants say that almost any brush with soft, rounded-end bristles will do if used with care and diligence. Here are some examples of the modern brush and the claims made for them:

Jordan V by Viadent. The sawtooth "V" tufts are "designed to clean better between teeth." The handle is "like [a] dental instrument."

Oral-B Indicator. With "bristles [that] show when to replace." The blue band fades after about three months of brushing—to remind you to buy a new brush. Of course, if you must have a reminder, you could jot down the date on a calendar.

Aquafresh Flex. Flexible neck works like a "shock absorber" to reduce pressure and "prevent gum irritation." Handle has nonslip grip. Angled, tapered head "helps clean hard to reach areas."

Colgate Plus. Diamond-shaped head "narrows . . . for easy access to back teeth and areas between teeth." Brush "works like a dental tool to fight bacterial plaque at home."

Reach. Long, narrow head "helps clean a broad surface area." Handle is "angled . . . [to] clean most tooth surfaces—even back teeth."

Crest Complete. "Because teeth aren't flat," crinkle-cut profile can "get further between teeth." Tapered head and neck "for easy access to back teeth"; rubber-grip handle is "for better control."

Colgate Precision. "Triple-action bristles clean . . . where plaque accumulates." Angled outer bristles are for gumline; long inner bristles are for between teeth; shorter bristles for tooth surfaces.

MOUTHWASHES

Mouthwash manufacturers make serious medicinal claims as well as hygienic ones. *Listerine*, the leading brand, claims an antiseptic formula that not only banishes bad breath but also reduces plaque and gingivitis, a mild and reversible gum disease. Another brand says nothing about breath at all, but boasts that it "removes more plaque than brushing alone"—and leaves teeth looking "whiter and brighter."

Nevertheless, breath, not health, seems to be the first priority where mouthwash is concerned.

GETTING RID OF BAD BREATH

You don't need to rinse with a mouthwash to quell oral odors. Brushing your teeth also rids the mouth of bacteria and their malodorous by-products, at least temporarily. Even drinking a glass of water can freshen the breath somewhat.

But while many things can help a little, nothing is completely effective against bad breath. For one thing, its causes are just too diverse. In addition to the bacteria that cause "morning breath," they include:

- Smoking, chewing tobacco, and drinking alcohol.
- Aromatic compounds in foods like garlic and onions, which enter the bloodstream and are carried to the lungs, then exhaled.

- Gum disease, especially when accompanied by bleeding gums.
- Local respiratory tract infections, such as chronic bronchitis or sinusitis with postnasal drip.

To combat odors from so many sources, mouthwashes rely in part on their ability to cover odors with pleasant-smelling ingredients.

Mouthwashes may differ in their ability to kill odor-causing bacteria or neutralize malodorous compounds. But Consumers Union's tests couldn't demonstrate those differences.

MOUTHWASH AND PLAQUE

Toothpaste's abrasives and detergents help scrub the coating from teeth, and floss can take off even more plaque from tooth surfaces a brush can't touch. But many people don't brush and floss conscientiously enough.

Some rinses, with proven plaque-fighting chemicals, can help finish the job. They're adjuncts to brushing and flossing, not substitutes for them. By killing the oral bacteria that produce plaque, such rinses can help keep plaque from forming in the first place. Twice-a-day rinsing, the typical regimen, can also reverse gingivitis (swollen and inflamed gums that bleed easily), which is brought on by unchecked plaque.

The American Dental Association has a system for reviewing chemical plaque-fighters, much like the program it established 30 years earlier to validate claims that fluoride toothpastes prevent tooth decay. To earn the ADA antiplaque seal, a manufacturer must submit substantial evidence that its product is safe and effective in the long term. Two basic types of rinse earned the seal: One type uses plant extracts; the other, a chemical created in the laboratory.

From stronger to weaker, the plaque fighters are:

Peridex. This is a prescription-only rinse with the ADA seal. The active ingredient is chlorhexidine, a broad-spectrum antimicrobial agent. Studies show the rinse reduces plaque by 40 to 50 percent or more, with a 30 to 50 percent reduction in gingivitis. It has a lingering bitter taste and stains teeth brown to varying degrees. (A dental cleaning easily removes the stain.) It's fairly expensive: $15 to $20 per 16-ounce bottle.

Listerine. This 113-year-old brand and other brands with copycat for-

Alcohol in Mouthwash

Nearly all mouthwashes also contain a potentially troubling ingredient: alcohol, an antiseptic and the vehicle that dissolves and delivers other ingredients.

The mouthwashes' alcohol content ranges from 6 percent, by volume, to nearly 27 percent. Alcohol in high concentration creates a burning sensation in the mouth; regular use can dry out the mucous membranes and aggravate existing inflammations.

More troubling, research from the National Cancer Institute has linked alcohol in mouthwash to mouth and throat cancers.

But the NCI has not recommended that people change their mouthwash use based on the research. For one thing, the study was retrospective—it relied on participants' reports of their past activities, which are not always accurate and which may not have covered all the crucial variables.

Oral cancer, too, is relatively uncommon. By NCI estimates, there will be some 30,000 new cases diagnosed this year—far fewer than the 181,000 new breast cancers, the 168,000 new lung cancers, or the 132,000 new prostate cancers. Further, three-quarters of oral cancers are directly attributable to smoking or to drinking alcoholic beverages, which have effects that far overshadow any possible risks of mouthwash.

The link between alcohol-containing mouthwash and oral cancer is not yet conclusive. But it is cause for concern. If you are concerned, find a mouthwash that is low in alcohol yet effective against plaque and with a flavor and "feel" you like.

mulas rely on four substances that are "essential" oils or derived from them: thymol (from thyme oil), eucalyptol (eucalyptus oil), menthol (from peppermint oil), and methylsalicylate (wintergreen oil). The rinses typically reduce plaque by 20 to 35 percent, with similar improvements in gingivitis.

Until 1991, *Listerine* was the only nonprescription rinse with the ADA

Listings of Mouthwashes

◉ Better ←→ ◓ ○ ◒ ● Worse

Product	Price	Size, fl. oz. or oz.	Cost per oz.	Alcohol	Short-term freshening	Flavor	Aftertaste/afterfeel	Color	Comments
Rinses									
Act Fluoride	$3.81	18	21¢	6%	◉ [1]	Sweet, spearmint	Sweet/cooling	Green	A,B,C,E
Cepacol Mint	4.54	32	14	15	◓	Spearmint, peppermint	Bitter/cooling	Green	—
Close-Up Anti-Plaque	2.29	12	19	15	◉ [1]	Cinnamon, peppermint	Sweet/cooling	Red	—
Colgate Fluorigard	3.59	18	20	6	◉	Sweet, spearmint	Sweet/cooling	Green	A,C
K Mart Antiseptic	1.84	32	6	27	◉ [1]	Eucalyptus	Bitter/burning	Amber	D,F,I
K Mart Mint	1.82	32	6	19	◓	Spearmint, peppermint	Mint/cooling	Green	J
Lavoris Mint	3.17	32	10	6	◓	Spearmint, peppermint	Mint/cooling	Green	—
Listerine Antiseptic	4.19	32	13	27	◉	Eucalyptus	Bitter/burning	Amber	D,F,I
Listermint with Fluoride	4.36	32	14	7	◉	Sweet, spearmint	Sweet/cooling	Green	A,E
Plax Anti-Plaque Soft Mint	4.01	24	17	7	◉ [1]	Sweet, spearmint	Sweet/cooling	Green	—
Rite Aid Antiseptic	1.81	32	6	27	◉ [1]	Eucalyptus	Bitter/burning	Amber	F,I
Rite Aid Mint	1.99*	40	5	19	○ [1]	Spearmint, peppermint	Mint/cooling	Green	J
Scope Original Mint	4.47	32	14	19	◓	Spearmint, peppermint	Mint/cooling	Green	J,K
Signal	3.65	32	11	15	◓	Sweet, spearmint	Sweet/cooling	Green	E
Viadent Anti-Plaque	4.94	30	16	10	◉	Eucalyptus, mint, spice	Metallic/cooling	Amber	—

Other products

Binaca Frosty Peppermint	2.18*	0.2	5[2]	58[3]	○	Peppermint	Bitter/cooling	—	G,H
Certs Peppermint	.49	0.6	4[2]	—	○[1]	Peppermint, chalky	Sweet/cooling	White	—
Pep-O-Mint Lifesavers	.48	0.7	4[2]	—	◒[1]	Peppermint, chalky	Sweet/cooling	White	—
Tic Tac Fresh Mints	.48	0.5	1[2]	—	○	Vanilla, anise, mint	Anise/cooling	White	—

[1] *Product labeling makes no explicit claim about freshening bad breath.*
[2] *Cost for candy mints is for 1 mint; for* **Binaca** *aerosol, for 3 sprays per use.*
[3] *50% by weight, according to mfr.; roughly equivalent to 58% by volume.*

Listed by types; within types, listed alphabetically. As published in a **September 1992** report.

Price. The estimated average, based on prices paid nationally. An * denotes the price paid; an average wasn't available.

Size. The typical rinse comes in a 32-fluid-ounce bottle, other products in a small aerosol spray or a small package.

Alcohol. Percentage alcohol by volume, according to the company.

Short-term freshening. How well a product masked garlic odor in a panel of volunteers 10 minutes after eating pizza and using the product. The better products masked the odor completely, though the odor typically returned within an hour.

Flavor. Based on a sensory expert's description.

Aftertaste/afterfeel. A sensory expert's characterization of how the mouth felt after each product had been spit out.

Features in Common

Except as noted, all: • Rinses recommend a dose of 3 tsp. or less. • Are promoted to freshen breath.

Key to Comments

A–Contains fluoride to help prevent tooth decay.
B–Bottle has convenient dose-dispensing pump.
C–Has American Dental Association seal as an effective decay preventive.
D–Has American Dental Association seal for prevention or reduction of plaque and gingivitis.
E–Panelists liked flavor more than most.
F–Panelists disliked flavor more than most—burned more than most and was too medicinal-tasting.
G–Spray can ignite if exposed to open flame; no warning on label.
H–Harder than most to use for people with hand or arm limitations.
I–Dose is 4 tsp.
J–Dose is 6 tsp.
K–Panelists complained that the recommended dose was too much.

plaque-fighter seal. As of late 1992, a number of private-label amber antiseptic rinses had the seal, too. The formula's main drawbacks: its medicinal taste and powerful mouthburn.

Viadent. The rinse and the brand's toothpaste each contain sanguinaria, an extract of the bloodroot plant that fights plaque-causing bacteria. Several long-term studies of the toothpaste showed no significant plaque reduction. A six-month study in which people used both the toothpaste and mouthwash twice a day showed a 21 percent reduction in plaque, 25 percent in gingivitis.

Cepacol. This rinse contains the antiseptic cetylpyridinium chloride. One six-month study reported a 14 percent reduction in plaque, with a 24 percent decrease in gingivitis. (Briefer studies have shown greater reductions.) *Scope* and some generic mouthwashes also include cetylpyridinium chloride. But neither *Scope* nor *Cepacol* were promoting themselves as plaque fighters in the final months of 1992.

For mouthwashes, the FDA considers an antiplaque claim "therapeutic," since antiplaque rinses could theoretically cure gingivitis chemically. (In contrast, antiplaque claims on toothpaste are "cosmetic" in the FDA's book, because they are generally based on the paste's ability to help scrub off plaque above the gumline mechanically, not on any chemical action.)

RECOMMENDATIONS

Don't count on mouthwash to freshen your breath for very long. Consumers Union's sensory tests with garlic found only short-lived protection at best. Bad breath typically returned sometime between 10 minutes and an hour after rinsing.

Good oral hygiene—regular toothbrushing and flossing, periodontal treatment where necessary—should go a long way toward combating bad breath. However, chronic bad breath that persists even after toothbrushing may be a symptom of dental disease or a disease elsewhere in the body. Instead of relying on mouthwash to mask the problem, a person with persistent bad breath should be examined by a dentist and possibly by a physician.

Beyond temporarily freshening the breath, some mouthwashes deliver extra benefits. Fluoride rinses help protect teeth from decay, especially for cavity-prone people with receding gums or a reduced saliva flow. They can also be especially beneficial for people who use nonfluoride toothpastes. Mouthwashes with proven plaque-fighting formulas curb the oral bacteria that form plaque and can lead to gingivitis. Those are real benefits.

ORAL IRRIGATORS

Irrigators deliver a pressurized, pulsating stream through a thin nozzle that you direct against the teeth and gums. The devices flush out bits of food and other debris from between teeth or under dental work, a benefit for people with braces, crowns, implants, or nonremovable bridgework, who often find it difficult to clean their mouths with brush and dental floss alone.

Anyone planning to use an irrigator should first receive careful instruction from a dentist. One of Consumers Union's dental consultants cautioned that people with gum disease could wind up forcing debris *deeper* into a pocket, thus setting the scene for an abscess. Irrigators also have the potential to damage the cheeks and tongue. That's unlikely, however, if you have learned how to irrigate and use the lowest pressure setting that's effective, which is what the American Dental Association advises.

Oral irrigation, as an adjunct to regular brushing and flossing, can help people with gum disease as well. Irrigation helps gums by flushing out bacteria, their irritating by-products, and some plaque along with the food debris it dislodges. (Toothbrush bristles and dental floss cannot reach very deep.) An irrigator's stream can be directed not only above the gumline, but also below it.

The trouble spot where gum disease takes hold is called the "sulcus," the fold of soft tissue surrounding a tooth's crown. Normally, gum tissue follows a tight, arching contour around a tooth. But if plaque isn't brushed away scrupulously, deposits can extend downward into the sulcus below the gumline. Over years of neglect, plaque, bacterial toxins, and tartar can deepen the normally shallow crevice to form a deep and festering pocket that can eventually undermine the tooth's attachment. The cleaner the gum margin, the slimmer the chances that periodontal disease will develop.

Some oral irrigators offer two kinds of nozzle tips—blunt tips for general use and more pointed tips to focus the flow into the sulcus or a pocket. The sulcus tips slow the flow of liquid, which can save money if you're irrigating your teeth and gums with mouthwash.

If you use that tip with a mouthwash or medicated rinse, you could consume more than a dollar's worth of rinse to irrigate the whole mouth. But you probably wouldn't want to irrigate every tooth. Your dentist will probably tell you to use the special rinse on only the most diseased areas. That's the fastest and most cost-effective approach.

FEATURES

Usually more money buys more features—a bigger reservoir, a small spare reservoir, extra snap-on nozzle tips, handier controls. But the irrigators look and work pretty much alike. Here are some similarities and differences:

Controls. All provide a graduated flow control to adjust the force of the irrigation stream. The best arrangement is a large button dial on the handset that alters pressure when turned and that temporarily stops the flow when depressed. The layout lets you do everything one-handed—you can pass the handpiece from one hand to the other without spraying the bathroom walls.

Reservoir. Reservoir capacity ranges from about 12½ ounces to 35 ounces. You might have to refill the smallest tank to do a thorough job. Some tanks, when inverted, double as a dust cover for the unit.

Tips. Most of the irrigators include four regular tips, color-coded for different family members' use. Extra tips are available by mail for a dollar or two apiece, though tips are durable and generally don't wear out.

RECOMMENDATIONS

Oral irrigators are a specialized tool. They're useful mainly for people who have trouble keeping their dental work clean and for those with gum disease, who will benefit most by irrigating with an antimicrobial rinse. Most

Ratings of oral irrigators

⊙ Better ◓ ○ ◒ ● Worse

Brand and model	Price	Reservoir, fl. oz.	Dimensions (WxDxH), in.	Overall performance	Cleaning	Instructions	Ease of use	Advantages	Disadvantages	Comments
				Panel judgments						
Water Pik Professional Dental System WP-32W	$60	35	7x4x7½	◓	◓	⊙	◓	A,B,F	—	*A,E,H*
Water Pik Family Dental System WP-30W	70	35	7x4x7½	◓	◓	⊙	◓	F	—	*E,H*
Water Pik Personal Dental System WP-20W	55	25	5½x4x7½	◓	◓	⊙	◓	F	a,b	*B,E,H*
Conditionally Acceptable										
■ *The following models were judged Conditionally Acceptable due to excessive electrical leakage in the tests. They should only be used with their wall mount.*										
Colgate Via-Jet Periodontal Irrigator 7500	60	25	8½x4½x7	◓	◓	⊙	⊙	C,D	c	*A,C,F,H*
Sunbeam Dental Water Jet 6282-100	61	12½	8½x4¼x5½	○	○	◓	◓	E	d,e	*D,F,G,H*

Listed in order of overall performance, based on judgments of CU's user panel. As published in a **September 1992** report.

Price. Manufacturer's suggested retail.

Dimensions. The width and depth, plus the height in use, to the nearest quarter-inch. The tank on the *Water Pik WP-32W* and *WP-30W* detach and serve, inverted, as a dust cover. That reduces overall height three inches.

Panel judgments. Staffers tried each model at home for one week and judged key aspects.

Features in Common

Except as noted, all: • Supply 4 regular tips, which can be stored in or on base. • Have American Dental Association's seal as acceptable when used as an adjunct to brushing, flossing, and regular professional care. • Run on 120-volt AC. • Have continuous pressure-adjustment control. • Have control on handpiece to stop water flow temporarily without changing pressure setting. • Do not include wall mount. • Have adequately long power cord and water hose.

Key to Advantages

A–Includes secondary 10-oz. reservoir for periodontal rinses.
B–Sulcus (pointy) tips supplied have soft points, judged safer to use.
C–Large, clearly marked pressure-control knob.
D–Judged somewhat less noisy than most.
E–Tips are a bit easier to change than those on other models.
F–Reservoir has permanent volume markings in ounces and milliliters.

Key to Disadvantages

a–Provision for storing only 2 tips on base unit; 1 stores in handpiece, thus increasing overall height.
b–Hose connecting handpiece to base judged short, making unit less convenient to use than most.
c–Sulcus (pointy) tips supplied have hard points, judged more likely to scratch gums.
d–Stopping water flow temporarily at handpiece—to switch hands, say—requires user to change pressure setting.
e–Lacks markings on pressure-control knob to help reset pressure to accustomed level.

Key to Comments

A–Includes 2 regular (blunt) and 2 sulcus (pointy) tips, the latter for irrigation below the gumline or into periodontal pockets.
B–Includes 2 regular (blunt) tips only.
C–Includes wall-mounting hardware.
D–Wall mount must be ordered from the distributor for $3.25.
E–Wall mount must be ordered from mfr. for $2.75.
F–Lacks the American Dental Association seal.
G–Judged easier to use for people with limited use of fingers and wrist or difficulty grasping.
H–Replacement tip prices. **Water Piks:** Pik Pocket Tip PP-3, 2 for $10; Jet Tip JT-4, 4 for $4. **Colgate Via-Jet:** 4 for $5. **Sunbeam:** 2 for $5.

other people should be able to keep their teeth and gums healthy with routine brushing and flossing—and perhaps rinsing with an antiplaque mouthwash, if they need extra help. Some may use an irrigator simply because they like the feel—the "massage"—it provides.

TOOTHPASTES

You can buy dentifrice in a paste or a gel, packaged in a pump or a tube; buy a paste for kids, or one for older adults with sensitive teeth; buy a product with special bleaches, enzymes, or tartar-control ingredients, or one whose main ingredient is plain old baking soda.

Still, a toothpaste needs only simple ingredients to be effective: detergents and fine abrasives to clean the teeth, and fluoride to help keep cavities from forming. But toothpastes vary tremendously in their cleaning ability. And while most have enough fluoride to be effective, a few don't even contain enough to meet the U.S. Food and Drug Administration's proposed basic standards.

CLEANING EFFECTIVENESS

If your teeth were cleaned only when you went to the dentist, they'd become dingy again very soon. Less than a minute after teeth receive a thorough cleaning, a transparent film called the pellicle begins to coat the teeth and gums. The film, made of salivary proteins, acts as an anchor for the bacteria that form plaque; it also collects stains from food, drink, and tobacco.

Fortunately, such stains are usually superficial—they rarely penetrate tooth enamel. Brushing away the pellicle and whatever adheres to it can theoretically remove the stains. To remove pellicle effectively, however, requires the abrasives and detergents found in toothpaste; the mechanical action of the brush alone won't work as well. And toothpastes vary greatly in the cleaning potential of their ingredients.

The lightest shade you can expect to achieve with any toothpaste is the color of your teeth just after they have been professionally cleaned. (Cosmetic bleaching done in a dentist's office can actually lighten the enamel's hue, but the FDA and the American Dental Association have questioned bleaching's safety.

Laboratory tests showed a wide range of toothpastes' cleaning ability among the brands tested. The best-cleaning toothpastes removed almost all the stain the lab had cooked in.

For all their hype, the baking-soda toothpastes were disappointing in their ability to clean. The best netted only middling scores; others left the test teeth very brown, the stain mostly untouched. One problem is that baking soda starts as a decent if gentle abrasive, but dissolves in water and loses its punch.

ABRASIVENESS

Manufacturers walk a fine line with abrasive ingredients: Too gentle and a toothpaste doesn't clean well; too harsh and it can harm the teeth. The risk isn't to the enamel, but to dentin and cementum, far softer tissues that are exposed as the gums recede. Over time, harsh abrasives—or even a stiff toothbrush—can scrape dentin away, leaving teeth overly sensitive or more vulnerable to decay. Fortunately, the abrasives used nowadays are much gentler than those of a generation ago, and the risk of damage is less.

You don't necessarily need high abrasiveness for very effective cleaning. Excellent cleaners fall in both highly abrasive and moderate groups. The gentlest of the toothpastes did only a halfhearted cleaning job in Consumers Union's tests, or worse.

While most people can use even a highly abrasive toothpaste safely, people with significant gum recession should probably choose a dentifrice on the gentler side. You should ask your dentist's advice if you think you may have this problem.

Many people with receding gums find that their teeth are especially sensitive to temperature or pressure, and so may want to use a desensitizing toothpaste—one with special ingredients that block pain perception by nerves in the tooth.

Ratings of toothpastes

Product	Package	Size, oz.	Price	Cost per month	Cleaning	Flavor	Comments
Fluoride toothpastes—moderate in abrasiveness							
✓ Ultra brite Original	T	6.0	$ 1.56	$ .58	86	Peppermint	—
Gleem	T	7.0	2.23	.66	79	Spearmint/ peppermint	B
Caffree Regular	T	5.0	2.96	1.02	77	Mint	—
Crest Tartar Control Original	P	6.4	2.53	.73	77	Peppermint/ anise	B,D,E,H
Crest Tartar Control Fresh Mint Gel	T	6.4	1.99	.53	75	Mint	D,E
Colgate Tartar Control Gel	T	6.4	2.04	.57	74	Peppermint	B,D,E
Pearl Drops Spearmint	B	3.0	3.18	.49	74	Spearmint/ peppermint	—
Crest Tartar Control Original	T	6.4	2.00	.53	72	Peppermint/ anise	D,E
Ultra brite Gel Cool Mint	T	6.0	1.53	.52	72	Peppermint	B
Colgate Clear Blue Gel	T	6.4	2.06	.71	71	Spearmint	B,D
Crest Cool Mint Gel	T	6.4	1.99	.55	70	Wintergreen	D,G
Crest Regular	T	6.4	2.01	.59	69	Wintergreen	D,G
Crest Sparkle	T	6.4	2.03	.51	64	Tutti-frutti	D,G,J
Aquafresh Tartar Control	P	6.0	2.55	.68	63	Peppermint	D,H
Close-Up Tartar Control Gel	T	6.4	1.94	.67	63	Cinnamon	—
Close-Up Anti-Plaque	T	6.4	1.97	.62	62	Spearmint	—
Colgate Tartar Control Paste	T	6.4	2.04	.66	62	Peppermint	B,D,E
Tom's of Maine Cinnamint	T	6.0	3.29	1.07	62	Cinnamon	—
Aquafresh Tartar Control	T	6.0	1.97	.80	60	Peppermint	D
Aim Anti-Tartar Gel	T	6.4	2.24*	.79	58	Spearmint	B,G
Colgate Tartar Control Paste	P	6.4	2.53	.89	58	Peppermint	B,D,E,H
Aim Extra-Strength Gel	T	6.4	1.70	.44	57	Spearmint/ peppermint	B,D,G
Mentadent Fresh Mint	P	4.5	2.65*	1.09	57	Peppermint	I,K,L
Slimer Gel	T	3.0	$ 1.79*	$1.04	57	Tutti-frutti	B,J
Arm & Hammer Baking Soda Fresh Mint Gel	T	6.3	3.26	1.12	55	Peppermint	B,L

	Package	Size, oz.	Price	Cost per month	Cleaning	Flavor	Comments
Oral-B Muppets Gel	P	4.6	2.09	.63	52	Tutti-frutti	H,J
■ *The following two products were downrated because they failed fluoride tests.*							
Aquafresh	T	6.4	1.98	.79	56	Peppermint	A,D,G
Aquafresh Extra Fresh	T	6.4	1.92	.81	53	Peppermint	A,D,G
Fluoride toothpastes—high in abrasiveness							
Close-Up Paste	T	6.4	1.92	.64	85	Peppermint	—
Topol Spearmint Gel	T	2.7	3.28	1.77	82	Spearmint	B,D,G
Topol Spearmint	T	6.4	5.12	1.32	76	Spearmint	B,D,G
Close-Up Mint Gel	T	6.4	1.92	.64	72	Peppermint	—
Aim Regular-Strength Gel	T	6.4	1.68	.55	70	Spearmint	G
Pepsodent	T	6.4	1.41	.39	58	Wintergreen	—
Fluoride toothpastes—low in abrasiveness							
Colgate Baking Soda	T	6.3	3.54*	1.22	51	Peppermint	B,G,L
Colgate Regular	T	7.0	2.08	.74	50	Peppermint	D
Colgate Junior Gel	T	7.7	2.05	.44	39	Tutti-frutti	B,D,J
Colgate Peak	T	6.3	2.78	.97	29	Peppermint	B,G,L
Arm & Hammer Baking Soda Fresh Mint	T	7.0	3.24	1.26	28	Peppermint/ baking soda	B,L
■ *The following three products were downrated because they failed fluoride tests.*							
Rembrandt	T	3.0	10.16*	4.73	53	Wintergreen	A
EpiSmile	P	4.0	11.00*	3.90	51	Soapy	A,H,I,L
Aquafresh for Kids	P	4.4	2.05	.89	39	Tutti-frutti	B,D,J
Non-fluoride toothpastes—moderate in abrasiveness							
Sensodyne Original	T	4.0	3.87	1.29	80	Peppermint	A,C,F
Sensodyne Gel	T	4.0	3.88	1.34	48	Spearmint	A,C,G
Non-fluoride toothpastes—low in abrasiveness							
Viadent Original Anti-Plaque	T	7.0	4.68	1.40	53	Wintergreen	A
Denquel	T	3.0	3.02	1.77	37	Peppermint	A,B,C,F,G
Butler Protect Gel	T	3.0	2.88*	1.11	20	Wintergreen	A,B,C,F

Listed in groups based on laboratory tests of fluoride and abrasiveness. Within groups, listed in order of cleaning ability. Toothpastes with the same cleaning ability are listed alphabetically. As published in a **September 1992** report.

Product. For several brands, variations in formula (paste, gel, tartar control, children's, pump, or tube) were tested for fluoride, abrasiveness, and cleaning ability. The variations sometimes affected test results. Except as noted, all fluoride toothpastes contained sufficient available fluoride to meet proposed FDA standards when tested as purchased and after accelerated aging.

Package. Toothpastes come in tubes (**T**), pumps (**P**), or a squeeze bottle (**B**).

Price. The estimated average, based on prices paid nationally. An * indicates the price paid; an average national price wasn't available.

Cost per month. An estimate based on brushing with one-half inch of toothpaste twice daily.

Cleaning. Scored on a 100-point scale, based on laboratory brushing tests with badly stained teeth. A clean, unstained tooth would get a score of 100; a stained, uncleaned tooth, a score of 0. Products scoring 80 or higher removed practically all stain from the teeth. Those scoring 40 or lower were judged fair or poor at cleaning.

Key to Comments

A–CU's dental consultants recommend using a fluoride mouth rinse with this dentifrice, which contained insufficient fluoride or none at all.
B–Unlike most toothpastes, carries an expiration date.
C–Labeled for use on "sensitive" teeth.
D–Carries American Dental Association seal as an effective decay preventive.
E–Carries ADA seal for tartar reduction above the gumline.
F–Carries ADA seal as an effective desensitizer for teeth sensitive to heat, cold, and pressure.
G–Because of product's consistency and packaging, easier to use than most toothpastes by people with hand or arm limitations.
H–Because of product's consistency and packaging, harder to use than most toothpastes by people with hand or arm limitations.
I–Contains bleach, which might irritate the mouth with regular use.
J–Marketed as a children's toothpaste.
K–More packaging material than other products.
L–Contains baking soda, a mild abrasive.

FLUORIDE

During childhood, fluoride from drinking water, diet, or vitamin supplements helps growing children build teeth that are better able to resist decay. After the permanent teeth have grown in, fluoride in toothpastes and mouth rinses continues to protect the tooth surfaces—in both children and adults.

Acids from food, drink, and the activity of oral bacteria can eat into tooth enamel. Fluoride on the tooth surface helps repair early damage by speeding the return of minerals to the tooth before the decay process gets very far.

Most cavities form in the crowns of teeth. But older people, with receding gums, also develop "root caries": cavities at the base of the teeth, where the cementum and dentin are exposed. Fluoridated toothpaste can help prevent this problem as well as incipient decay in the enamel.

A few toothpastes aren't made with fluoride, including some brands for sensitive teeth. It's worth looking for one that is, since people often have sensitive teeth because they have receding gums, and thus run a higher risk of root caries if they don't get adequate fluoride protection.

ADA Seals

To get the American Dental Association's seal of approval on a toothpaste, mouthwash, or toothbrush, a manufacturer must submit convincing research—often clinical studies conducted at universities—to demonstrate its product is safe and effective and does what it is supposed to. And the company must play by ADA rules for advertising and packaging. In general, the ADA seal is a reliable endorsement of a product's performance and the accuracy of its claims. While there are good products that do not carry the seal—simply because they have not applied for it—the ADA seal is a consistent indicator of a product's effectiveness.

RECOMMENDATIONS

If possible, everyone should brush at least twice a day with a fluoride toothpaste. If your teeth and gums are in good shape, you can brush with just about any fluoride dentifrice. Find one with a taste and a price that are to your liking.

People with receding gums should choose a toothpaste of moderate or low abrasiveness to avoid abrading the exposed roots of their teeth. The gentlest products, however, won't leave teeth looking as clean as do products with more powerful abrasives.

If your teeth are particularly sensitive—a problem that often goes with receding gums—you may need to try a desensitizing toothpaste. If you use a desensitizing toothpaste that doesn't contain fluoride, rinse with a fluoridated mouthwash.

OTHER PERSONAL CARE

CONTACT-LENS MAINTENANCE

The price of wearing contacts is the bother and cost of keeping them clean. The price of laxity, however, can be uncomfortable or damaged lenses and even damaged eyes.

Corneal infections are the most dreaded complications of lens wear. They usually begin with a break in the cornea that allows microorganisms on a dirty lens to penetrate corneal tissue. If untreated for just a day or two, the infection can scar the cornea enough to cause permanent vision loss in the affected eye.

A less serious but more common hazard is giant papillary conjunctivitis, an inflammation of the lining of the upper eyelid. The person may have to stop wearing contacts for months for the condition to heal.

LENS CARE

Poor lens care is a major cause of contact-lens problems. So is confusion. Common errors include using the wrong cleaning solutions, reusing disinfecting solution, and skipping some lens-care steps altogether. Or wearers may diligently perform the main steps—cleaning and disinfecting—but then store their contacts in a soiled lens case. Others may neglect to wash their hands before handling their lenses, or they may put makeup on just before inserting them, then transfer some to a lens.

Researchers in one study found "a disturbingly high frequency" of contaminated lens cases among both soft-lens and rigid-lens wearers. Of 94 cases tested, 46 percent were contaminated. Another study found contamination in 60 percent of the lens cases. Many studies have now linked incidents of corneal infection to microorganisms that were found in patients' lens cases.

With so many competing products available, moreover, it's easy to make mistakes in the search for bargains. Products in one brand line aren't necessarily compatible with those in another. A mix-and-match approach can result in ruined lenses. So it's important to know your options.

WHAT TO DO

When you buy contact lenses, your practitioner will usually give you a starter kit for cleaning and disinfecting the lenses. A typical kit contains a complete lens-care system, which includes a lens case, a daily cleaner, a saline rinse, a disinfectant, and a weekly enzyme cleaner. Solution makers commonly charge practitioners a nominal price for the kits, usually $1 to $5 each. The idea is to make the contact wearer comfortable with using a particular company's lens-care system for as long as the lenses last.

In one sense, that's not a bad idea. Sticking to one system avoids incompatibility problems. Each company has to prove to the U.S. Food and Drug Administration (FDA) that the products in its lens-care system work together safely and effectively.

With few exceptions, however, any FDA-approved soft-lens care system can be used with any brand of soft lenses. If the system in the starter kit turns out to be impractical, you can switch to a different one (but take certain precautions discussed later in this section).

Generally, casual switching of products between systems is inadvisable, but there is one major exception. Most people can buy saline strictly on the basis of price or convenience.

DAILY CLEANING

Daily use of a cleaning solution may be the most important step in lens care. Electron-microscope studies show that deposits begin forming on a clean lens within minutes after it's put in the eye. Tears contain some 60 different proteins, and most of them will stick to contact lenses. If the proteins are not removed regularly, they can dull your vision, ruin your lenses, and irritate your eyes.

Some cleaners can be used for both rigid and soft lenses, but most are specific for one or the other. Soft-lens cleaners can damage rigid lenses and vice versa.

Effective cleaning requires thorough rubbing of the lens with a drop or two of cleaner. The next step—washing off the soapy residue—is equally important but often slighted by soft-lens wearers trying to save on saline. Unrinsed cleaner is carried over to the disinfection stage, where it may be baked on the lens (in heat disinfection) or react with a chemical disinfectant and damage the lens.

Weekly cleaning with an enzyme product removes the protein deposits that daily cleaning misses.

Cleaning with an enzyme product breaks up protein deposits but doesn't actually wash protein remnants from lenses. So it's a good idea to use a daily cleaner and rinse after enzyming. This washes off the protein as well as the potentially irritating enzyme.

According to surveys of lens wearers, many believe that cleaning disinfects lenses. It doesn't. You need to put the lenses through a separate disinfection process.

KILLING MICROBES

Disinfecting a contact lens, which kills microorganisms attached to it, is crucial for preventing infections, especially with soft lenses. The water in soft lenses makes them ideal breeding grounds for microbes of all kinds.

Rigid lenses, which contain little water, offer a less inviting environment. Thorough cleaning can sweep microbes from their hard surface. Disinfecting rigid lenses is a relatively simple process, usually involving an overnight soak in a conditioning solution.

Cleaning Contact Lenses with Salt Water

Saline is used for rinsing lenses. You also store lenses in it and use it to clean off enzymes; if you heat-disinfect your lenses, you cook them in it.

Homemade saline should not be used for contact-lens care. Using homemade saline for other lens-care purposes has been linked with a rare but severe corneal infection caused by an amoeba. In one study, 21 to 27 infected lens wearers had used homemade saline. It's safer to use commercial saline, which is available with or without preservatives.

Preserved saline is safe to use for at least several weeks after the container is opened. It's usually cheaper than unpreserved saline, which typically comes in single-use dispensers or aerosol cans to prevent contamination.

Until several years ago, the main preservative in saline was thimerosal, which caused eye irritation in a significant number of users. Most companies have since reformulated their products with two gentler preservatives, sorbic acid or potassium sorbate. The newer preservatives haven't eliminated eye irritation completely, but most people can now use preserved saline without difficulty.

The premium price of aerosol salines buys the convenience of an aerosol spray and freedom from contamination. The can's pressurization keeps unpreserved saline entirely free of microorganisms.

You can usually switch from one brand of saline to another, choosing strictly on the basis of price or convenience. If you're sensitive to thimerosal or other preservatives, however, check the label before purchasing.

One survey found that more than 15 percent of soft-lens users don't use an FDA-approved disinfection system. Instead, they simply soak their lenses in saline. Effective disinfection of soft lenses requires using one of three types of disinfection systems: heat, chemical, or hydrogen-peroxide disinfection.

Disinfecting with heat. When soft lenses were first introduced in 1971, heat was the only way to disinfect them. You soaked your lenses in saline and then put your lens case in a "cooker." Heating is fast—in 30 minutes your lenses are ready to wear again. But it does have drawbacks.

Unless you clean the lenses scrupulously, heating can bake deposits onto them. Repeated heating may shorten lens life by weakening the plastic, and using a cooker may be inconvenient when traveling.

On the plus side, heat disinfection doesn't involve the use of potentially irritating chemicals, and heat is the cheapest method. Heating is also the only technique proven effective against a type of amoeba that causes a rare but severe corneal infection. In soft-lens wearers, the infection is usually linked to the use of homemade saline. However, people who wear soft lenses in hot tubs or when swimming, or who rinse their lenses in tap water, are also at risk, a risk that heat disinfection can substantially reduce.

Nowadays most soft-lens wearers use one of two "cold disinfection" alternatives: chemical disinfection or hydrogen-peroxide disinfection. (While hydrogen peroxide is a chemical, the method leaves no chemical residue on the lens.)

Disinfecting with chemicals. In chemical disinfection, microorganisms are killed by soaking lenses in a solution. Such solutions contain chemicals that are gentle to sensitive eye tissue but strong enough to kill microbes. Only a few chemicals can perform this balancing act.

The first chemical disinfectants contained thimerosal and chlorhexidine. They killed microbes but also caused eye irritation in 15 to 30 percent of users. Now there are second-generation chemical disinfectants that are gentle to the eyes and simple to use, but they may leave a chemical residue, causing sensitivity problems in some users. And the disinfectants, while effective, are not as strong as hydrogen peroxide. For these reasons, hydrogen-peroxide disinfection is preferable.

Disinfecting with peroxide. Hydrogen peroxide is the leading method of disinfection. It offers two advantages over chemical disinfection: It is itself a powerful disinfectant, and it can be neutralized, so that no potentially sensitizing residue remains on the lens.

The major drawback of peroxide is the need to neutralize it, which makes the process more complex (and usually more expensive) than with chemical disinfectants. Forgetting to neutralize—a mistake that is possible with some peroxide systems—can cause intense pain when a lens containing peroxide is inserted into the eye.

A number of peroxide-disinfection systems are available. While each calls for soaking the lenses in 3 percent hydrogen peroxide, the various systems neutralize the peroxide differently.

In deciding between a peroxide or a chemical system, consider how frequently you wear your lenses. If you're an occasional wearer, then peroxide might not be a good choice. Once the peroxide is neutralized, lenses become vulnerable to contamination. With a chemical disinfectant, however, your lenses are protected against contamination for as long as they sit soaking in your lens case.

CHANGING BRANDS

You can generally switch from any lens-care system to any other approved for your lenses. Before switching, though, soft-lens wearers should first "purge" their lenses, especially if their current system is chemical disinfection.

Purging involves a few simple steps: Clean the lenses as usual, then soak them in distilled water for at least two hours or preferably overnight (the soaking swells the lenses, squeezing out chemical residues); finally, soak the lenses in saline for about two hours. The procedure may not be necessary when switching from some peroxide systems, but it's still a worthwhile precaution. Clean and disinfect your lenses before using them again.

You can also change from peroxide or chemical disinfection to heat, but switching from heat to chemical disinfection may cause a problem. If protein deposits have been baked onto a lens, the protein may absorb the chemicals and cause irritation.

CLEANING THE LENS CASE

Whatever system you choose can easily be compromised if your lens case is contaminated with microorganisms. Wash out the case with hot water every day, letting it dry, upside down, on a clean paper towel or napkin.

You should also sterilize the case once a week. Heat water to a boil in a saucepan. Take the pan off the burner and drop in your lens case (minus the lenses, of course). Leave it in for 20 minutes and then let it dry. As an alternative, make a solution of one part bleach and 10 parts water. Pour it into the case and let stand for 20 minutes. Rinse the case thoroughly with hot water or as directed by the manufacturer.

Another neglected lens-care step is handwashing. Lenses function as superb magnets for whatever you have on your fingers—grime that can ruin them or bacteria that can infect your eye. Always wash your hands before handling your lenses.

Unfortunately, some soaps can be worse than no soap at all. Pump-liquid soaps may contain beeswax or emollients such as lanolin, which can leave oily, tough-to-remove residues. Soaps with cold cream, cocoa butter, or heavy fragrances can also cause problems. You can buy soaps specially formulated for use with contacts or simply use a cheaper, bland soap such as *Ivory.*

FACIAL CLEANSERS

The main purpose of a facial cleanser is to remove makeup and grime. Soap and water do that, of course, but too much soap can remove a skin's natural oils, leaving it rough, chapped, and tender. Soap makes dry skin drier still. Soap and water also have less clout than cleanser at removing heavy makeup.

A typical cleanser, whether cream or lotion, contains water; glycerin or other moisturizers; oils, fats, or greases (to give the product the right consistency and to help loosen grime); detergents (to wash away grime); preservatives (to forestall spoilage); and dyes and scent (to make it look and smell good).

The archetypal cleanser is the traditional "cold cream" that you massage into your skin, then wipe off. *Pond's Cold Cream* and its descendants—including wipe-off lotions—are still very popular. Years ago, however, *Noxzema* cream in the blue jar pointed the way toward a revolutionary alternative; a less greasy substance you can wash off with water. Today, there are as many wash-off creams and lotions as there are those that you have to wipe off. There are also creams and lotions that you can remove either way. The results of use tests conducted by Consumers Union showed that preferences for cleansers specified by their makers for normal, dry, oily, or "combination" skin seemed to have no connection with skin type: Some women with dry skin preferred oily-skin products; some with normal skin liked dry-skin formulations, and so on.

PREFERENCES

An effective cleanser should be easy to apply and remove, take off makeup efficiently, smell pleasant, feel good on the skin during use, and leave the skin feeling nice.

The panelists judged some of the cleansers quite inconvenient to apply. One product was "like a paste," said a panelist; another was "like olive oil."

Some cleansers were hard to remove, according to the panelists. Removing some of the wash-off products occasionally took more than a dozen rinses, they said.

Preferred cleansers left the skin feeling nice ("smooth" or "creamy"), but some others left the skin feeling slightly coated, or dry and stiff. And some left the skin feeling greasy.

Most products have a scent, ranging in type from medicinal through spicy to floral. Some cleansers claim to be fragrance-free, but most of those have an "accidental" smell from ingredients not added for their fragrance, which you may or may not find pleasing.

Smell seemed to play an important if unconscious role in panelists' judgments of overall quality: When a panelist scored a product low in smell, she generally gave it a low overall score.

COST, SIZE, QUALITY

Cleansers come in a variety of sizes. The price range is astonishingly wide, as it often is in the world of cosmetics.

Price per ounce can vary considerably with container size.

FACIAL TISSUES

Tissues are used to handle all sorts of jobs—to wipe eyeglasses, remove makeup, stand in for a napkin or a towel. But you expect most from a tissue when your nose runs nonstop and your eyes water. A tissue shouldn't shred when you sneeze into it, yet you don't want one so harsh and scratchy that it chafes your nose. And you want something fairly economical. (If the tissues are packed in a box to match your decor, so much the better.)

QUALITY

Consumers Union tested tissues for sneeze resistance, wet strength, and softness. Since people can't be expected to sneeze on demand or to sneeze exactly the same way time after time, CU invented a mechanical sneezer to test tissues. The most sneeze-resistant tissues usually withstood the test just fine. But the worst were almost always shot through.

To measure strength when wet, CU testers clamped each tissue in an embroidery hoop, dampened it with a measured amount of water, then poured a slow, steady stream of lead shot onto the tissue. The strongest ones held more than 10 ounces of shot before they broke; they are the tissues you can count on to handle the most demanding jobs without disintegrating. The weakest tissues ruptured under about one ounce of weight. The thickest tissues tested were the three-ply, which weren't the strongest. Several two-ply varieties were just as strong—some were even stronger.

Manufacturers often make facial tissues in more than one plant around the country to cut down on shipping costs. This practice could create variations in the same brand of tissue purchased in different areas. With few exceptions, however, the tissues bought from stores in the East, South, and West were quite consistent.

RECOMMENDATIONS

It doesn't make much sense to spend a lot of money on a throwaway product like facial tissue. But it does make sense to buy tissues that are reasonably soft, suitably strong, and low in price. The softest tissues are obviously the most soothing for a prolonged cold or bout of hay fever. Those with only average softness are fine for everyday use, however.

HAND SOAPS

You can wash your hands for a penny with most soaps, but some designer brands can cost up to 20 cents or 30 cents per wash.

Here's what a soapmaker can do to make a penny's wash seem worth a nickel, a dime, or a quarter:

- Add fancy perfume. In its natural state, soap smells somewhat like the fat in meat. Fragrance masks this odor. Some soapmakers think that if they mask the odor well enough, it will upscale their product from the supermarket shelf—where soap can cost a dollar or less per bar—to the beauty counter at department stores, where you can easily pay $15 a bar.
- Appeal to health. The package may claim that the soap is "hypoallergenic" or "noncomedogenic" (that means the soap won't clog pores and promote blackheads, or comedones). A manufacturer may promote a soap's mildness to dermatologists, or the soap may come in several formulations for different skin types.
- Promise beauty. Manufacturers pledge that added emollients—bath oil, moisturizing cream, lanolin, vitamin E—will soften and condition skin. (As the Better Business Bureau reports, no soap can be truthfully

represented to keep skin young, and none may be advertised "as a cure, remedy, or competent treatment" for any skin disease.)

- Prevent embarrassment. Some brands claim that they're able to keep body odor at bay. These deodorant soaps usually include an antibacterial agent. (Perspiration itself doesn't smell; body odor is caused by bacteria that act on perspiration.) All provide some protection against unwanted odors because all soaps float off bacteria along with dirt and grease.

PERFORMANCE

Consumers Union found that all the soaps tested by a panel were at least good at cleaning or in the way they left hands feeling. But some clearly performed better than others. Liquids generally didn't feel as good on the skin as bar soap, probably because they're more likely to contain detergent, which tends to feel harsher than soap.

Since the 1950s, some soaps have included detergents, which work better than soap in hard water. (Soap combines with the minerals in hard water, leaving a bathtub ring; detergents tend not to form such scum.) Most liquid products are basically detergent, not soap.

Soap and detergent can dry the skin because they remove its natural oils. Once its oil coating is gone, the skin gives up water readily. For reasons not entirely understood, elderly people are particularly vulnerable. But even young people can suffer from dry skin, especially in winter, when humidity outdoors is low and central heating makes the indoors dry as a desert.

Most soaps have emollients, which may help seal in moisture. If you have dry skin, however, don't look for some magic soap formula to provide relief. Apply baby oil or a moisturizing cream after bathing, while the skin is still damp.

People with oily skin can wash often without fear of dryness. They should, in fact, stick with soaps that lack emollients.

Check labels. Some liquid soaps contain preservatives such as formalin (formaldehyde) and methylparaben. According to Consumers Union's medical consultants, a small percentage of people could become sensitized to those additives, which can cause inflammation.

RECOMMENDATIONS

It makes no sense to pay more than a penny a wash for soap.

On average, liquid soaps are slightly more expensive to use than bars, and their plastic containers often leave more packaging waste. (For many liquids, a pump refill is available, but then the refill bottle is tossed out.)

TOILET TISSUES

Whatever the price per roll, you expect certain basic qualities in this homely but indispensable product. The tissues should be tough, especially when they're wet, so they don't fall apart in use. And yet they should break up quickly when flushed, to avoid clogging. They should be soft and absorbent.

Some tissues come in single rolls, some in packages of up to 12 or more. Four-packs are the most popular. Some tissues are scented. Scent serves no practical purpose in bathroom tissues, and it may be irritating to some people.

TISSUE QUALITY

The stronger the tissue, the less likely it is to break or tear in use. Wet strength is far more important than dry strength.

Two-ply tissues are stronger as a group, but there are some strong single-plies, too.

Most tissues are soft enough for all but sensitive individuals. Most people won't find even the roughest tissues objectionable. Two-ply tissues are generally softer than single-ply.

Bathroom tissues should absorb moisture quickly and thoroughly. Two-ply models soak up a drop of water within five seconds or less. Most single-ply tissues are not quite as absorbent.

Tissues should break up promptly when flushed away. If they don't, a slow toilet may back up. Tissues are likely to disintegrate less quickly in a low-flow toilet than in a conventional one, since each flush uses much less water.

CONVENIENCE

A package should be easy to open, the roll should be easy to start, and tissues should be easy to tear off.

Plastic packages with perforations around the top are easiest to open.

On some rolls, the first few sheets stick to the ones underneath, an annoyance when you begin using the roll. On others, the end of the first sheet hangs free, providing a pull tab that's easy to grasp. Sometimes the tab works nicely; sometimes it shreds before freeing the next sheet.

Most two-ply models are relatively easy to detach, thanks to their adequate perforations. By contrast, some single-ply products are flimsy and tend to tear raggedly.

RECOMMENDATIONS

No tissues have all four qualities: soft, strong, easy to tear, and cheap. Some qualities are mutually exclusive. For example, softness generally doesn't go with strength.

Then again, perhaps all the fuss about softness is unnecessary. Most people would find even the harshest of the tissues tested unobjectionable.

TOILET TISSUES AND RECYCLING

Recycling conserves the vast amounts of energy and water that go into converting trees to paper. It reduces the amount of toxic chemicals released into the environment. It also lessens the burden on overflowing landfills.

Many bathroom tissues contain some recycled paper, but the manufacturers rarely advertise this.

Recycled paper generally includes two basic types, known as "preconsumer" and "postconsumer" waste. The former consists of trimmings at paper mills, printing overruns, and other paper that has never reached con-

Ratings of Toilet Paper

◉ ◓ ○ ◒ ●

Better ← → Worse

Listed in order of estimated quality, based primarily on wet strength and softness. Products judged equal in estimated quality are bracketed. As published in a **September 1991** report.

Product. Popular national and regional brands were tested.

Cost per 100 sheets. To the nearest cent, based on the average price paid for a 4-roll package, except where noted.

Sheets in roll. Manufacturer's claimed number, which is often less than determined by actual count.

Plies. Each roll has either 1 or 2 plies, or layers. All tissues were tested the same way, regardless of plies.

Strength. This is a measure of the tissues' resistance to bursting under pressure—a good indication of overall strength. **Wet strength** was tested by securing a sheet of tissue in an embroidery hoop, dampening it, and pouring lead shot onto the center. When the tissue broke, the amount of shot that fell through was weighed. For **dry strength,** a dry tissue was secured in the embroidery hoop with a test tube over the center of the tissue to concentrate the load. Lead shot was poured into the tube until the tissue ruptured. Again, the shot was weighed to determine the test score.

Softness. A trained panel felt the tissue with their hands and judged the softness subjectively.

Absorbency. The rate at which a tissue absorbed a given amount of water. For each product, a sheet was secured in a hoop and the time noted for a drop of water to be absorbed completely.

Disintegration. How quickly a tissue came apart in swirling water. Rapid disintegration may reduce chances that a sluggish toilet will clog your plumbing. A single sheet of tissue was inserted into a laboratory beaker containing about a pint of water, and a magnetic stirrer swirled the water at a uniform speed. The testers recorded how long the tissue took to break up. The tissues were also flushed in a low-flow toilet and the results observed through a clear glass pipe.

Tearing ease. The various rolls were tested in two types of dispenser and judgments made of how easy it was to tear tissues off the roll. The rolls were mounted so they spun both ways, dispensing tissues up over the top and down from under the bottom of the roll. (People who own a playful cat often prefer the latter method.)

Product	Cost per 100 sheets	Sheets in roll	Plies	Strength: Wet	Strength: Dry	Softness	Absorbency	Disintegration	Tearing ease	Comments
Lady Lee Wonder Soft (Lucky Stores)	10¢	300	2	◉	◉	◒	◉	◉	◓	—
Marina	13	300	2	◓	◉	◒	◉	◉	◉	—
Charmin	12	300	1	◓	◒	◓	◉	●	◉	E,M
White Cloud, Spring Breeze Scent	16 [1]	250	2	○	◒	◉	◉	◉	◉	E,F,M
MD	12	300	2	◓	◓	○	◉	◓	◉	—
Skaggs Alpha Beta	11	300	2	◓	◉	○	◉	◉	◉	—

Truly Fine (Safeway)	12	300	2	◓ [3]	○	◒	◉	◉	◉	—
Seventh Generation	12 [2]	500	2	○	○	○	◉	◉	◉	A,B,J,M,P
Charmin Free	13 [1]	300	-	◓	◒	◓	◉	●	◉	M
Envision	11 [2]	500	2	◓	◒	○	◉	◉	○	A,B,M,O
Soft'N Gentle	9	300	2	◓	◓	◒	◉	◉	○	I,L
Quilted Northern	12	300	2	○	◓	○	◉	◉	◉	—
Aurora	13 [1]	300	2	○	○	○	◉	◉	◉	—
Kleenex Premium	10	300	-	○	◒	○	◉	◉	◉	M
Coronet Angel Soft	11	300	2	○ [3]	○	◒ [3]	◉	◉	◉	M
Cottonelle Hypo-Allergenic	12	300	2	○	○	○	◉	◉	◉	D
Cottonelle	12	300	2	○	○	○ [3]	◉	◉	◉	E
Nice and Soft	11	300	-	○	◒	◒	○	◉	◉	—
Stop & Shop	9	300	2	○	○	◒	◉	◉	◉	—
Delsey	10	300	2	○	○	◒	◉	◉	○	I
Pathmark	10	300	2	○	◒	◒	◉	◉	◓	L,N
E.S.P.	10	300	2	○	○	◒	◉	◉	◉	A
Charmin Care	23	200	1	●	◒	◓	◉	◉	◉	C,M
Kroger	8	300	2	○	○	◒	◉	◉	◉	A
Coronet	10 [4]	280	2	○ [3]	○	◒	◉	◉	◓	—
Waldorf	10	350	1	◒	◒	○	◉	◉	◉	—
Grand Union	13	300	2	○	○	◒	◉	◉	◉	A
Green Forest	12	300	2	○	○	◒	◉	◉	◓	A,H
Banner	9	350	1	◒	◒	○	◓	◓	◉	M
Marcal Sofpac	10	280	2	○	○	◒	◉	○	◓	A,G,L
Cottonelle Convenience Pack	13 [5]	300	1	◒	◒	○	◉	◉	◉	E
Albertson's	10	300	2	◒	○	○	◉	◉	◉	—
Big'N Soft	11 [1]	300	2	◒	○	◒	◉	◉	◉	—
A&P	9	300	2	○	○	◒	◉	◉	◉	A

	Cost per 100 sheets	Sheets in roll	Plies	Wet	Dry	Softness	Absorbency	Disintegration	Tearing ease	Comments
Scottissue	6	1000	1	○	◒	◒	◒	◉	◉	L
Family Scott	9	350	1	○	◒	◒	◒	◓	○	—
Marcal 1000	5 [2]	1000	1	○	◒	◒	●	◉	◉	A
Always Save [6]	6	400	1	◒	◒	◒	○	◉	○	—
Tree Free	7 [1]	500	1	○	◒	◒	◒	◉	○	A
No Frills	6	400	1	○	◒	◒	◒	◓	○	L,N
Delta	9	350	1	●	●	◒	○	◉	○	—
Cost Cutter (Kroger)	6	350	1	●	◒	◒	○	◉	○	A,I,L,M
Scotch Buy (Safeway)	7	350	1	●	◒	◒	●	◉	○	A
C.A.R.E.	7 [2]	1000	1	●	●	◒	●	◉	◉	A,K,M

[1] *Based on average price of 6-roll package.*
[2] *Based on average price of single roll.*
[3] *Varied significantly among samples bought in different states.*
[4] *Based on average price of 8-roll package.*
[5] *Based on average price of 12-roll package.*
[6] *Data are for samples bought in Missouri. Those bought in New York average 89 cents for a package of 4 and scored ◒ for absorbency and disintegration.*

Features in Common

All rolls: • Range from about 4 to 4½ in. in dia. • Have a core about 1½ in dia. and fit standard dispensers.

Except as noted, all: • Are unscented and untreated with lotion. • Are made of paper that has been bleached, a process that could be harmful to the environment.

Except as noted, none: Are made of recycled paper.

Key to Comments

A–Made of recycled paper.
B–Made of unbleached paper.
C–Treated with lotion for sensitive skin.
D–Claims to be hypoallergenic.
E–Scented.
F–Available scented and unscented.
G–Plastic wrapper of 8-roll pack can be reused as storage or shopping bag.
H–Rolls sold in Missouri have 360 sheets.
I–Ease of tearing varied significantly from sample to sample.
J–Sheets measured about ¾-inch shorter than others.
K–Rolls judged hard to start.
L–Ease of starting varied significantly.
M–Wrapper judged especially easy to open.
N–Wrapper judged especially hard to open.
O–Mail-ordered from Co-Op America, 2100 M Street, Suite 403, Washington, D.C. 20036.
P–Mail-ordered from Seventh Generation Prods., 49 Hercules Drive, Colchester, Vermont 05446.

sumers; the latter is made up of newspapers, stationery, and other paper used and salvaged by consumers.

Logically, virgin-wood fiber should be reserved for copying paper, photo paper, and other fine papers at the top of the paper chain.

Preconsumer waste is best used in products that can be recycled again. For toilet paper and other products at the bottom of the paper chain, postconsumer waste is more appropriate.

The bleaching of bathroom tissues, disposable diapers, coffee filters, and other throwaway paper products is a matter of environmental concern. Manufacturers are determined to spare you the sight of paper containing wood-colored pulp.

TIPS FOR CLEANING A VARIETY OF HOUSEHOLD ITEMS

Acetate fabric. Dry cleaning is safest for this delicate fabric even if there are laundering instructions on the care label. Laundering must be done very carefully. Avoid wringing or twisting garments. Dry acetate items by draping them over a clothesline.

Air conditioners. Clean a window air conditioner's filter once a month or change it during the air-conditioning season to keep the machine's efficiency as high as possible. When cleaning or changing the filter, vacuum clean any visible cooling coils. (Be careful not to cut yourself on sharp edges.)

Plastic foam filters can be washed at the kitchen sink, using dishwashing liquid and water. Condenser coils facing outside also need cleaning before hot weather sets in, but the unit may have to be removed from the window to do the job. In very sooty areas, or when the air conditioner is in a window over a heavily trafficked street, you may need to hire a professional firm that does steam cleaning.

Aluminum scuffs. Some sinks, especially older ones with a bit of their enamel worn off, tend to collect scuff marks from aluminum pots and pans. A good cleanser should remove these marks readily after covering the stain with it for a few minutes.

Appliance exteriors. Many kitchen and laundry appliances have a baked enamel surface that scratches quite easily, unlike the glass-hard porcelain enamel finish that is common on kitchen ranges as well as some washing machines or other appliance tops. Never use an abrasive cleaner on baked enamel. Soap and water should do the job. If this doesn't work, a liquid all-purpose cleaner can help, but check the label instructions to be sure the manufacturer states that it is safe to use on painted surfaces. Otherwise, use a product made especially for baked enamel finishes, one that combines cleaning and waxing in one operation.

Asphalt tile. Damp mop for day-to-day cleaning. Don't use solvent-based wax; the solvent can soften the tile.

Auto carpeting, upholstery, and mats. A plug-in, lightweight, hand-held vacuum cleaner works best. A cordless model with rechargeable batteries is less powerful but may work well enough on loose surface litter.

Barbecue grills. If you run a gas barbecue for about 15 minutes at the highest heat setting—after you finish cooking—most grills look reasonably clean but will still need some wire-brushing to get rid of any heavy residue. When using a charcoal barbecue, let the grill stand over the coals for about 20 minutes after cooking to achieve similar results. Any remaining baked-on dirt should yield to additional wire-brushing and to an abrasive powdered cleaner.

Bathroom fixtures. Bathroom cleaners can discolor aluminum and brass—especially brass. Rinse off excess cleaner immediately to prevent or minimize the problem.

Blenders. Glass containers stay better-looking longer than plastic ones because they resist scratching and staining. A glass container should also be dishwasher safe; a plastic container probably should not go into a dishwasher. It might soften or melt if placed too close to the machine's heating element.

Butcher block. *See* Wood work surface.

Carpet grit. Use a full-size upright vacuum cleaner or canister model with a power nozzle.

Cat litter box. Avoid using chlorine bleach for cleaning: Fumes are created through a chemical reaction between the bleach and residual ammonia remaining in a litter box after it has been emptied.

China dishware. It's best to wash fine china by hand with dishwashing liquid. Harsh dishwasher detergents can wear away the overglaze and metallic decorations on some fine china, and fine china can be easily chipped or broken by forceful water or jostling among pots and pans. Everyday china can be washed in the dishwasher.

Citrus juicer. The easiest-to-clean juicer has the cone, strainer, and juice container as a single unit. Models with several pieces have to be taken apart, washed, dried, and put back together. It's helpful if the pieces can be put into a dishwasher; check the manufacturer's instructions.

Clothes dryer. Clean a dryer's lint screen after each load. This will maintain high drying efficiency and will help to prevent excessive heat buildup. Vacuum clean any visible lint buildup in other parts of the machine but leave any disassembly to a service technician.

Coffee maker. The carafe and brew basket of a drip-type coffee maker should be cleaned after every use, because dried coffee oils can ruin the taste of even the best blend. Coffee taste may also be improved by using a special coffee-maker cleaner sold in supermarkets and hardware stores. Because minerals accumulate in the tank and tubes of automatic-drip units, it's important to clean them now and then, especially if they are used with hard water. As a substitute for a commercial cleaner, try running white vinegar diluted with water through the machine. It's a chore, but worth the trouble.

Computer monitor. *See* Television set.

Continuous-cleaning oven. The porous finish of a continuous-cleaning oven is supposed to gradually dissipate light dirt at normal cooking temperatures. But major spills won't go away. You have to wipe them up right after they happen. Minor spills are slowly eliminated, partly because they spread out on the finish, which is mottled, thereby helping to disguise patches of dirt.

You can protect the most exposed surface from becoming soiled in the first place by covering the oven bottom with aluminum foil, but be careful to avoid blocking any vents in a gas oven or short-circuiting an electric element.

Countertop. Never use an abrasive cleanser on a plastic-laminate surface. Clean these easy-to-scratch areas with the gentlest product possible. Hot utensils can cause hard-to-remove marks and, even worse, loosen the bond between the countertop surface and the base material. In the bathroom, liquid cleaners should be rinsed off to prevent damage to the countertop finish.

Curtains. Vacuum clean thin fabrics at a reduced suction setting to prevent the fabric from being drawn into the cleaner's nozzle.

Dehumidifier. Vacuum the coils at least once a year, more often in a dusty environment. This will help maintain the appliance's performance.

Delicate fabrics. The less time some delicate fabrics spend in water, even cold water, the better.

You may find that a liquid dishwashing detergent is as effective as a special-purpose product.

Dish sanitizing. Some dishwashers have a final rinse cycle that uses extra-hot water, and their makers may refer to protection against colds and flus. In fact, once you put "sanitized" dishes into the cupboard, household microbes quickly settle on them—the same microbes that are on everything else in the house.

Disinfecting. It's really not possible to prevent the spread of germs in the house by using a disinfectant. When a medical problem requires using a germicide, ask a doctor for advice on how to proceed.

Dust. A little bit of furniture spray polish on a rag makes the rag tacky enough to pick up more dust than a dry cloth.

Electric blanket. Follow the manufacturer's instructions for laundering (usually a cold or warm wash and low-heat machine drying or, even better, line drying). Never have an electric blanket or pad dry-cleaned; dry-cleaning chemicals can damage the wiring.

Electric range tops. Electric elements are all self-cleaning since spills burn off quickly. If you soak an electric element in water, it may become damaged.

Clean under the control knobs by pulling them off. Use care when scrubbing around the control panel: The markings can often be rubbed off with steel wool or an abrasive powdered cleanser.

You can raise or remove the cooktop to clean beneath it. But some electric ranges have a fixed cooktop; in that case, you have to poke your hand through the burner holes. Clean drip pans and reflector bowls with the least abrasive cleanser that will keep them looking up to par. A new spare set of drip pans or reflectors is handy for making the cooktop presentable at a moment's notice.

Fan. Dirty fan blades impair air-moving efficiency and also detract from the appliance's appearance. Clean metal blades carefully to prevent bending them, which can cause unwanted vibration when the fan is turned on. A whole-house or attic fan's louvers and screening should be brushed and vacuumed at least once a season to keep airflow at the maximum possible rate.

Floor cleaning. A lightweight upright vacuum cleaner works well for picking up loose dirt from bare floors. For stains and adherent soil, however, use a damp (not wet) sponge mop or its equivalent.

Floor wax buildup. Try a wax remover. Use fine steel wool for stubborn spots.

Food processor. Simple, clean lines make for easy cleaning. Use a damp sponge for gaps around switches and trim.

Freezer. Self-defrosting is available in some upright models: You can skip the manual defrosting chore and just swab down inside surfaces with a cleaning solution of baking soda (bicarbonate of soda) and water.

A chest freezer has a smooth interior and removable wire baskets or dividers instead of shelves. Use a windshield ice scraper to remove frost and hasten defrosting. An upright freezer requires more patience because you must wait for the ice to melt around the cooling coils in the shelves. If you use a tool to scrape and pry ice away to speed the process, the result could be damage to the refrigeration system that is expensive to repair.

Defrost when the food supply is low. Transfer remaining food to the refrigerator's freezer or cooling compartment. Or wrap food in layers of newspaper for insulation while you defrost. If you pick a very cold winter day, you may be able to store the food outdoors while you defrost. But be wary of animal predators.

Furniture. The original oil or lacquer finish on a piece of furniture provides the best protection. Clean up spills quickly, before they have a chance to attack the finish. Use the softest cloth possible for dusting.

If you apply polish each time you dust, excessive wax buildup can result, causing loss of the wood's natural beauty plus difficulty in getting the kind of luster you really want. Don't wipe against the grain. Use soft insulating pads under hot, heavy, or sharp objects or containers. Treat dents or burns with steam from a steam iron, applied through several thicknesses of dampened brown wrapping paper. Consecutive applications can swell the wood sufficiently to bring it up to the surrounding level.

Furniture nicks and scratches. Some polishes are colored to match the furniture wood, and thereby mask the marred area, but the color match must be accurate for cover-up to work well.

Garbage disposer. Most manufacturers suggest allowing a disposer to run—or at least allowing the water to run—for 30 to 60 seconds after grinding is finished. Some also suggest purging the disposer by filling the sink halfway with water, removing the drain stopper, and turning on the machine for a few seconds.

Glass-fiber fabric. This material is resistant to soiling and can be very decorative. It is fragile and should be carefully hand-laundered and line-dried.

Glassware. It is best to wash crystal glassware by hand; there's a possibility of chipping and breakage if you wash such items in a machine.

Greasy dirt on hard surfaces. Pine oil in some all-purpose cleaners helps penetrate and loosen greasy dirt.

Heater. Many space heaters have shiny reflecting surfaces to help direct the heat where you want it. If the shiny area becomes dulled, the heater will become less effective. After unplugging the appliance, vacuum any surfaces you can reach.

Heating pad. Never use a heating pad without its fabric cover. This helps to prevent skin burns as well as damage to a pad's waterproof exterior. Wash the cover when necessary. Throw away any pad that has frayed wiring, cracks in any portion of the waterproof cover or line cord, or holes in the cover.

Heating system. Vacuum radiators and fins regularly during the heating season to keep them at their maximum operating efficiency. Change or wash any filters in a warm-air heating system at least once during the heating season, as well as during the summer if the air ducts also serve as part of a central air-conditioning system.

Hot plate. Unplug before cleaning.

Humidifier. Molds and bacteria from humidifiers and vaporizers can trigger allergic symptoms. Although ultrasonic models do not emit fine microorganisms, they have been implicated in spraying fragments of bacteria and molds into the air. Therefore, like cool-mist and evaporative humidifiers, an ultrasonic humidifier should be scrupulously cleaned daily.

After unplugging and emptying the humidifier, clean it as directed by the manufacturer or, if there are no directions, rinse the tank with a solution of one tablespoon of chlorine bleach in a pint of water; for large units, use a cup of bleach in a gallon of water, then rinse the tank with fresh water.

A steam vaporizer, the kind that boils water and produces moisture in the form of steam, doesn't present problems of molds and bacteria. But a steam vaporizer must still be cleaned to keep it working properly. Rust accumulations in a steam vaporizer are harmless, but should be rinsed out periodically, particularly before storing the unit.

Humidifier dust. If you use a humidifier, you may be forever wiping up white dust that settles on furniture and other surfaces, even beyond the room in which the cool-mist or ultrasonic humidifier is located. Use only distilled water or demineralized water in cool-mist or ultrasonic humidifiers, particularly if you live in a hard-water area.

Insect killers. First unplug the appliance. It's usually difficult to poke through the outer screen or blow through it with a vacuum cleaner's exhaust. It's much easier to disassemble the unit, at least to the extent of removing the sides so that the grid can be properly brushed off.

Linen. This is a durable fabric whose appearance and "feel" improve with laundering. Linen that has been chemically treated for wrinkle resistance may not be able to withstand hot-water washing.

Lint on garments. A washing machine's lint filter helps, but tumbling in a clothes dryer may be even more effective. It's worth trying a lint roller or even wrapping Scotch-type sticky tape around a hand, sticky side out, and patting the garment to remove the lint.

Litter on carpeting and hard-surface floors. Use a lightweight suction vacuum cleaner. Reserve uprights and power brushes for cleaning deep in a carpet's pile.

Microwave cookware. Except for the browning dishes and the crevices on some trivets, cleaning microwave cookware should be easy with just plain soap and water. Some plastic utensils have a nonstick finish. This is usually unnecessary, since sticking food is seldom a problem in microwave cooking. The nonstick finishes are probably a drawback because they scratch easily and look worn quickly. Browning dishes sear food and accumulate a fair amount of burned-on soil that requires some cleaning effort to remove.

Microwave oven. Wipe the inside with plain water, or water with a bit of dishwashing liquid. Spills and spatters are generally easy to wipe up with a damp (not wet) sponge. Keep the oven clean to prevent odors from developing. Pay particular attention to the door and the door seal. They should be kept scrupulously clean to help maintain the seal's tightness, thereby keeping any microwave leakage to the lowest possible level.

Mildew around the house. Mildew has an unpleasant odor and appearance. It's a common household mold that thrives in dark, damp, poorly ventilated places—and it can be easier to prevent than to eliminate. Chlorine bleach, diluted according to label directions, is a good mildew remover. The chemicals in moth flakes and pellets are hazardous to humans, but used judiciously in enclosed spaces, they can help to keep mildew under control.

Mildew can also be controlled by lowering the humidity in a closed-in space such as a closet. During the spring and summer, when mildew growth is greatest, use a continuously burning 60-watt bulb in a large closet to raise the temperature slightly (and thereby lower the humidity). A smaller bulb can be used in a smaller enclosure. Be certain that the bulb is well away from any stored articles. The electricity cost is about $3.50 a month, at national average rates, plus the price of a bulb once a month, assuming a bulb life of 750 hours.

Mildew in bathrooms. Specialty bathroom cleaners contain chlorine bleach, an effective mildew fighter. But undiluted chlorine bleach is the best and cheapest mildew fighter. Thoroughly rinse any mildewed surface washed with bleach. Never mix bleach with other cleaning products. Bleach reacts with many acidic and alkaline household cleaners and can produce very hazardous gases.

Nylon. White nylon items should be washed separately because of nylon's tendency to pick up colors from other items in a laundry load. Oily substances can stick to nylon; treat these stains quickly, before they have a chance to set.

Oven. See Continuous-cleaning oven *and* Self-cleaning oven.

Painted surfaces. All-purpose cleaners should be tried on an inconspicuous area first. Cleaners containing pine oil can be damaging to paint.

Polyester. Fabrics containing polyester fibers have a strong affinity for oily substances. Treat oily stains as soon as possible after you notice them. Unfortunately, even quick attention may not result in satisfactory stain removal.

Porcelain enamel bathroom fixtures. Sinks, bathtubs, toilets, and other plumbing fixtures are generally made of metal with a heavy outside layer of glasslike porcelain. Porcelain can tolerate abrasive cleansers without wearing off, but the shiny finish will be gradually destroyed, making the fixture less resistant to staining and therefore more difficult to clean. Stick to nonabrasive cleansers on new or nearly new fixtures.

Porcelain enamel kitchen fixtures. Treat these items as gently as possible to avoid unsightly scratches that can attract dirt and make future cleaning increasingly difficult.

Portable food mixers. Crevices and grooves trap food and dirt. A dampened old toothbrush can help.

Refrigerator/freezer. The condenser coil, which helps disperse heat, is outside the cabinet, where it tends to collect dust. Dust lowers the appliance's efficiency and raises the cost of running it. The condenser should be cleaned once or twice a year, particularly before the onset of hot weather, because high outside temperatures impose special demands on a refrigerating system.

It's easy to clean a back-mounted condenser once you pull out the refrigerator. But in many models, the coil is mounted in a compartment underneath the cabinet. Clean this area by using a condenser-coil cleaning brush (available in hardware and appliance stores) and a vacuum cleaner's crevice tool. Most manufacturers tell you to clean from the front, a task made more difficult if the coil is under a shield and toward the refrigerator's back. Cleaning the coil from the back after you remove the cardboard "service access" cover is a bit easier, once the appliance has been wrestled from its normal position.

The drip pan under a refrigerator can develop odors from food spills that drip into it from inside the refrigerator. If possible, check it from time to time, and rinse the pan with water.

Cleaning inside the refrigerator is best done with the mildest possible detergent or just a damp sponge. Try to avoid scratching soft plastic surfaces. A solution of baking soda and water is probably enough to do the job if water alone doesn't work. It's particularly important to keep the door seal (gasket) clean: Dirt buildup impairs the gasket's ability to keep in the cold air.

Rust. Only the special-purpose cleaners discussed on page 45 are likely to be effective on rust or green metallic deposits.

Self-cleaning oven. Use the self-cleaning cycle as often as necessary. The energy cost (using national average rates) is about the same per cleaning as an application of a chemical cleaner in an oven without the self-cleaning feature.

The self-cleaning cycle turns the most stubborn spills into a powdery gray ash residue. At the end of the cycle, simply wipe off the residue.

The self-cleaning cycle produces smoke and fumes, which exit through a vent on the backguard of gas models or under a rear element of electrics. If there's a loose duct from the oven to the rear element, hard-to-clean dirt may be deposited under the cooktop during the cleaning cycle. Ventilate the kitchen during the self-cleaning cycle to prevent smoke and fume particles from being deposited on the kitchen's walls and ceiling.

A self-cleaning oven's door and frame usually need some scrubbing outside the door seal, where vaporized soil can leak through. Use the mildest nonabrasive cleanser. Avoid scrubbing the gasket itself, except very gently with a wet, slightly soapy sponge.

Shaver. Men's electric shavers need daily cleaning. Unclip the blade cover. Shake and brush clippings from the cutters and the underside of the head. Once every week or two, the shaver should be cleaned thoroughly to help maintain its ability to operate satisfactorily, a job that usually involves removing, disassembling, brushing, and refitting the cutters and the head.

Silk. Garments made of silk usually require dry cleaning because water and silk are often not compatible. However, there are some silk garments that can tolerate washing in water. Be guided by care labels.

Slow cooker. Avoid an abrasive cleaner or steel wool in favor of a sponge, cloth, or plastic scrubber. Washup is easiest with an appliance that has a removable liner that can be immersed. If the liner is not removable, take care not to wet any electrical parts of the cooker.

Smoke detector. To keep detectors operating properly, vacuum them yearly, cleaning with the vacuum wand from a full-powered canister cleaner, if possible. If a detector has a fixed cover, pass the wand across the cover's openings. If a detector's cover is removable, *gently* vacuum the sensor chambers.

Spots on glassware and dishes. This is a particularly annoying problem in areas of the country that have hard water. Try switching to a name-brand detergent (rather than a store brand); if you are already using a name-brand detergent, try adding a rinse agent. These products help to reduce spotting. Many dishwashers have dispensers for such additives.

Stainless steel flatware. Scratches or surface imperfections tend to affect the stain resistance of stainless steel tableware adversely. Consequently, flatware should not be cleaned with scouring powder or steel wool. It is advisable to wash stainless steel soon after using it to minimize any possible staining.

Steam iron. If an iron's soleplate has a nonstick finish, any adherent starch or dirt should come off easily by wiping with a damp sponge. For an iron without a nonstick finish, clean with soap and water or a fine metal polish. Avoid any abrasive that causes scratching. When the soleplate is clean, run it over a piece of wax paper (at a low heat setting) to coat a scratched soleplate. This should make the iron easier to push.

Television set. A television's screen attracts fingerprints, but even more of a nuisance is its tendency to accumulate dust and grime as a result of static electricity. With the set turned off, use glass cleaner sparingly. Wet a rag or paper towel with the cleaner rather than spraying it, and thereby avoid getting cleaner on the cabinet.

Toaster, toaster oven, toaster oven-broiler. Clean the crumbs from these appliances often enough to prevent an accumulation that will smolder. Too many crumbs may also impede the operation of door-opening mechanisms.

A "continuous-clean" interior is supposed to rid itself of grease and grime at normal cooking temperatures. This doesn't seem to work very well, however, although a continuous-clean finish's dull, usually mottled surface may present a cleaner appearance for a longer time than an ordinary finish will. In the long run, a continuous-clean finish may be something of a disadvantage since its rough, soft surface eventually makes cleaning very difficult.

Vacuum cleaners. Clumps of dust or other debris can clog a vacuum cleaner's hose. One way to dislodge them is with a broom or mop handle inserted into the hose, or else with a straightened garment hanger used *very carefully* to prevent puncturing the hose cover. Change the paper bag or clean a cloth bag as soon as the cleaner's suction drops noticeably, even if the bag doesn't seem full. Small quantities of fine, dense dirt can reduce a bag's efficiency and consequently a cleaner's suction.

Vaporizers. See Humidifier.

Vinyl and vinyl-composition floor. Damp mop for day-to-day cleaning. Self-polishing water-based wax is best for providing luster (depending on whether the floor has a "permanent" glossy finish).

Waffle maker. The bits of food that stick to nonstick grids should be easy to dust off with a pastry brush when the grids are still slightly warm from cooking. When you want to wash away excess oil, dunk removable grids in a sinkful of warm, sudsy water. (Never dunk the appliance itself.) Flat grids for grilling usually require thorough cleaning—sometimes soaking—to remove hamburger grease or sticky cheese. Most manufacturers recommend washing the grids by hand rather than in a dishwasher.

Washing machine. Follow the manufacturer's instructions for cleaning underneath the agitator or cleaning a lint filter. Sponge off detergent accumulations from around the top of the machine.

Reserve the hot water setting for very dirty laundry loads. Warm or cold water should do well for most clothes—it saves energy and helps to maintain the finish on clothes that are permanent-press. Slow agitation and spin speeds help to minimize wrinkling and are necessary speeds for washing delicate items.

Water heater. To lengthen tank life, drain off some hot water periodically to keep sediment from accumulating at the bottom of the tank. In areas with hard water, draining is best done every month. Where the water is soft, every three or four months should be enough.

Wood work surface. Butcher blocks and other wood work surfaces used for food preparation should be cleaned thoroughly after each use to minimize bacterial growth. It's a good idea to get into the habit of using one side of a portable wooden cutting board for vegetables and fruits, and the other side for meats, thereby avoiding excessive bacterial contamination of both sides. Portable or not, scrub the board with hot water and detergent after each use. Be particularly attentive to any deep scratches where bacteria can accumulate.

Wool. Dry cleaning is the safest method, unless the item has a care label stating that it is machine washable. If it says the wool can be laundered, *use only cool or cold water,* and minimum agitation and spinning to prevent shrinkage and matting of the wool fibers. Do not use bleach.

STAIN REMOVAL CHART FOR FABRICS

Quick action is often the key to success with stain removal. Many a tie or blouse has been saved by dipping the corner of a napkin in some water and treating the stain immediately. Gather all the materials mentioned in the following Selected Glossary of Materials and keep them in a place where you can locate them quickly. The editors' cleaning consultant suggests the charted methods for a variety of fabrics and fiber combinations; however, it is impossible to predict the circumstances of a particular stain. If in doubt, pretest the method on an inconspicuous area of the item to be cleaned. Be certain to follow the manufacturers' instructions and cautions on any product used in the stain removal process. For washable items the fabric should be laundered promptly after treatment. For nonwashables the treated fabric should be damp-sponged with cool water to remove any residue from the stain removal process (assuming the fabric will tolerate water). Check the care label. If it reads "Dry Clean Only," use water with caution or not at all.

Dry cleaning will remove many stains from washable as well as nonwashable garments; however, the cost of professional dry cleaning should be weighed against the value and age of the article.

SELECTED GLOSSARY OF MATERIALS

Absorbent. Any dry powder that will soak up excess liquid associated with the stain. Absorbents allow removal of the staining liquid without rubbing or other action that might spread the stain. Cornstarch or talcum powder can be used to absorb many staining liquids. Use only enough absorbent to soak up the liquid. Available in variety stores and supermarkets.

Alcohol. Use only pure denatured alcohol, applying with an eyedropper to the stain while holding an absorbent pad under the stained area. Denatured alcohol is available at many hardware and paint stores. Caution: Denatured alcohol is both flammable and poisonous. Use in a ventilated area, away from heat or flame, and store carefully.

Do not use rubbing alcohol, which can't be used on nonwashable fabrics and may contain other substances that interfere with stain removal.

Ammonia. Can be used as a mild bleach for some stains; its chemistry allows it to work where other bleaches may be ineffective. Apply sparingly using an eyedropper. Any household ammonia will work. Dilute one part ammonia with five parts water, and apply only in a well-ventilated area. Caution: *Never* mix ammonia with either chlorine bleach (or any products containing chlorine bleach) or vinegar.

Bleach. Bleaches are not stain removers. They are color removers—the idea (once you've removed the bulk of the staining substance) is to select a bleach that will remove the color in the stain and not the dyes in the fabric.

Start with a weak agent, such as lemon juice or white vinegar diluted with water (1:1). If you need more cleaning action, try a 3 percent solution of hydrogen peroxide. If that fails, use a nonchlorine bleach. Use chlorine bleach (diluted with water—see instructions on the bottle) only as a last resort. Chlorine bleach can destroy silk and wool and, most likely, will remove some of the color from the fabric. All of the above are available in supermarkets or drugstores.

Bleaches should be applied sparingly and only to the stained area. Use an eyedropper to control the amount of bleach applied to the spot. Caution: *Never* mix chlorine bleach, or products containing chlorine bleach, with ammonia or vinegar.

Note that the Stain Removal Chart recommends the mildest bleaches (vinegar or lemon juice). Move on to the stronger substances only if necessary to remove color from a stain. You may find that certain color stains (red, for instance) need stronger bleaches.

Combination solvent. A commercial product that is sprayed on or rubbed into the affected area. These are generally classified as laundry boosters and contain solvents for both oil- and water-based stains. Most supermarkets stock a few brands along with other cleaning materials.

Soon after treatment, the fabric should be either laundered or rinsed. Use only enough of the product to remove the stain. Treat the stain, check, and re-treat if necessary.

Detergent. Any liquid detergent, such as the type used to wash dishes, will do. The undiluted detergent should be worked into the stain and allowed to rest for a few minutes before rinsing.

Digestant. An enzyme available in pure form (such as pepsin and amylase) or as a component of some laundry products. If the enzyme-containing product is dry, mix with water to form a paste (1 tablespoon powder to 1 tablespoon water) and apply to the stain. If in liquid or paste form, apply directly. Keep the treated area moist and allow at least a half hour before laundering or rinsing. Caution: Do not use on wool or silk.

Glycerin. A heavy alcohol that has the ability to mix with some stains without spreading them, it is especially useful in treating some ink stains. Carefully work undiluted glycerin into the stain and then continue treatment as directed in the Stain Removal Chart.

Glycerin can be found in most drugstores. A number of people have used glycerin suppositories in lieu of the liquid form.

Oil solvent. Liquid products described as "dry cleaning" solvents contain volatile organic compounds and require careful attention to the manufacturers' instructions for safe use. Apply as directed, and allow the area to dry thoroughly before any additional treatment. Use of any volatile solvent requires caution: Apply only in a well-ventilated space or, if possible, outdoors. These products are available in most hardware stores. Be sure to avoid products containing perchlorethylene, which is considered quite hazardous.

Petroleum jelly. Useful for assisting with the removal of bacon grease, motor oil, suntan lotion, and other oil-based stains.

Stain Removal Chart for Fabrics

The procedures in this chart have been tested and shown to work in most instances. As it is impossible to test all treatments on all fabric and blend combinations, no warranty of any kind is made as to the effectiveness of the treatments suggested in any particular situation. The editor, cleaning consultants, and publisher are not responsible for any adverse effects resulting from the use of the treatments in this chart.

Stain	Supplies	Steps to Stain Removal
Ashes, soot	Detergent, ammonia	**All fabrics**—Carefully brush off or remove using masking tape (stronger tape can pull the fabric). **Washables**—Moisten stained area with water, apply detergent and a few drops of ammonia, launder. **Nonwashables**—Moisten, apply detergent, rinse thoroughly.
Baby formula	Digestant, detergent, water, oil solvent	**Washables**—Moisten the spot with cool water, apply digestant, keep moist. After 15 minutes, rinse with plenty of water. **Nonwashables**—Sponge with water/detergent mixture, allow to dry, then treat with an oil solvent.

Stain	Supplies	Steps to Stain Removal
Bacon grease	Absorbent, combination solvent, petroleum jelly, oil solvent	**Washables**—Use an absorbent to remove as much grease as possible, then apply a combination solvent followed by petroleum jelly. **Nonwashables**—Treat with an oil solvent.
Ballpoint pen ink	Glycerin, detergent, oil solvent	**Washables**—Apply glycerin, treat with detergent, rinse. **Nonwashables**—Apply glycerin, then treat with an oil solvent.
Barbecue sauce	Water, glycerin, combination solvent, white vinegar	**Washables**—Rinse with cool water, apply glycerin and a combination solvent, rinse again. **Nonwashables**—Apply mixture of ½ white vinegar, ½ water, blot dry, then apply plain water, blot dry again.
Beer	Cool water, white vinegar, digestant, bleach	**Washables**—Blot with dry cloth, rinse with cool water and vinegar, rinse, apply digestant. If needed, try nonchlorine bleach. **Nonwashables**—Use cool water and vinegar, rinse.

Stain	Supplies	Steps to Stain Removal
Candle wax	Boiling water, warm iron, white vinegar, bleach Warm iron, oil solvent	**Washables**—Scrape wax off fabric, spread fabric over bowl, pour boiling water through fabric from a height of 12 inches, apply vinegar or bleach to remaining stain. **Nonwashables**—Sandwich fabric between paper towels, use warm iron. Apply oil solvent to any remaining stain. Bleach if necessary.
Cheese sauce	Combination solvent, digestant, oil solvent	**Washables**—Apply combination solvent, wash in cool water, apply digestant if needed. **Nonwashables**—Sponge with warm water, use oil solvent.
Chewing gum	Peanut butter, ice, hammer, combination solvent, oil solvent, cool water	Soften the bulk with peanut butter, then remove or freeze with ice. Break with hammer. To remove remaining gum: **Washables**—Rinse with cool water, use combination solvent. **Nonwashables**—Use combination solvent and cool water, rinse, try oil solvent if needed.

Stain	Supplies	Steps to Stain Removal
Chili	Cool water, combination solvent, white vinegar, oil solvent	**Washables and nonwashables**—Rinse with cool water, use combination solvent, apply vinegar if needed. Let fabric dry and use oil solvent for grease stain. Try hydrogen peroxide (carefully applied) on any remaining color.
Chocolate	Absorbent, digestant, oil solvent	**Washables**—Apply absorbent, then oil solvent; use digestant for any remaining stain. **Nonwashables**—Dry-clean the garment.
Coffee	Combination solvent, boiling water, oil solvent, vinegar, glycerin	**Washables**—Combination solvent, rinse, spread fabric over bowl, pour boiling water through fabric from a height of 12 inches. Use oil solvent on dry fabric for cream stains, use vinegar if needed. **Nonwashables**—Use glycerin, then oil solvent.
Cooking oil, butter	Absorbent, combination solvent, oil solvent	**Washables**—Apply combination solvent, launder, dry, use oil solvent if needed. **Nonwashables**—Use an absorbent, brush off, then use an oil solvent.

Stain	Supplies	Steps to Stain Removal
Cranberry juice	Water, glycerin, combination solvent	**Washables**—Sponge off with cool water. Spread fabric over bowl, pour boiling water through fabric from a height of 12 inches. Apply glycerin, rinse, use combination solvent. Bleach to remove any remaining color. **Nonwashables**—Sponge with plain water.
Crayon	Boiling water, vinegar or lemon juice, bleach, warm iron	**Washables**—Scrape off fabric, spread fabric over bowl, pour boiling water through fabric from a height of 12 inches, use vinegar or lemon juice. Bleach if needed. **Nonwashables**—Sandwich fabric between paper towels, use warm iron.
Dog stains	Combination solvent, detergent, vinegar	**Washables**—Scrape off fabric, use combination solvent, wash with detergent. Use vinegar if needed. **Nonwashables**—Dry-clean the garment.
Dried blood	Cool salt water, ammonia, digestant, bleach	**Washables**—Soak several hours in salt water, rinse, soak in ammonia/water, rinse, use digestant. Bleach if needed.

Stain	Supplies	Steps to Stain Removal
		Nonwashables—Dry-clean the garment.
Fecal matter	Combination solvent, detergent, vinegar	**Washables**—Scrape off fabrics, use combination solvent, wash with detergent, use vinegar if needed. **Nonwashables**—Dry-clean the garment.
Glue (white)	Warm water	**Washables**—Soak in very warm water until the glue softens. **Nonwashables**—Dry-clean the garment.
Grape juice	Water, glycerin, combination solvent	**Washables**—Sponge off with cool water, spread fabric over bowl, pour boiling water through fabric from a height of 12 inches. **Nonwashables**—Use glycerin, then combination solvent.
Grass	Alcohol, vinegar, bleach, water	**Washables**—Sponge with alcohol or rinse with vinegar, use bleach if needed. **Nonwashables**—Sponge with vinegar, then plain water.
Gravy	Absorbent, cool water, digestant	**Washables**—Use absorbent, soak in cool water, then use digestant.

Stain	Supplies	Steps to Stain Removal
	Oil solvent	**Nonwashables**—Use oil solvent.
Ground-in dirt	Combination solvent, bleach Detergent, oil solvent	**Washables**—Use combination solvent, wash with bleach. **Nonwashables**—Spot-clean with detergent, use oil solvent on dry fabric.
Hot fudge	Absorbent, oil solvent, digestant	**Washables**—Scrape off fabric, use absorbent, brush off, use oil solvent, apply digestant if needed. **Nonwashables**—Use absorbent, brush off, use oil solvent.
Ice cream	Combination solvent, liquid soap, oil solvent	**Washables**—Use combination solvent. **Nonwashables**—Sponge with liquid soap/cool water, rinse, use oil solvent if needed.
Iron scorch	Fine sandpaper, cool water, vinegar, bleach	**Note**—Severe scorch cannot be completely removed, particularly on synthetics. **Washables**—Brush or rub surface with fine sandpaper, wash, and bleach remaining stain with water and vinegar (1:1).

Stain	Supplies	Steps to Stain Removal
		Nonwashables—Brush or rub surface with fine sandpaper, sponge bleach on remaining stain.
Ketchup	Cool water, vinegar, combination solvent, digestant	**Washables**—Rinse with cool water, use combination solvent, rinse, use vinegar if needed, or use digestant. **Nonwashables**—Use combination solvent, then vinegar, rinse.
Lipstick	Oil solvent, liquid soap, ammonia	**Washables**—Use oil solvent. If needed, use liquid soap mixed with ammonia, rinse well, repeat if necessary. **Nonwashables**—Use oil solvent.
Liquid ink	Glycerin, ammonia, alcohol, combination solvent, bleach, hydrogen peroxide	**Washables**—Apply glyceri let stand 30 minutes, mix combination solvent w ammonia, apply, wa bleach if needed. **Nonwashables** alcohol, then peroxide, r

Stain	Supplies	Steps to Stain Removal
Marker ink	Glycerin, ammonia, alcohol, combination solvent, bleach, hydrogen peroxide	**Washables**—Apply glycerin, let stand 30 minutes, mix combination solvent with ammonia, apply, wash, use bleach if needed. **Nonwashables**—Sponge with alcohol, then hydrogen peroxide, rinse.
Mascara	Bleach, oil solvent, combination solvent	**Washables**—Use combination solvent, then wash, use bleach if needed. **Nonwashables**—Use oil solvent.
Mildew	Chlorine bleach, liquid soap	**Washables**—Add bleach to soapy water. **Nonwashables**—Dry-clean the garment.
Motor oil	Absorbent, combination solvent, petroleum jelly Oil solvent	**Washables**—Use an absorbent to remove as much oil as possible, apply a combination solvent followed by petroleum jelly, wash. **Nonwashables**—Treat with an oil solvent.
Must	Liquid soap	**Washables**—Apply liquid soap, wash in cool water.

Stain	Supplies	Steps to Stain Removal
	Absorbent, glycerin, alcohol	**Nonwashables**—Use absorbent, sponge on glycerin, let stand for 30 minutes, rinse, apply alcohol/water, rinse.
Nail polish	Acetone, bleach	**Note**—Acetone is available at paint supply stores. Follow cautions for use and storage; it is highly flammable. Do not use acetone on fabrics containing acetate. **Washables**—Treat stain with acetone, use mild bleach if needed. **Nonwashables**—Treat with acetone, bleach with vinegar and water (1:1).
Newsprint	Glycerin, oil solvent	**Washables**—Apply glycerin, rub in gently, remove with oil solvent, launder. **Nonwashables**—Apply glycerin, rub in gently, remove with oil solvent.
Orange juice	Water, glycerin, combination solvent, vinegar	**Washables**—Sponge with cool water, spread fabric over bowl, pour boiling water through fabric from a height of 12 inches. If fragile, use glycerin, then use combination solvent.

Stain	Supplies	Steps to Stain Removal
		Nonwashables—Sponge with vinegar/water, then plain water.
Paint (dried)—oil or latex	Mineral spirits, liquid soap	**Note**—Dried latex paint may not be removable. **Washables**—Soak stained area with mineral spirits, apply liquid soap. **Nonwashables**—As above, but do not launder; rinse stained area with water.
Paint (wet)—latex	Liquid soap	**Washables**—Apply liquid soap, rinse with water, repeat as needed. **Nonwashables**—As above, but do not launder.
Paint (wet)—oil	Mineral spirits, liquid soap, oil solvent	**Washables**—Soak with mineral spirits, apply liquid soap, rinse with water. **Nonwashables**—Apply mineral spirits, then oil solvent.
Peanut butter	Combination solvent, digestant Oil solvent	**Washables**—Use combination solvent, rinse, use digestant for remaining stain, rinse thoroughly. **Nonwashables**—Scrape off excess, treat with oil solvent.

Stain	Supplies	Steps to Stain Removal
Pencil	Eraser, liquid soap, ammonia Oil solvent	**Washables**—Use clean eraser, apply liquid soap/ammonia, rinse. **Nonwashables**—Use oil solvent.
Perfume	Glycerin, vinegar	**Washables**—Apply glycerin, rinse with water, bleach with water and vinegar (1:1). **Nonwashables**—As above, but omit laundering. Carefully rinse out water/vinegar bleach.
Perspiration	Ammonia, vinegar, oil solvent	**Washables**—Treat with ammonia/water mixture, rinse, follow up with vinegar/water mixture, dry, use oil solvent if needed. **Nonwashables**—Dry-clean the garment.
Rust	Salt, vinegar, lemon juice, bleach	**Washables**—Use paste of salt/vinegar, let stand 30 minutes, wash. Use paste of salt/lemon juice, rinse, use bleach if needed. **Nonwashables**—Dry-clean the garment.

Stain	Supplies	Steps to Stain Removal
Salad dressing	Absorbent, combination solvent, liquid soap, oil solvent	**Washables**—Apply absorbent, remove. Apply combination solvent, rinse. Apply liquid soap, rinse. **Nonwashables**—Apply absorbent and remove. Use oil solvent on remaining stain.
Shoe polish	Combination solvent, liquid soap, vinegar Oil solvent	**Washables**—Apply combination solvent, rub in liquid soap, rinse. Remove any remaining color with water and vinegar (1:1). **Nonwashables**—Apply oil solvent.
Sour cream	Cool water, combination solvent, oil solvent, absorbent	**Washables**—Sponge with cool water. Use combination solvent, then wash, use oil solvent if needed. **Nonwashables**—Use absorbent for several hours, follow with oil solvent.
Soy sauce	Cool water, vinegar, combination solvent Oil solvent	**Washables**—Rinse with cool water, apply combination solvent, wash, use vinegar/water if needed, rinse. **Nonwashables**—Use oil solvent.

Stain	Supplies	Steps to Stain Removal
Strawberry jam and other fruit jams and jellies	Combination solvent, water, glycerin, vinegar	**Washables**—Scrape off jam, rinse, use combination solvent. If stain remains, spread over bowl, pour boiling water through fabric from a height of 12 inches. If garment is fragile, use glycerin, rinse, use combination solvent. **Nonwashables**—Sponge with vinegar, sponge off with water.
Suntan lotion	Absorbent, combination solvent, petroleum jelly, vinegar, oil solvent	**Washables**—Apply absorbent, remove. Follow with combination solvent and petroleum jelly, then launder. If necessary, bleach with water and vinegar (1:1). **Nonwashables**—Apply oil solvent. If necessary, bleach with water and vinegar (1:1).
Tea	Combination solvent, oil solvent, water, vinegar, glycerin	**Washables**—Spread fabric over bowl, pour boiling water through fabric from a height of 12 inches, use combination solvent/cool water, use oil solvent if needed, rinse with vinegar/water, plain water. **Nonwashables**—Use glycerin, let stand 30 minutes, rinse with cool water.

Stain	Supplies	Steps to Stain Removal
Urine	Ammonia, vinegar, digestant	**Washables**—Treat with ammonia/water mixture followed by a mixture of vinegar and water, rinse, use digestant if needed. **Nonwashables**—Use a vinegar/water mixture, then rinse.
Wine, red	Cool water, salt, boiling water Oil solvent, vinegar	**Washables**—Sponge off with cool water. Spread fabric over bowl, pour salt on stain, then pour boiling water through fabric from a height of 12 inches. If garment is fragile, pour salt on stain, moisten with water, let stand, then scrape off and rinse. **Nonwashables**—Use oil solvent, use vinegar/water, then rinse.

INDEX